THE
INNER GUIDE
MEDITATION

THE
INNER GUIDE
MEDITATION

A Spiritual Technology
for the 21st Century

Edwin C. Steinbrecher

SAMUEL WEISER, INC.

York Beach, Maine

First published in 1988 by
Samuel Weiser, Inc.
P. O. Box 612
York Beach, Maine 03910-0612
www.weiserbooks.com

08 07 06 05 04 03 02 01 00
15 14 13 12 11 10 9 8 7

1st Edition: *An Excerpt from "The Guide Meditation,"* April, 1975,
         private printing, Santa Fe, NM.
2nd Edition: *The Guide Meditation: The Manual on Theory and
         Technique,* July, 1975, private printing, Santa Fe, NM.
3rd Edition: *The Guide Meditation,* 1977, private printing, Santa
         Fe, NM.
4th Edition: *The Inner Guide Meditation,* 1978, Blue Feather Press,
         Santa Fe, NM.
5th Edition: *The Inner Guide Meditation: A Transformative Journey
         to Enlightenment and Awareness,* 1982, The Aquarian Press,
         London, England.

Library of Congress Catalog Card Number: 85-51591

ISBN 0-87728-657-4
BJ

Cover illustration is a painting titled *Aquarius Rising.*
Copyright © 1988 Joe Rizzo. Used by kind permission.

Printed in the United States of America

The paper used in this publication meets the minimum requirements of the
American National Standard for Information Sciences—Permanence of
Paper for Printed Library Materials Z39.48-1992(R1997).

Contents

Acknowledgments

Grateful acknowledgment is made to Inner Traditions International, Ltd., 1 Park Street, Rochester, VT 05767; Oxford University Press, 200 Madison Avenue, New York, NY 10016; Princeton University Press, Princeton, NJ 08540; the Sabian Publishing Society, 2324 Norman Road, Stanwood, WA 98292; and to Mitch Walker/Treeroots Press, P. O. Box 684, Berkeley, CA 94704, for their kind permissions to utilize materials from their respective publications.

I would also like to thank all the people and groups, past and present, who have helped in their many and varied ways to produce this present work. Special thanks to my parents, Edwin E. and Helen S. Steinbrecher, to my God-mother, Josephine M. Siska — the real founder of D.O.M.E. — who introduced my family to astrology and metaphysics, to David Benge, Maggie Bott, Stephen P. Connors, Maryanne Hastings, Michael Sean Tierney, and John Woodsmall of D.O.M.E., the Inner Guide Meditation Center, for their inspiration and support over the years, to Steven Hechter for always appearing to help edit and advise just when I have to get a new edition out, to Leigh McCloskey, Carol Hurd Rodgers and Sheila W. Ross for their beautiful artwork for this book, to Karl T. Tani for both his graphics and his tarot illustrations, and to my five known Inner Guides, Aman, George, Ta, Emily and Simon.

Foreword

The investigation of the inner world of the soul has long been the special province of what is known as occultism. Some forms of religion have also attempted much the same task — especially the Eastern ones — limited, however, by some original revelation which hampered the free reign of scientific method. It is only in relatively recent times that some schools of modern psychology have turned their attention to that same area, and in the process of doing so developed their own peculiar techniques. The latter, curiously enough, bear many resemblances to the more archaic methods that are referred to as occult.

The author of this little handbook on meditation deserves an enormous amount of credit for first having approached the possibility of such methods through the medium of analytical psychology, the method of Carl G. Jung. Since Steinbrecher was an astrologer years before becoming an analyst and, it did not take him long to perceive relationships and thus to attempt some kind of unification of these different sets of ideas and techniques. So his handbook describes an amalgam of Jung's use of creative imagination, astrology and the tarot. The author evidently knows what he is doing, for he has evolved a viable system of self-discovery with all sorts of fascinating overtones and undertones.

The book is clearly written, the technique vividly and plainly described so that there is little room for misunderstanding as to what the author means. The meditation often yields up entirely new and unexpected types of information and interpretation relative to the meaning of the tarot, for example, and their relation to the planetary symbols — and in turn to the psycho-physical structure of the student.

Steinbrecher's directions are unambiguous and should be intelligible to anybody with the least capacity for imaginative or occult work. I am certain this book, from the very tentative first edition of only a few years ago to the umpteenth yet to come, will go down in occult history as one of the most significant contributions to meditation in modern times. Edwin Steinbrecher deserves any praise and commendation that is handed out to him, for he has labored long and patiently in this field especially to make *The Inner Guide Meditation* the classic that it is well on its way to becoming.

Israel Regardie
Sedona, Arizona
1983

Preface to Revised Sixth Edition

It is now eighteen years since I discovered the Inner Guides as entities specific to each person and more than ten years since the first edition of *The Inner Guide Meditation* made its appearance in the world. My view of the meditation continues to evolve and expand. In a time when many systems for interacting with archetypes and working on the inner planes abound, I continue to regard the work with the Inner Guide and archetypes as the safest and most specific way available for touching Spirit and for learning the spiritual physics that governs everything in each of our perceived realities. I see the book as a primer for the 21st century shaman and the meditation as a spiritual technology for a technician of the sacred.

A shaman is one who works with super-nature, that which is beyond, but which interacts with and affects the physical plane. The shaman of today no longer requires the rigid doctrines and outdated traditions of other ages and times. The shaman is free — wherever he or she resides — to discover, test and develop his or her own unique spiritual path by working with personal Inner Guides. And the developed shaman, perhaps evolving into priest or priestess, is urgently needed for this post-Christian spiritual era we find ourselves in. Exclusive religious forms and bibles interpreted dogmatically have had their day. The time for outer gurus and hierarchical spiritual structures is done. We have left the influence of the autocratic Fish of the first phase of our Piscean Age, and we now can flow with the friendly Fish of the second phase.

Revisions and additions to this work will necessarily continue until my death, since the wisdom given by interaction with the archetypes and the knowledge others bring from their own inner experiences continue the revelatory process. I feel like a man polishing a gem to enable it to reflect and refract more Light.

May this book continue to reach and touch the lives of all of you who have asked for a way to journey within to your own spiritual sources. Blessed be your knowledge of Spirit. Sacred is your Path.

Edwin C. Steinbrecher
D.O.M.E.
The Inner Guide Meditation Center
Los Angeles, California
November, 1987

D.O.M.E.
Dei Omnes Munda Edunt

All the Gods and Goddesses
bring forth the worlds

Initiators' Creed of D.O.M.E.

This I know: the flow of universal energies through me and my response to this flow create my personal reality. Bringing myself and these energies into harmony heals my experienced world. The inner worlds generate the outer world, and the source of all is within. The Inner Guides are our teachers and advisors in our personal quests for wholeness and spiritual enlightenment. Work with these inner teachers in the Inner Guide Meditation facilitates achievement of these goals. Each of us carries total responsibility, without blame, for the world that is individually experienced and cannot disclaim responsibility for any portion of it. Work with the Inner Guide can bring this world into a state of harmony and balance. To kill, injure or cause harm, either physical or psychological, to a fellow being injures and causes harm to the individual God-flow. Expansion of individual consciousness expands the consciousness of all beings.

Turn inward for your voyage!
For all your arts
You will not find the Stone
In foreign parts.

> *Angelus Silesius,*
> *Alchemist*

Part 1

BASIC CONCEPTS

Introduction

Times of great change are times of stress for both individuals and collective groups of people. As a child during the Great Depression and as a teenager during World War II, I was impressed by the struggle of the people around me to find meaning and significance for their lives, to rise above the mundane or the tragic in personal quests for Spirit. But I also saw that the tools and paths offered to these people didn't seem to work for them in their everyday lives. Then the horror of Korea and Vietnam demonstrated that war was obsolete, that the polarization of Good and Evil of World War II was done and that nothing could ever be black or white again. Everything had become some shade of grey with no one being right, no one being wrong. The late 60's and early 70's brought with them a great variety of spiritual tools and teachers. Too many of these seemed to be a way to run away from life and problems, of separating the spiritual from daily life, instead of bringing the two together. I didn't want once-a-week spirituality. I wanted Spirit to infuse my life twenty-four hours a day, every day. And, when my wanting was at its most intense, I discovered my Inner Guide; then the meditation slowly came together from different parts of my life and experience.

The Inner Guide Meditation is the product of the mingling of a number of spiritual and philosophical streams: astrology, tarot, alchemy, analytical psychology, qabalah and the Western Mystery Tradition, which contains the Judaeo-Graeco-Christian spiritual heritage of the West. From this synthesis of potent currents comes a spiritual technology in which the Guides—humanity's lost teachers—appear, fresh, alive and waiting to serve the individual spiritual quest; to lead us toward the "Kingdom of Heaven" to be found within each of us. The Inner Guide Meditation is a transformative process that assimilates the disparate energies which exist

Figure 1. The Guides—humanity's lost teachers—appear, fresh, alive and waiting to serve the individual spiritual quest; to lead us toward the Kingdom of Heaven to be found within each of us. Engraving by Gustave Doré from Dante's *Inferno*.

in the human psyche into the unified wholeness that is the enlightened being inherent in each of us. This unification ends the illusions which cause separation, guilt, fear and judgement. With the mediation of the Inner Guides, problems once unapproachable and unchangeable become fulfilling challenges, bringing forth productive and creative life responses.

Astrology provides the only available "road map" of the inner and outer worlds that I have been able to find. An astrological chart diagrams the multi-dimensional physics of the unconscious. It shows the structural relationships among the reality-creating, reality-sustaining energies each of us carries. The tarot provides pictures of these energies, each containing living aspects of Spirit, so that our individual egos can experience and comprehend them. Both alchemy and analytical psychology furnish us with conceptual methods through which we can assimilate these particular energies, allowing us to understand and incorporate within ourselves the living substance of our individual world perceptions. The qabalah and the Western Mystery Tradition give us time-tested tools with which to work and experiment in the inner dimensions. And our Inner Guides give us the love, teaching, guidance and necessary protection as we follow the path of our individual and collective Becoming.

Analytical psychology is the system of thought and therapeutic practice developed by the Swiss psychiatrist, Carl G. Jung, Sigmund Freud's pupil and protégé. The psychological terms used in this book, such as *ego, Shadow, active imagination, persona, collective unconscious, Self, projection, anima, animus and archetype* were, in the main, developed by Dr. Jung, and I am deeply indebted to this great, courageous innovator for them. In his *Two Essays on Analytical Psychology* Jung says:

> The experience of the archetype is frequently guarded as the closest personal secret, because it is felt to strike into the very core of one's being. . . . [These experiences] demand to be individually shaped in and by each man's life and work. They are images sprung from the life, the joys and sorrows, of our ancestors; and to live they seek to return, not in experience only, but in deed. Because of their opposition to the conscious

mind they cannot be translated straight into our world; hence a way must be found that can mediate between conscious and unconscious reality.[1]

The Inner Guide Meditation gives each of us that way.

The Archetypes

Living energies that contain ideas and information are called archetypes. They are specific patterns of instinctual behavior and thought, the forces that make up the collective unconscious — the impersonal part of humanity's psyche that all of us share. These archetypes *automatically* project themselves *outwardly* from within us onto whatever "screens" are available. The man we dislike instantly, "love-at-first-sight," a fondness or antipathy for dogs or cats, a peace-inducing picture of Buddha or some favorite landscape or poster, the *Playboy* centerfold, the bag lady, the frocked priest, *Whistler's Mother* — each of these images acts as a screen for forces that live in us; and each draws the energies to itself which fit. Powered by some unknown central Sun within us, these energies are living, intelligent forces which have particular life functions and which weave the fabric that we regard as our personal realities. They somehow attach themselves, without our conscious awareness, to everything we meet in the world we call real. Attaching themselves to inanimate objects, the archetypal energies infuse these objects with positive or negative "meaning," creating what we identify as our "lucky" coins or the "personalities" of our automo-

---

[1] *The Collected Works of C. G. Jung*, ed. Herbert Read, Michael Fordham, Gerhard Adler, William McGuire; trans. R. F. C. Hull, Bollingen Series XX, vol. 7, *Two Essays on Analytical Psychology*, © 1953, 1966 by Princeton University Press, pp. 78–79, used by permission.

biles. Attaching or projecting themselves onto living entities, they both influence the behavior of those entities and draw back onto themselves a corresponding projection, *always* functioning as a two-way street — therefore, "If I'm projecting on you, then you're projecting on me."

These archetypes are the life energies that pour out of us unceasingly night and day, asleep and awake, influencing everyone in our lives and causing us to be influenced in return. They mold and change our behaviors. They shape the very structure of our lives, but remain invisible to normal ego consciousness, almost always functioning beneath the level of ego awareness. In each human being they constellate in an individual and unique pattern. They form the "machinery of the universe," shaping and reshaping our realities. They are the energies that cause change and fluctuation in our affairs and relationships. These processes are unknown to each of our personal egos, that person we see when we look into our mirrors. By "ego" I mean the persona or mask each of us wears, that body-mind being that includes our physical vehicles, how we think about ourselves and how others define us.

If you have ever seen someone's ego or personality undergoing a Jekyll/Hyde transformation when he or she becomes "high" or drunk, or seen someone become psychotic or "freak out" on drugs to the point where he or she becomes someone or something else, you have witnessed one or more of the archetypes or the Freudian "id" displacing or taking over the normal ego. In these situations the person becomes flat and two-dimensional for the ego loses its stability and sinks into unconsciousness. In schizophrenia, for instance, the usurping archetype in control seeks only its own gratification, while the other inner archetypal energies starve. This is, perhaps, why schizophrenia is usually a deteriorating disease unless the other archetypal forces can be brought back into balance and a strong ego resurrected. The inner archetypes must be in balance, each working with the others and with the ego, for harmony to exist in the life.

Once archetypes have projected out onto the screen of an object, situation or person, they resist removal from the screen until their needs have been satisfied. As an extreme example, if the alcoholic can resist that first drink, he or she may be able to control

the archetypal forces; if not, the unleashed power of the unconscious archetype projected onto the alcohol is in control. If the first
action in any compulsive behavior chain can be avoided, the acting
out of the compulsion may be inhibited, giving more time for the
development of new habit patterns that can transform the compulsion into behavior more useful to the individual.

Hence the archetypes are those energies which create and sustain our personal realities — aspects of God, if you will, that are
experientially available to each and all of us.

The Tarot

The tarot cards are the most easily obtainable set of picture symbols of archetypal energies available to Westerners. The tarot deck
has seventy-eight cards which are divided into two sections: the
Major Arcana or Trumps consisting of the twenty-two main
images, and the Minor Arcana containing the remaining fifty-six
cards. These cards of unknown origin appeared in Europe around
the end of the 13th century. They are the ancestors of our modern
playing cards. The Major Arcana contain images of twenty-two
universal archetypal forces. These are named the *Fool*, the *Magician*, the *High Priestess*, the *Empress* or *Queen*, the *Emperor* or
King, the *High Priest* or *Hierophant*, the *Twins* or *Lovers*, the
Chariot, *Strength*, the *Hermit*, the *Wheel of Fortune*, *Justice*, the
Hanged Man, *Death*, *Temperance*, *Old Pan* or the *Devil*, the
Lightning-Struck Tower, the *Star*, the *Moon*, the *Sun*, the *Last
Judgement* or *Resurrection* and the *World*. They relate astrologically to the twelve signs of the zodiac, the eight planets (excluding
Earth), the Sun and the Moon. (It is interesting to note that the
architects of the tarot provided images or slots for Uranus, Nep-
tune and Pluto, although these planets were not discovered until
more than four hundred years after the tarot's initial appearance,

Uranus being discovered in 1781, Neptune in 1846 and Pluto in 1930.)

In his *Archetypes of the Collective Unconscious,* Carl Jung refers to the pictures of the tarot as being descended from archetypes of transformation.[2] These twenty-two symbolic pictures are images of archetypal energies which project out of each of us to establish and sustain the reality we perceive around ourselves—the form of each individual world, its characters, and the human relationships we experience. (This is most apparent to anyone versed in the art and science of astrology.)

These archetypal energies exist in what physicists and brain scientists refer to as a *primary frequency realm.* Karl Pribram, a neuroscientist from Stanford University in California, theorizes a "primary reality" which is a "frequency domain," an "invisible matrix," that produces the universe as a hologram. The twenty-two archetypal energy–forms pictured in the tarot are the specific energies that come from this primary frequency realm to create and sustain the holographic universe we perceive.

Astrology

A natal horoscope calculated for the year, month, day and exact minute of an individual's birth at the exact latitude and longitude of the birthplace provides the blueprint of that individual's life experience—the plot for the "movie"—the world, both inner and outer, through that specific individual's eyes. Over the days and months and years, the inner cycles that correspond to the planets' movements in the heavens activate components in that individual

---

[2]*The Collected Works of C. G. Jung*, trans. R. F. C. Hull, Bollingen Series XX, vol. 9, part 1, *Archetypes of the Collective Unconscious* (Princeton, NJ: Princeton University Press, 1969), p. 38.

blueprint, causing the movie to live itself out. Not only can a competent astrologer recount your life events from your natal horoscope; he or she can also describe what is taking place or has taken place in the lives of everyone you are related to through blood, law or role relationship. For example, the astrologer can describe your eldest sister's current marriage crisis, dates of recent chaos or luck in your own love area, your third child's difficulties at school, or the erratic behavior of your employer—all from *your own natal pattern*, without knowledge of any of these other people's lives or birth patterns. He or she can describe the personalities and physical characteristics of parents, aunts, uncles and vaguely remembered distant relatives you might not have seen since childhood. The astrologer can tell of troubled areas in the lives of first and second

Table 1. Symbols and Rulerships of the 12 Signs of the Zodiac.

Sign	Element	Ruler
Aries ♈	Cardinal fire	Mars ♂
Taurus ♉	Fixed earth	Venus ♀
Gemini ♊	Mutable air	Mercury ☿
Cancer ♋	Cardinal water	Moon ☽
Leo ♌	Fixed fire	Sun ☉
Virgo ♍	Mutable earth	Mercury ☿
Libra ♎	Cardinal air	Venus ♀
Scorpio ♏	Fixed water	Pluto ♇
Sagittarius ♐	Mutable fire	Jupiter ♃
Capricorn ♑	Cardinal earth	Saturn ♄
Aquarius ♒	Fixed air	Uranus ♅
Pisces ♓	Mutable water	Neptune ♆

Table 2. Symbols of the Planets.

Sun	⊙	Jupiter	♃
Moon	☽	Saturn	♄
Mercury	☿	Uranus	♅
Venus	♀	Neptune	♆
Mars	♂	Pluto	♇

cousins in remote parts of the world. In fact, the astrologer can give intimate life details and concise dates — past and present — about anyone in your family or any close associate after whom you choose to inquire — again, all from your own horoscope, not from the horoscopes of your relatives or associates.

When a stranger — the astrologer — is able to deliver this sort of accurate personal information, it illustrates that some sort of machinery is at work in which you, yourself, are the major cog. It soon becomes apparent that more than coincidence is involved.

How are you connected to brother Joe's broken leg? What is your relation to sister Jan's religious conversion? Are *you* to blame for the "bad" things described in your horoscope that occur in your life? Are you to be credited with the "good?" And if you *are* somehow connected to all these events and people, as the astrologer will have demonstrated, can *you* make things better for all concerned?

Astrology is a language of symbols. It allows you to make connections and see relationships that are invisible or obscure in other systems of thought. Some basic symbols used in astrology are shown in Tables 1 and 2.

If anyone ever says to you that he doesn't believe in astrology, you can be sure that he never has studied it; he's just being superstitious. Even superficial study with a competent astrologer will quickly demonstrate the truth of this ancient science.

Projection

The theory of solipsism states that nothing can be known and verified except through the perceptions of the *knower*, the individual ego. If we begin with this philosophical view and look for verification of the theory, we will find that astrology furnishes evidence that this may well be so. A correct horoscope describes *everything* in a person's life, all that will occur and be perceived throughout the person's lifetime, the person's total subjective reality, manifesting according to the person's degree of consciousness. However, until the person *experiences* how the perceived reality is being created, how the sources of that reality create *through* the person from some inner place of origin, there is no way to understand the different ways many people's realities fit and work together.

Let us return to the twenty-two archetypal forces that the tarot images represent. These forces or energies are projecting out from each of us all of the time, establishing the realities we find ourselves experiencing. If one of these archetypes is repressed, pushed away from the level of ego consciousness into the dark depths of the psyche, it is rendered "negative" or "evil" to our ego judgments. It then functions as a negative hook or magnet for experience in our outer worlds, drawing to us or to our "parts" (those to whom we are related in some way) the very quality we had attempted to avoid through repression.

If one considers them as the pure energy which they are, none of the archetypal forces is or can be essentially "good" or "evil." They are *neutral*, but potent, energies capable of presenting themselves as either. It is their degree of repression or suppression, if any, that makes them appear as "good" or "bad," "positive" or "negative," "plus" or "minus," as they project out into our lives, creating the realities we experience. The level at which our egos assimilate or reject them determines how we judge the manifestations they create. If we change the ego relationship to the archetypal force within ourselves, we will change the projected "screen" as it exists in our outer worlds. What we label "evil" or "bad" are those forces within ourselves that we have pushed into unconsciousness, which then act on those receptive or needful screens in our environments. The illusion of "evil" is created by the repression of energy. "Evil" is unconsciousness. Those who are concerned about its prevalence in their lives might well attempt to seek the source within themselves. "Evil" results from ignorance of the way the multi-dimensional laws of the Universe work.

The psychoanalytical school of psychology regards repression as an essential defense mechanism which the ego uses unconsciously to reject from awareness any disagreeable or painful ideas, feelings, desires, memories or impulses, so that the ego can cope with its world. But this doesn't work. The repressed material then exteriorizes and has to be dealt with in the outer world.

Here is an astrological example. The planet Mars (called *The Lightning-Struck Tower* in tarot) has to do with our instinctual animal vitality. It signifies much sexual force and aggressive life "go" energy. If it is *suppressed*, that is, the forces symbolized by this planet are suppressed, or consciously excluded from awareness, the usual manifestation in us will be irritability or anger, temper or "pushiness." If Mars exists as a *repressed* force within — for example, if it is located in the 12th section (or *house*) of a horoscope where those forces *which we are born with as repressed factors* reside — it can act as a negative magnet in our realities and draw extreme anger or violence down upon us. It may cause health or work traumas in our partners' lives, without any ego awareness of participation in or connection to those traumas.

Jesus taught, "The Kingdom of Heaven is **within** you." However, we keep looking everywhere but within for our solutions and our peace. The process of receiving from within is the major key to expanding consciousness, but we are conditioned from childhood to look without. Our parents, our teachers and our peers dismiss the inner worlds with such typical responses as: "It's only your imagination," or "Be realistic — quit dreaming," or "You're just putting yourself on." The "imaginary" playmates of sensitive children are discouraged, ignored or "trained" out, causing the children to lose their keys to the inner worlds, perhaps forever. How many of our evangelists, gurus, rabbis, priests or spirit guide channelers encourage this individual quest within, this inner search for the Kingdom of Heaven? Such a quest might weaken or remove their own imposed authority, the authority of their own personal "king"-dom. Everyone is encouraged to understand and believe through another's experiences or dogma — few of us are encouraged to

Figure 2. The *Tower* is associated with the planet Mars and has to do with our instinctual animal vitality. It signifies much sexual force and aggressive life ''go'' energy. Illustration from the tarot deck in *Seed*, Crown Publishers, New York, 1969. Used by permission.

embark on our own inner journeys, to establish our own spiritual individualities. We tend to look for our teachers or gurus in the outer world — few look within where this teacher actually exists.

Projection is the unconscious phenomenon which acts to transmit our inner archetypes onto the available screens in our outer worlds. This can be most easily noted in those people and things one actively dislikes or hates. Whatever is uncomfortable to the current ego generally becomes repressed. It gets pushed down into the darkness within us where we become unaware of it. But this process does not get rid of the problem. Instead, the repression, which is an expenditure of *directional* psychic energy (*down*, away from the ego, away from the light of consciousness into the darkness of unconsciousness), acts as a magnet. This magnet then draws from the outer world those very qualities our egos have rejected, because the force being pushed away *will have its equal expression in some way*. Since some kind of outer screen is always available to us, projection takes place. The outer screen presents the hook or passive psychic structure to which the "hang-up," neurosis, or unconscious material attaches itself by the mechanism of projection. The receiver fills with the qualities and energies of the repressed material causing our egos to react with "hate" or "dislike." For instance, the paranoid personality has submerged an archetype having to do with aggression and unconsciously projects it out into his world. He then believes everyone is attacking him.

Some projections are considered "good" or desirable by the social norms or current standards of the collective unconscious which condition the values and beliefs that our egos hold. Falling in love, as opposed to *loving*, is one of the most prevalent forms of "approved" projection in human society. It is Nature's trick that brings couples together to perpetuate the species. When we "fall in love," we experience the projection of some *ideal* archetypal part of ourselves onto the screen of another person who serves as a receiver for that ideal. The archetype imposes on the "loved one" a whole range of potential desires, behavior patterns, emotional responses and psychological "sets," all nourished by the psychological expectations of the person projecting the archetype. "Falling in love" is literally loving a part of oneself which the projection process places on the screen of another being. This displacement and reception of a part of one's being causes the bliss of love, if the other willingly

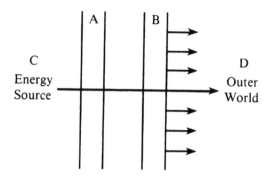

Figure 3. Diagram of the mechanics of the process of projection.

receives and responds to it, or the pain of love, if the other rejects or only partially accepts the projection. "Falling in love" makes demands on the other, willing or unwilling. "Loving," on the other hand, is free and giving; it requires nothing in return, has no expectations, accepts the other without judgment or reservation, and wants only that which can be freely and willingly given out of the other's Self. The relationships where "falling in love" turns into "loving" as the initial projection wanes are those that endure with the greatest depth and beauty.

Projection sends component energies of the Self, the central part of each of us, out into the world. When these energies remain unconscious to the person projecting them, the result is a loss of psychic energy and freedom. When the energies are made conscious (with ego and Self being brought into balance through the ego's willingness to serve as vehicle for the Self), the result is a free individual who radiates light and love into the world. In contrast, when two individuals are involved in a deeply repressed projection, both experience a curtailment of the freedom of their individual egos and subsequent energy loss. You can be sure that you are involved in a deep-seated unconscious projection with any person whose mere physical presence exhausts you for no apparent reason. Most often this "exhaustion relationship" can be found with a member of your immediate family, usually one of your parents. Experiment the next time you encounter such an individual. Don't *expect* the old responses and behavior. Let the person be *new*, and send love out of your heart *consciously*. Love is the greatest freeing energy we have. You may be surprised at the results for you both.

Figure 3 is a diagram of the mechanics of the process of projection. Let us call A the blueprint or "set film strip" of an individual: in astrology this would be symbolized by the natal horoscope of the person. Let B represent the ego structure which is being constantly shifted and modified by the forces activating it from A: this B in astrology would be the rising sign or Ascendant of a horoscope. Together A and B constitute the moving film or inherent flowing pattern of a life. As long as the source energy, C, flows unconsciously along our nerve channels from within to without through this film, *free will remains an ego illusion*. But when, through meditation, the ego attempts to move along these same flow channels *back* toward its own source or center (C in the diagram), an assimilation and consciousness of these source-energies begins, and one can then make real choices and become truly free. Freedom is *impossible* so long as we think of D, the outer world and its elements, as the source or basis of our realities. It is only when we learn that the foundation of our realities lies within that we find ourselves on the road to individual freedom and consciousness, no longer able to take the role of victim of circumstances. How long have we heard of the "Kingdom within" without really understanding what this means? Free will is not a "given." It must be earned, and the price of consciousness and free will is the death and rebirth of the current ego.

Assume for a moment that the unconscious contains various adjacent levels. Let us say that there are four levels, each containing a greater degree of darkness (unconsciousness) as they exist in a progressive relationship away from the awareness of the ego. In these four successive levels of the unconscious live all the energies that create and sustain our experienced realities. Here lie our psychic capabilities, the body's abilities to maintain and repair itself, the monitor of breathing and heart action, our forgotten memories, our latent dreams, the central Sun or Source we each carry — all that we are unaware of. The unconscious is both a storehouse and a center of creation, a place of secrets and hidden things, of joy and terror.

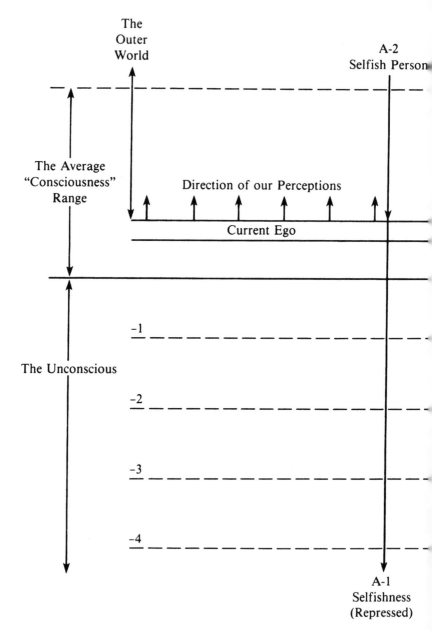

Figure 4. The projection process illustrating a repression of an energy constellation.

Figure 4 is an example of the projection process illustrating a repression of an energy constellation, the quality called *Selfishness* (A-1 in the diagram), into the darkness of the unconscious. Let us say that an individual has this quality repressed within at the level called Minus 4 in the diagram, the level furthest from ego awareness where the deepest repressions dwell. A directional expenditure of psychic energy is required to keep it pushed to this depth, away from any ego awareness. A balancing component of some sort from the outer world is required to stabilize the negative energy at the depth of unconsciousness. The psychic radar which exists in all of us searches our environments and draws to us from the outer world (A-2) the person or persons who have the need to live out this quality of selfishness and will accept the projection of this energy constellation from us because of their corresponding unconsciousness.

All of our repressed or suppressed energies take on the qualities of the levels of darkness in which they exist. The qualities of the level of unconsciousness in which they live within us determine how they manifest out in our worlds. When we push our own creative energies away from the awareness of our egos, we will draw to ourselves creative people who will live those energies out for us. When we push our hate into the darkness, we will draw the hateful into our worlds so that those energies can have their expression. All that we brand "bad" or "evil" in our worlds act as mirrors of our own unconsciousness. Jesus' advice to "Love thine enemies" is good contemporary advice, for nothing heals and brings forth our negative parts transformed, within and without, as does the power of love.

You *yourself* hold the unique key to your own self development and spiritual evolution. No one outside you holds that key. To change anything in your personal reality effectively or permanently, you must seek the cause of its current reality manifestation at its point of origin, or as close to that point as you are able to, within yourself. As long as unconscious projection is taking place, everyone in your outer world is literally some part of yourself functioning as the perceived ego of the other—*all* are actors in the movie *you* are starring in, taking their positive and negative roles to fit *your* particular movie script. Your current ego (what you presently consider yourself to be) acts as a membrane between the

Figure 5. The unconscious is both a storehouse and a center of creation, a place of secrets and hidden things, of joy and terror. Engraving by Gustave Doré from Milton's *Paradise Lost*.

forces flowing out of you onto your world and the forces flowing back onto and into you from the other projecting entities in your personal reality. Until you can experience how your projecting energies are affecting others, you will never understand how their projections are affecting you in turn.

Active Imagination

Active imagination, an ancient metaphysical meditation tool redis-covered by Dr. Jung just before the beginning of World War I, is the primary technique utilized in the Inner Guide Meditation. In his discussions of alchemy, Jung compares the process of active imagi-nation to the production of the Philosopher's Stone of the alche-mists. He describes the process in *Mysterium Coniunctionis*:

> [Active imagination] . . . is a method which is used spontane-ously by nature herself or can be taught. . . . As a rule it occurs when the analysis has constellated the opposites so powerfully that a union or synthesis of the personality becomes an imper-ative necessity. Such a situation is bound to arise when the analysis of the psychic contents, of the patient's attitude and particularly of his dreams, has brought the compensatory or complementary images from the unconscious so insistently before his mind that the conflict between the conscious and the unconscious personality becomes open and critical. When this confrontation is confined to partial aspects of the unconscious the conflict is limited and the solution simple: the patient, with insight and some resignation or a feeling of resentment, places himself on the side of reason and convention. Though the unconscious motifs are repressed again, as before, the uncon-scious is satisfied to a certain extent, because the patient must now make a conscious effort to live according to its principles and, in addition, is constantly reminded of the existence of the

repressed by annoying resentments. But if his recognition of the Shadow is as complete as he can make it, then conflict and disorientation ensue, an equally strong Yes and No which he can no longer keep apart by a rational decision. He cannot transform his clinical neurosis into the less conspicuous neurosis of cynicism; in other words, he can no longer hide the conflict behind a mask. It requires a real solution and necessitates a third thing in which the opposition can unite. Here the logic of the intellect usually fails, for in a logical antithesis there is no third. The "solvent" can only be of an irrational nature. In nature the resolution of opposites is always an energic process: she acts *symbolically* in the truest sense of the word, doing something that expresses both sides, just as a waterfall visibly mediates between above and below. The waterfall itself is then the incommensurable third. In an open and unresolved conflict dreams and fantasies occur which, like the waterfall, illustrate the tension and nature of the opposites, and thus prepare the synthesis.

This process can, as I have said, take place spontaneously or be artificially induced. In the latter case you choose a dream, or some other fantasy-image, and concentrate on it by simply catching hold of it and looking at it. You can also use a bad mood as a starting-point, and then try to find out what sort of fantasy-image it will produce, or what image expresses this mood. You then fix this image in the mind by concentrating your attention. Usually it will alter, as the mere fact of contemplating it animates it. The alterations must be carefully noted down all the time, for they reflect the psychic processes in the unconscious background, which appear in the form of images consisting of conscious memory material. In this way conscious and unconscious are united, just as a waterfall connects above and below. A chain of fantasy ideas develops and gradually takes on a dramatic character: the passive process becomes an action. At first it consists of projected figures, and these images are observed like scenes in the theatre. . . . As a rule there is a marked tendency simply to enjoy this interior entertainment and to leave it at that. Then, of course, there is no real progress but only endless variations on the same theme, which is not the point of the exercise at all. What is enacted on the stage still remains a background process; it does not move the observer in any way, and the less it moves him the smaller will be the cathartic effect of this private theatre. The piece that is being played does not want merely to be watched impartially, it wants to compel his participation. If the observer understands that his own drama is being performed on this inner stage, he cannot remain indifferent to the plot and its denouement. He will notice, as the actors appear one by one and the plot thickens, that they all have some purposeful relationship to his conscious situation, that he is being addressed by the unconscious, and that it causes these fantasy-images to appear before him. He therefore feels compelled, or is encouraged . . . to take part in the play and, instead of just sitting in a theatre, really have it out with his alter ego. For nothing in us ever remains quite uncontradicted, and consciousness can take up no position which will not call up, somewhere in the dark corners of the psyche, a negation or a compensatory effect, approval or resentment. This process of coming to terms with the Other (the other half or Shadow side of ourselves) in us is well worthwhile, because in this way we get to know aspects of our natures which we would not allow anybody else to show us and which we ourselves would never have admitted. It is very important to fix this whole procedure in writing at the time of its occurrence, for you then have ocular evidence that will effectively counteract the ever-ready tendency to self–deception. A running commentary is absolutely necessary in dealing with the Shadow, because otherwise its actuality cannot be fixed. Only in this . . . way is it possible to gain a positive insight into the complex nature of one's own personality.[3]

Here Jung outlines the technique of active imagination, although he presents it within the structure of an analytical relationship between doctor and patient. The technique is a process of interacting with and gradually assimilating, as a result of these

[3] *The Collected Works of C. G. Jung*, ed. by G. Adler, M. Fordham, and H. Read; trans. R. F. C. Hull, Bollingen Series XX, vol. 14, *Mysterium Coniunctionis*, © 1963 by Bollingen Foundation, reprinted by permission of Princeton University Press.

interactions, those parts of ourselves that our current egos are ignorant of or have only partially assimilated. It is an invaluable experiential process, and in the Inner Guide Meditation it brings back to the Guide that energy and wisdom which up to now we have projected out from within us onto analyst, priest, guru, psychic or spirit guide channeler.

Becoming Conscious

Plato's "Allegory of the Cave" from *The Republic* beautifully illustrates aspects of the process of projection and of becoming conscious. Here Socrates speaks to Glaucon:

"Imagine the condition of men living in a sort of cavernous chamber underground, with an entrance open to the light and a long passage all down the cave. Here they have been from childhood, chained by the leg and also by the neck, so that they cannot move and can see only what is in front of them, because the chains will not let them turn their heads. At some distance higher up is the light of a fire burning behind them; and between the prisoners and the fire is a track with a parapet built along it, like the screen at a puppet-show, which hides the performers while they show their puppets over the top."

"Now behind this parapet imagine persons carrying along various artificial objects, including figures of men and animals in wood or stone or other materials, which project above the parapet. Naturally, some of these persons will be talking, others silent."

"It is a strange picture," he said, "and a strange sort of prisoners."

"Like ourselves," I [Socrates] replied; "for in the first place prisoners so confined would have seen nothing of themselves or of one another, except the shadows thrown by the fire-light on the wall of the cave facing them, would they?"

"Not if all their lives they had been prevented from moving their heads."

"And they would have seen as little of the objects carried past."

"Of course."

"Now, if they could talk to one another, would they not suppose that their words referred only to those passing shadows which they saw?"

"Necessarily."

"And suppose their prison had an echo from the wall facing them? When one of the people crossing behind them spoke, they could only suppose that the sound came from the shadow passing before their eyes."

"No doubt."

"In every way, then, such prisoners would recognize as reality nothing but the shadow of those artificial objects."

"Inevitably."

"Now consider what would happen if their release from the chains and the healing of their unwisdom should come about in this way. Suppose one of them was set free and forced suddenly to stand up, turn his head, and walk with eyes lifted in the light; all these movements would be painful, and he would be too dazzled to make out the objects whose shadows he had been used to seeing. What do you think he would say, if someone told him what he had formerly seen was meaningless illusion, but now, being somewhat nearer to reality and turned towards more real objects, he was getting a truer view? Suppose further that he were shown then various objects being carried by and were made to say, in reply to questions, what each of them was. Would he not be perplexed and believe the objects now shown to him to be not so real as what he formerly saw?"

"Yes, not nearly so real."

"And if he were forced to look at the fire-light itself, would not his eyes ache, so that he would try to escape and turn back to the things which he could see distinctly, convinced that they really were clearer to him than these other objects now being shown him?"

"Yes."

"And suppose someone were to drag him away forcibly up the steep and rugged ascent and not let him go until he had hauled him out into the sunlight, would he not suffer pain and vexation at such treatment, and, when he had come out into the light, find his eyes so full of its radiance that he could not see a single one of the things that he was now told were real?"

"Certainly he would not see them all at once."

"He would need, then, to grow accustomed before he could see things in that upper world. At first it would be easiest to make out shadows, and then the images of men and things reflected in water, and later on the things themselves. After that, it would be easier to watch the heavenly bodies, and the sky itself by night, looking at the light of the moon and stars rather than the sun and the sun's light in the day-time."

"Yes, surely."

"Last of all, he would be able to look at the sun and contemplate its nature, not as it appears when reflected in water or any alien medium, but as it is in itself in its own domain."

"No doubt."

"And now he would begin to draw the conclusion that it is the sun that produces the seasons and the course of the year and controls everything in the visible world, and moreover is in a way the cause of all that he and his companions used to see."

"Clearly he would come at last to that conclusion."

"Then if he called to mind his fellow prisoners and what passed for wisdom in his former dwelling place, he would surely think himself happy in the change and be sorry for them. They may have had a practice of honoring and commending one another, with prizes for the man who had the keenest eye for the passing shadows and the best memory for the order in which they followed or accompanied one another, so that he could make a good guess as to which was going to come next. Would our released prisoner be likely to covet those prizes or to envy the men exalted to honor and power in the cave? Would he not feel like Homer's Achilles, that he would far sooner 'be on earth as a hired servant in the house of a landless man' (Achilles' statement in Hades) or endure anything rather than go back to his old beliefs and live in the old way?"

"Yes, he would prefer any fate to such a life."

"Now imagine what would happen if he went down again to take his former seat in the cave. Coming suddenly out of the sunlight, his eyes would be filled with darkness. He might be required once more to deliver his opinion on those shadows, in competition with the prisoners who had never been released, while his eyesight was still dim and unsteady; and it might take some time to become used to the darkness. They would laugh at him and say that he had gone up only to come back with his sight ruined; it was worth no one's while even to attempt the ascent. If they could lay hands on the man who was trying to set them free and lead them up, they would kill him."

"Yes, they would."[4]

What we perceive in our outer realities are but shadows cast by inner images, made visible by some unknown light or central Sun within. "It's all in your head, y'know," said The Beatles. Perhaps not exactly in our heads, but somewhere within us or through the doors of ourselves lie the sources that present these animated shadows to us, that project on the world through a kind of holographic film strip each of us possesses or is. Also, we each have an inner liberator who will release us from our chains, and who will teach us to recognize those shadow-making images as he leads us toward the realization of Source. And, as he leads us toward that Source, he helps us become gradually more accustomed to the light, taking care that our inner eyes not be blinded. (Projection doesn't end with becoming conscious, or we would have no outer reality to experience. It just becomes conscious to the ego.)

"Shadow" pictures of Jesus and the Virgin on an old woman's living room wall seem to speak to her, giving her advice on her life affairs, consoling her in her griefs. A "shadow" Venus in a Botticelli *Birth of Venus* art print on a young man's bedroom wall presents an echo, whispering of the delight of womanhood and promising life's pleasures. A "shadow" masquerading as a shopkeeper's first dollar bill, framed and mounted above the shop counter, tells him of money to come, of stability, of business growth. A "shadow" presenting itself as a statue of Satan commands the "black magician."

These are all shadows in the exact sense that Plato speaks of them, but each individual will swear to their reality. All feel the source of the communication to be the image they can see or touch or imagine in their outer worlds. Each will argue for the validity of his or her particular "shadow" on the wall of his or her own "cave."

---

[4]Plato *The Republic*. trans. F. M. Cornford (New York: Oxford University Press, 1945), p. 227–231. Used by permission.

Figure 6. We each possess an inner liberator, who will release us from our chains. Engraving by Gustave Doré from *The Doré Bible Gallery*.

Just as a motion picture projector projects its images upon a screen, these shadows on which the individuals focus merely serve as screens for living forces being drawn or projected out from each of the people. From the old-woman, the shadow images of Jesus and Mary draw energies from the unconscious dealing with love and motherhood. Out of the young man, a force or energy having to do with the pleasure principle and physical love is pulled. The shopkeeper projects an organic growth force, and the black magician, a force dealing with power and paranoia. Because they are uneducated about how projection works, neither the old woman, the young man, the shopkeeper or the black magician is aware of the inner sources that the shadow images draw from and focus upon the outer world images or forms.

The Initial Experiments

In 1969 I was in Jungian analysis with an analytical psychologist in Los Angeles, California. It was going slowly, as analysis usually does. The analyst went off to Zurich on some business, and I was left with the forward-impelling inertia of someone whose unconscious has been activated.

I had been using the "active imagination" technique in my analytical sessions through my own insistence, going back to dreams and finishing or reworking them. I was fascinated by the living experiences I had while exploring my psyche. The analyst had emphasized the dangers of the active imagination process — of repressed unconscious forces that might overcome the ego and usurp it, of the terror that an encounter with repressed energy forms could trigger. But fire is fascinating to the unburned.

In the analyst's absence, I was experimenting with astrological and tarot imagery (I was an astrologer by profession at that time), attempting to puzzle out the psychological "physics" involved in getting information from the tarot cards. I deduced that the accu-

Figure 7. The archetype associated with Capricorn in astrology and with *Old Pan* or the *Devil* in tarot is one of the most severely repressed archetypes in Western civilization. Because of this, it is usually represented by ugly, threatening, or frightening forms. As our materialism and ignorance of spiritual law evolves into wisdom and understanding, our inner perception of this energy form will correspondingly evolve and change. Illustration of *D'Evil* from the tarot deck in *Seed*, published by Crown Publishers, New York, 1969. Used by permission.

rate data I was able to obtain from these readings must have its origins somewhere deep within my psyche. If, say, the *High Priestess* card could "tell" me of events happening in a distant city by projecting an energy force with this particular information from within me out onto a card screen, then how much more accurately could "she," the archetypal force of the *High Priestess*, communicate with me face to face in the inner world through the process of active imagination?

I had also at the time just finished reading Richard Wilhelm's translation of the Chinese classic, *The Secret of the Golden Flower*,[5] in which the secret seemed to be to "circulate the light backwards," or, as I interpreted it, to force the mental energy back along the same channels or nerve pathways that the projection energy flowed out on.

I attempted to do this in my imagination by inventing a staircase that would take me within to those archetypal images I was seeking. And it worked! I reached a room at the bottom of my stairway, thought of the *High Priestess*, and she was *there*, a *living* presence in that inner world, different from the picture on the tarot card, but without a doubt the *High Priestess* as a reality within me. And the experience seemed to be happening *there*, in some other dimension or reality, totally unconnected with the *here* of the normally experienced outer world.

I was delighted with my new toy. It had a reality and a freshness I hadn't experienced since childhood, and there was no doubt about the experiential "realness" of it. I was with the *Sun*, and my body became warm and relaxed. The *Magician* taught me things I had never heard in my outer reality. The presence of the *Fool* would cause a "pins and needles" sensation in my limbs.

But then I had an experience that acutely demonstrated the analyst's warnings about the dangers of active imagination as it is practiced in analytical psychology. I was inside the room where I came into contact with the archetypal forms when an image of *Old Pan* or *Devil* appeared, unsummoned and unwanted. It was a classic Christian devil with an emanation of "evil" as real as the beneficence I had felt when interacting with the archetype of the *Sun*. I

---

[5]Richard Wilhelm and C. G. Jung, *The Secret of the Golden Flower*, (New York: Harvest, 1970).

tried to end the experience by opening my eyes, but I discovered that I was unable to move or perform this simple feat. I was paralyzed. I began to panic. I seemed to be frozen in the chair. The *Old Pan* entity became even more menacing than before, placing himself in my inner world between me and the stairway to the outer world and safety. The panic finally subsided (although not the fear), and I further tried to maneuver to the stairway around the figure, but to no avail. This entity of the inner world blocked my every move whenever I attempted the stairs. He did not advance toward me, but remained as a moving barrier to any possible exit. It even crossed my mind that I might be discovered by someone in the outer world who might think I had become catatonic, who might take me off to the nearest psychiatric hospital. I couldn't even call out to try to communicate my situation to anyone who might be within hearing.

Finally, I was able to calm myself and concentrate on my outer body sufficiently to try to move a finger on my right hand. Using all my will and ignoring the *Old Pan* figure entirely, I managed this feat, and it broke the state in which I had been locked. The experience was so frightening, however, that I decided then and there never again to attempt another venture into the realms of the inner worlds without the presence of a trained analyst.

A few months passed. Fear weakened with this passage of time, and curiosity increased. There *had* to be some *safe* way to go back "down there" without having to be dependent on an analyst's presence. It was so like a foreign country whose laws and customs I did not know. This analogy triggered the thought that perhaps "guides" existed there as they do in other foreign countries, their roles being created in response to travelers' needs. Throughout the myths, poetry, fairy tales and spiritual literature of the world, guides in some form have been spoken of or referred to—the spirit guides of trance mediums, the "still, small voice within," the *daemon* or tutelary spirit of the Greeks, the Guardian Angel we hear of in childhood, Dante's Virgil, Alice's White Rabbit, the Guides mentioned in the writings of Agni Yoga, the "Guardians" of the Pueblo Indians of North America. Perhaps if I attempted the descent once more . . .

All proceeded as before: I found my inner stairway and cautiously descended. I reached the bottom. The room was deserted.

Standing close to the stairs, I called out for a guide to appear. At first nothing happened, but then a feeling of love and warmth touched me from my left. Slowly I moved away from the staircase through an opening that I now noticed on the left. I passed through the opening, and, to the right of it, I saw an old, old man standing. He was dressed in striped robes of muted colors, had white whiskers, was of medium height and wore a turban. Kindness and gentleness radiated from him. I asked if he were a "guide." He responded that he was *my* Inner Guide and that his name was "Aman." I told him of my terrifying experience with the *Old Pan* energy, and he explained that it was my fear that had made the experience so potentially dangerous. I asked him if he could truly guide and teach me in this strange, beautiful, but frightening, inner world and if he could protect me from such experiences as I had had with *Old Pan*. He stated simply that he *had* always tried to guide and protect me and always would if I requested and allowed him to do so. And so began the inner adventure and the beginnings of true choice and freedom in my life.

I was at this time a conventional astrologer, delineating horoscopes for those who were referred to me, many by Jungian analysts. This became increasingly frustrating for me. It was like telling someone about the *trap* he or she had been born into without being able to give any key for transcending it. All that was given was a new rationalization system through the vocabulary of astrology — a novel, new mind game.

It was during this same time period that I was also experimenting with the tarot cards. It occurred to me that, as the twenty-two tarot images correspond to the primary astrological factors (twelve zodiacal signs, eight planets, the Sun and Moon), the entire horoscope or solar system birth pattern might be re-translated and expressed in terms of these tarot forms. Perhaps one could resolve the energy conflicts described in the horoscope by *arbitrating* the "quarrels" (astrological "hard angles" and polarizations) between the archetypal energies in the inner world, by allowing antagonistic energy systems to begin touching each other and restructuring their relationships and energy flows.

I did this re-translation with my own horoscope as the base. Where the planet Uranus was in 90° relationship (or *square* aspect) to the planet Saturn, I interpreted it as the *Fool* (Uranus) and the

Figure 8. The planet Uranus is associated with the archetype of the *Fool*, and the astrological sign of Sagittarius is symbolized by the horse. From 1981 to 1988, Uranus in Sagittarius brings the promise of new freedoms and ideas in philosophy, religion, meditation and ways of exploring within oneself. This illustration is "The Fool on the Horse—I," by Carol Hurd Rogers, 1983, in the D.O.M.E. collection. Used by permission.

World (Saturn) being antagonistic. Where Saturn was in a 180° relationship (or *opposition* aspect) to the planet Pluto, I transposed it to the *World* (Saturn) and the *Last Judgement* (Pluto) being polarized, and so on with all the so-called "afflictions" or "hard angles" in my natal pattern. I then attempted the arbitrations.

It was during this initial arbitration phase that I experienced the difference between *ego* and *non-ego* elements in my own psyche. My imagination took on a life of its own. Conflicting archetypal forms would not be pushed into agreement or easy reconciliations. Where I had supposed, "I'm making most of this up," I soon found experiences full of surprises. It became dramatically clear to me that these were *living* entities I was dealing with, and that my ego could not get them to cooperate or come together just because I thought they should or asked them to. They seemed to be separate, sometimes alien, entities totally unlike any familiar aspect of myself. They had their own likes and dislikes, interests and aversions, moods and temperaments. Their behaviors, as I observed and interacted with them, were often completely unpredictable. Occasionally they were hostile to me. Sometimes they totally ignored my presence, and only with the greatest effort could I attract their attention and get them to communicate with me. To get behavior change or cooperation from them, *I* usually had to agree to make changes in my outer world, modify my behavior or agree on new actions. They were most explicit about the changes they required from me or from my life in exchange for their cooperation or assistance.

As this inner process went on, I began to notice new phenomena occurring in my outer world. Those people in my life whom my ego regarded as negative or destructive began to change for the better or go out of my life. It seemed that everyone around me was suddenly beginning to "get it together" as I continued to do the inner work. Problems that had been with me since childhood began to drop away. There was usually no high drama in this; I would just notice one day that a life-long problem had not occurred for a long time, and as more time passed, there was no recurrence of it. It had quietly disappeared.

As an example, up to this time I had an incurable "sweet tooth." I kept a bowl of different kinds of candy in almost every room of my house. One day it occurred to me that I hadn't bought any new candy for a long time. The bowls of candy were starting to collect dust. My sweet tooth had gone away! And I wasn't aware of ever *wanting* it to go away. Through meditation with the archetypes, the need for candy was being filled in some new way.

It occurred to me that perhaps others could contact their Inner Guides, so I began trying to get others to their Guides at the conclusion of my horoscope readings. At first I had limited success because of my own tentativeness, but then the Guide contacts increased as did my own confidence in demonstrating and working with the meditation. Friends volunteered time to talk out their inner workings to me, and I began to get a concept of the archetypal forces as collective entities.

I also began to receive feedback from others who were working on their own with their Guides. They were beginning to get the same kinds of positive life changes and experiences that I had noticed, which were often more dramatic than mine. Reports came of physical healings, mended marriages and spiritual breakthroughs. The common thread throughout seemed to be an alteration, often drastic, of the life values, and an active new spiritual force that gave freshness, meaning and depth to the individual life. And the meekest, mildest appearing Guides would become strong and protective when danger threatened on the inner planes. The Guide was all that was needed for inner world protection and safety. I was relieved that no one would be in danger of experiencing the horror of my initial encounter with the *Old Pan* archetype.

After a few years of helping others find their Inner Guides, I received the astrological surprise of my life. I began to notice a remarkable similarity between one area of the horoscopes of the individuals I worked with and their descriptions of the Guides they contacted in their inner worlds. I discovered that *the personality and physical appearance of one's first Inner Guide always corresponds to the ninth house (or horoscopic section) of the natal pattern* (when Koch birthplace house cusps, not Placidean, are used). This is traditionally the section called the *House of God and Religion* and the area describing your philosophical and spiritual views, as well as your own ability to act as a guide or way-shower for others. In addition, "false" guides, those inner entities who sometimes appear and represent a personification of an individual's mind or rationalization system, were also described in the natal pattern by the third house. That we are so completely programmed, internally as well as externally, came as an astonishing revelation. However, this new insight gave the ability to distinguish the true Guide from the false to anyone versed in astrology. My confidence in the entire meditation increased, making the Guide contact easier for me to initiate. It also showed that the horoscope is a literal road map of the inner world's inhabitants, geography and physics, and a tool which can be verified by your own personal psyche.

The positive reports continued to reach me. Often frightening material, such as I had experienced with *Old Pan*, was reported. The presence and advice of the Guide in each case enabled the individual not only to face the unconscious material that the image represented, but also actually to deal with and transform it. Usually the previously threatening or horrifying image healed over time and became a comfortable or enjoyable presence. As the archetypal image in the inner world was healed, all that it had projected upon in the outer world simultaneously healed or changed. "Negative" relatives would surprisingly change their behaviors. Sudden insight would replace persistent misunderstanding. Hates or objects of hatred would vanish or change. All the screens that the previously "good" or "evil" archetypal energy had projected upon received the new projection and were transformed.

These sudden outer changes initially produced a common reaction in those experiencing them, including myself. It all seemed "too fast." A resistance to sitting down to work with the Guides and the archetypes would develop and would last until our egos got used to the outer changes and assimilated them. Each of us had to reconsider beliefs about reality and how it worked. For example, if I could meditate in a chair in Sante Fe, New Mexico, working on an archetypal energy within me that corresponded to my oldest brother in my horoscopic pattern, and have that brother go through sudden positive change fifteen hundred miles away at the same time that the archetype that I project on him (according to astrological theory) changes in my inner world, something is erroneous in the way we've been taught that reality works. Somehow the energies *I* carry are *making* the world I occupy and experience. Not "I," the current ego, but "I" as a totality. The realization also came that if what I see in my outer world is negative or destructive, this archetypal interaction, with the Guide present, is a process by which I can change or heal the outer reality. By searching out and healing that inner part of myself which participates in the particular manifestation of negativity or unconsciousness, my outer world improves. I understood that no one can do anything harmful or destructive to anyone else unless the inner unconscious projections of *both* parties set them up to do so. There is no one to blame for anything that happens to us. No one is a victim. The *totality* of each person creates the reality that person experiences. Our negative experiences of an individual are the inescapable results of our own unconsciousness in thought, word and deed.

The inner work changes the outer world, literally and for the better. At this time I began to understand the Inner Guide Meditation as a spiritual tool that Western culture could use for its own healing. It begins as an action-oriented, result-based process which can be tested against and verified by experience and by the natal horoscope symbology, and it progresses according to an individual's developmental needs. It answers specific questions, aims at specific life targets — a Western method of meditation for the West. And it is a meditation which can be used in the midst of life — on the subway or train, while waiting in the car, during the lunch or coffee break, alone in a motel.

Since its discovery in 1969, thousands of people from all walks of life have been initiated by me and by other trained initiators who follow the horoscopic road map and help others into the inner dimensions with the Inner Guide Meditation. No psychotic breaks or other negative experiences have been reported. The inner world remains a world with its own peculiar dangers, but the presence of the Guide allows these dangers to be dealt with safely. The Guides restrain us from going faster in our interactions with the internal energies than our egos (which include our physical bodies) can handle and absorb, often refusing to take us into certain inner world areas or suggesting that a specific archetypal form be avoided at the ego's first request — or perhaps suddenly pulling us away from one of the inner forms in mid-sentence. When things are happening too fast in our inner or outer lives, the Guides may suggest just sitting or talking with them at the inner meeting place rather than interacting with any of the archetypes. The Guide may give a quieting *mantra* or teach a centering ritual or exercise. My initial Guide usually had me sit with my feet in a cool forest brook, close my eyes and let my mind quiet during these times in my life.

What happens in the interaction with the archetypal figures is that the interaction itself — just the fact of being with or touching one of the archetypal forms — starts the assimilation of its energy by the ego so that the archetype's negative-seeming projection ability is lessened. The more you work with one specific archetype in the inner world, the more you will find yourself becoming free in the area of life that archetypal energy governs in your particular pattern.

Let's take the *High Priestess* for an example. The more time you spend with that form in the inner world and the more positively the image presents itself to you as you interact with it, the more you will notice a corresponding change in those individuals who accept and live out your *High Priestess* projection — the nourishers, sustainers, protectors and mother figures in your life. You will notice a new emotional relationship with your own mother which contains greater freedom, love and individuality for each of you.

It's the same with the twenty-one other tarot archetypal energy forms. A greater amount of friendliness and love in the relationship between you, the current ego, and a particular archetypal part of yourself will correspond with an improvement in your ego's relationships to those who are screens or projection receivers for that force or principle in the outer world. "As above, so below," goes the ancient Hermetic axiom, or, to paraphrase, "As within, so without." If you want to know *how* you're doing, look at the outside world around you. *That's* how you're doing.

Since discovering the Inner Guides, information about them seems to be everywhere I look. Jung found Philemon, a "guide" of sorts, as he reports in his *Memories, Dreams, Reflections*,[6] but didn't, to my knowledge, develop and incorporate the Guide into his active imagination methods. In the literature of magic, Guides are mentioned and used. They appear in the fairy tales and myths of all human cultures. Everyone knows the concept of the Guardian Angel. Italy's most famous poet, Dante Alighieri had his Inner Guides Virgil and Beatrice and describes his inner journeys in *The Divine Comedy*. The spirit guides mentioned by Spiritualists and others contacting the inner planes seem often to be true Guides. But the physics of where they exist seems to have been misunderstood,

---

[6]C. G. Jung, *Memories, Dreams, Reflections*, ed. A. Jaffee (New York: Vintage Books, 1965), p. 182f.

Figure 9. Those individuals who accept and live out the *High Priestess* archetype in their lives are the nourishers, sustainers, protectors and mother figures. Trump of the *Priestess* from Aleister Crowley's Thoth Tarot Deck, published by Samuel Weiser, Inc., York Beach, ME, and U.S. Games Systems, Inc., Stamford, CT. Used by permission.

their existence being projected outside of the person channeling the spirit as often as not. The Inner Guides sometimes show up spontaneously in LSD experiences, as John C. Lilly reports in his *The Center of the Cyclone*,[7] or in other altered states of consciousness experiences, and some children know them as "invisible friends." The *daemon* of Plato seems to be the same as the Inner Guide. The *Oxford English Dictionary* defines the Greek word *daemon* as "an attendant, ministering, indwelling spirit; a genius," "a tutelary spirit." In Plato's *Symposium*, Diotima speaking to Socrates describes them:

> They are envoys and interpreters that fly between heaven and earth, flying upward with our worship and our prayers, and descending with the heavenly answers and commandments, and since they are between the two estates they weld both sides together and merge them into one great whole. They form the medium of the prophetic arts, of the priestly rites of sacrifice, initiation, and incantation, of divination and sorcery, for the divine will not mingle directly with the human, and it is only through the mediation of the spirit world that man can have any intercourse, whether waking or sleeping, with the Gods. And the man who is versed in such matters is said to have spiritual powers, as opposed to the mechanical powers of the man who is expert in the more mundane arts.[8]

And in the *Cratylus*, Socrates again speaks of a golden race of men who preceded our current race. He quotes a poem: "But now that Fate has closed over this race,/ They are holy daemons upon the earth,/Beneficent, averters of ills, guardians of mortal men." And follows this with: ". . . when a good man dies he has honor and a mighty portion among the dead, and becomes a daemon, which is a name given to him signifying wisdom. And I say too, that every wise man who happens to be a good man is more than human both in life and death, and is rightly called a daemon."[9]

---

[7]John C. Lilly, *The Center of the Cyclone* (New York: Julian Press, 1985).

[8]Plato, "Symposium," from *The Collected Dialogues*, trans. Michael Joyce (Princeton, NJ: Princeton University Press, 1971), p. 555.

[9]Plato, "Cratylus," from *The Collected Dialogues*, trans. Benjamin Jowett (Princeton, NJ: Princeton University Press, 1971), p. 435.

Figure 10. "The Guide and I into that hidden road now entered, to return to the bright world." Italy's famous poet, Dante Alighieri, describes his journeys to the inner planes with his Guide Virgil in his masterpiece, *The Divine Comedy*. Engraving by Gustave Doré from Dante's *Inferno*.

They appear to us in dreams if we give them no more direct access, and they function as conscience, intuition or hunches, often warning us of imminent danger. They say they are with us from birth and have been with us in other lives. The feeling of love and familiarity that comes from them is a reality which cannot be denied once felt.

Part of the difficulty in reaching the Inner Guide is that it is so simple. We live in a world which teaches us that for a thing to have value it should be difficult to achieve and take a long time to accomplish. The Inner Guide Meditation is both simple and easy, and it can be learned by most people in just a few attempts. The Guide waits for each of us, sometimes throughout an entire lifetime. Our collective belief that the outer material plane has more reality than the inner planes blocks our contact with our personal Guide figures. The Guides are so easy to get to that we've forgotten how. In the distant past the relationship to one's Inner Guide was probably so taken for granted that no one ever thought to write down how simple it is to do it.

False Guides and False Guidance

False, or ego, guides are a problem for people with resistance to their own transformation process. They also become a problem because of our naive ignorance about "inner speakers" and a lack of clear definition of who is who on the inner planes. First of all, let no one claiming psychic powers or claiming knowledge superior to your own tell you that your Guide is false, unless he or she is a trained Inner Guide Initiator with a currently dated Certificate of Qualification from D.O.M.E., the Inner Guide Meditation Center. If you do not have access to a trained D.O.M.E. Initiator, trust yourself. The information contained in this book is as complete as it can be at present. Be thorough in your reading and your under-

Figure 11. False or ego guides are a problem for people with resistance to their own transformation process. They also become a problem because of our naive ignorance about "inner speakers" and a lack of clear definition of who is who on the inner planes. Detail from an engraving by Gustave Doré from Coleridge's *The Rime of the Ancient Mariner*.

standing of the material given herein. Take time to digest it all before beginning the initial Guide contact; especially study the Questions and Answers section that follows.

Second, the test of love is the test of the true Guide. If there is no consistent feeling of love and total acceptance from a figure you think might be your Inner Guide, you are probably working with a false guide. Go back to where you first encountered him. Feel beyond him to your right for the love from your true Guide. Your Guide will come when you let him. Just give him permission.

False guides are often judgmental of you or others. They will inflate your ego through flattery. They will encourage separative thinking, most often telling you that you are "right" and others are "wrong." They give little or nothing in terms of spiritual insight, and they subtly discourage ego change and growth, attempting instead to help the ego maintain its *status quo*. False guides seem to be reflections of the current ego, with all its defenses, opinions, rationalizations, denials and other problems. Your true Guide will probably, although not always, have a personality quite different from your own or that of a false guide. Your Guide's point of view will also be very different from yours. If you and a figure you think may be your Guide think exactly alike, this is probably a false guide.

Another way to see whether or not you have a false guide is to ask yourself if your life has changed for the better and moved toward Spirit since you began working with him. If there have been no positive changes in you and the people around you, you are probably with a false guide or are working very superficially with the archetypal energy forms.

If you have continued doubts about the figure you have contacted, who has presented himself to you as your true Inner Guide, you might write to D.O.M.E. Center with a description of the figure you have contacted along with a description of other figures you might have encountered when you first attempted to contact your Guide. Send this information along with an application for your horoscope and an Astrology-Tarot Equivalent Worksheet (see information at the back of the book), and the D.O.M.E. staff will check to see if the figure you are working with coincides with the description of your Inner Guide from your natal horoscope. Remember to include as many details about the figure as you can, e.g., appearance, personality, age, personal qualities, clothing, body type, hair, eye color and quality, ornaments worn, etc. If the figure wears a hooded robe, ask him to throw back the cowl so that you can get impressions of his head and perhaps see some details about his face, even though you might not see the whole face clearly.

Many people, when they have a false guide, simply lose interest in meditating. This is probably due to the true Guide's subtle protective influence.

There is another area in which false guides have become quite prominent. This is through a process known as "channeling." We are living in a time when many people seem to be channeling some entity or other from the inner planes. Much of this was brought to public attention in recent years through Jane Roberts' "Seth" books. "Seth," for a long time, channeled through Jane with information which seemed quite solid and which provoked much thought. But Seth was not Jane Roberts' true Inner Guide.

Your Inner Guide is described in your natal horoscope. The Guide's Ascendant or first house (what he looks like and what his personality is like) is the ninth house of your chart. From the painting of Seth by Jane's husband (from her description to him) which is shown in the early editions of *The Seth Material*,[10] it is apparent that Seth is Jane's Pisces Rising third house or false guide and not her Virgo Rising ninth house guide. Her true Inner Guide would have had the power to protect her on the inner planes (perhaps preventing her untimely death) and would have brought forth information more spiritual but, perhaps, less clever and entertaining.

When a true Inner Guide is initially contacted in the visualization process, it is usually difficult to see his face clearly, while the face of a false guide is usually quite clear. Why this is, I have no idea. Perhaps we see the true Guide's face when we stop trying to make up a face for him.

True Inner Guides *do not channel* through an individual (although the archetypes sometimes do). They exist to help the individual achieve his or her own personal spiritual path. They do

---

[10]Jane Roberts, *The Seth Material* (Englewood Cliffs, NJ: Prentice-Hall, 1972).

not exist to guide and counsel others, because those others have their own Inner Guides to teach them their ways to Spirit.

If anyone is channeling "guidance" for you or for a group which you are in, it would be useful to apply the following tests to the entity which is being channeled. True Inner Guides have the following traits:

1) A feeling of love for the individuals they teach and guide;

2) Never volunteer information unless first asked;

3) Generally don't make predictions for you or others;

4) Don't judge you or anyone else, nor do they take sides in disagreements;

5) Will not contact the dead for anyone but the individual whose Guide they are;

6) Will not give information about other people;

7) Do not manifest through automatic writing, ouija boards, channeling or trance states;

8) Are always accepting of where you are emotionally, physically, mentally and spiritually;

9) Don't lie or give inaccurate information, nor are they inconsistent;

10) Often answer questions with questions, teaching in the Socratic mode.

False inner guides are recognizable by the following:

1) Volunteer information freely, some of which may be valid. They are often very long-winded. Information from false guides fill many books while the true Guides practice economy of speech;

2) Judge you or others, or try to make you feel "evil," wrong, or guilty;

3) Communicate often in terms of separation and polarization, e.g. good vs. evil, right vs. wrong, the good guys vs. the bad guys;

4) May make you uncomfortable or ill, or draw illness and unfortunate outer world circumstances into your life;

5) Inflate the ego. They often make you feel that you are a "chosen one," a "walk-in," better, higher, more special or more spiritual than others;

6) Are often known figures from your own reality, e.g., famous gurus, saints, dead relatives, historical figures, or figures from your fantasy system, e.g., entities claiming to be from outer space or other galaxies, or they may be disincarnate entities or one of the archetypes, the latter being quite dangerous to sanity. In order to work with the archetypes safely, it is absolutely necessary to have the true Inner Guide, who has the ability to protect you from an overwhelming archetypal energy or to pull you out of the situation, if necessary;

7) Make the conditions of your life worsen;

8) Will lie or exaggerate, or are inconsistent;

9) Will flatter and agree with your ego's opinions; usually they are definite Yes-men or -women;

10) Are usually quite theatrical, making grandiose claims about themselves, and, when channeled, speak with strange accents and gesticulate in bizarre ways or cause strange body movements to occur in the naive channeler, who is generally sincerely ignorant of who or what is being channeled or the danger of the process he or she is involved in.

If a supposed guide exhibits any of the above behaviors, be sure that a false guide is in attendance.

In this time of dramatic changes, it is important to receive information from the inner planes which will aid us in our spiritual quests. Challenge and test all so-called "guides" which others may channel for you. Also challenge any information that "guides" of psychics or channelers may receive for you. Remember, true Guides do not channel information for others. My Guide is not here to teach you — your Guide is. False guides will channel for anyone.

Much silly information comes through false guides and incompetent or deluded psychics who pander to the spiritually ignorant through newspapers, books, and popular magazines. This usually does no great harm. But some information that does seem actually harmful and confusing to spiritual understanding and experience also often comes through, e.g., the channeling about "walk-ins" (another, "higher" entity taking over a person's body) and other erroneous material, or the many "divinely revealed" religions which create duality, wars, separation and hatreds in the name of God. Spiritual truth never comes as dogma. It always unifies. Hence it is imperative that tests be put to all channeled entities and to those who channel them. Anything real can stand testing—the real is not fragile. So don't be afraid to question and test. Don't give the power and ability to establish spiritual (or even mental and psychological) truths for yourself away to another. When you do, you only get unconscious elements of that outer person's ego—his or her problems, prejudices and opinions mixed in with the channeled information—and you serve neither the channeler nor yourself in any conscious way.

STOP!

BEFORE READING FURTHER IN THIS BOOK, STOP AND THINK. HAVE YOU UNDERSTOOD ALL THE INFORMATION AND CONCEPTS UP TO THIS POINT? IF ANYTHING UP TO NOW HAS BEEN VAGUE OR FUZZY, GO BACK AND RE-READ THIS FIRST SEC-TION BEFORE CONTINUING.

Remember that it is most important that your psycho-physical system be as purified as possible before attempting the Inner Guide Meditation. Stay off all drugs which might inhibit initial Inner Guide contact, especially cocaine or marijuana, and use no alcohol for at least two weeks before attempting the initial contact. Think of yourself as a temple being prepared and cleansed to welcome the arrival of a true and holy spiritual teacher.

It is also advised that before contacting your Guide initially, you read and absorb the remainder of this book. Much contained in the Questions and Answers section will help you with the initial contact and further your working with your Inner Guide. The Questions and Answers also contain important information that will let you get the "feel" of the meditation through questions and reactions others have had.

I would also advise reviewing this book at least monthly for the first three to six months of regular meditation. Many people have found re-reading invaluable. As you work with the meditation and evolve your own meditation rhythm, the reviewing or re-reading will cause you to be aware of material you may have not assimilated or didn't think you needed to remember during the early stages of your meditation practice.

Part 2

INNER GUIDE MEDITATION AND THE KUNDALINI EFFECT

How to Contact the Inner Guide

Read and follow these instructions carefully. When contacting your Inner Guide for the first time, try not to make it hard or think that you can't do it. A psychological state of ease and relaxation is helpful, though not necessary, for the experience. Sit in a comfortable, straight-backed chair, with your spine erect and both feet flat on the floor. Separate the two sides of the body (don't have your arms or legs crossed), with your thighs parallel to the floor and your hands resting lightly on the thighs, palms up and open. Or, if you prefer, sit on the floor in a yoga position with your legs crossed, arms resting on your thighs. Putting the thumb and first finger of each hand together, an Oriental *mudra*, seems to help achieve and maintain a good meditation level for some. Having the left palm up and the right palm down is helpful to others. Experiment to discover which body and hand positions work best for you.

There seems to be a specific motion sequence or "movement of the mind" that gets you most easily to your Guide. It is: *forward, then left, and then right.* A movement of forward, left and left tends to bring the false guide. The following visual sequence used for the initial Guide contact is one that has evolved through trial and error over the years. If it doesn't work easily for you, accept a structure that your own unconscious presents to you, or invent your own, but utilize the forward, left and right movement. There is no way to do it wrong if you follow these instructions.

Close your eyes, and invent a cave around you as if you have just walked into the cave and the entrance is at your back. Allow the cave to structure itself as it will, large or small, well-lighted or dim, smooth-walled or rough. Try to be like blank film receiving impressions. Accept these impressions uncritically as they come to you from this environment. Try not to edit what comes.

Be as *sensory* as you can. Is the cave moist or dry? Feel the weight of your body as you stand on the cave floor. What kind of floor are you standing on? Feel it with your feet. Is it flat and smooth or rough and uneven? Feel the texture of the floor under your feet. Is it sandy, rocky or gravelly? Feel the air around you. Are there currents, or is the air still? Smell the air. Notice the color impressions that come to you. Use all your senses.

Be sure you are observing and sensing this environment while being *in your body* and *looking out of your eyes*. Don't be watching an image of yourself! Should you find yourself watching yourself, get back into your body, keeping the point of view of your own eyes. If at any time during the meditation you do find yourself watching your own image, return to the viewpoint of your body until it becomes a habit. Feeling the touch of your feet on the ground in the inner world — and the weight of your body on your feet — will help keep you in your body, as does the active use of any of your senses, such as touching something and feeling what it feels like.

Keeping the point of view of your own eyes and body is one of the most important aspects of the Inner Guide Meditation. For a long time I couldn't understand why some people weren't getting life results while others were. Then, one of the people who got no changes mentioned that he was watching himself and his Guide as if he were watching himself in a film. That was the key. He was "unplugged." If you are only *watching* the meditation process and not actively *in it with all your senses*, the meditation becomes no different than a fantasy or day-dream. You may well get information, but nothing will change, heal or transform in your life. Being in your body is essential.

When you can feel yourself in the cave, even though things may still be vague at this point, *move forward and to the left*, away from the entrance further into the cave, and find some kind of doorway or opening there on the left that will lead you out into a landscape. Many people find an actual door in the cave wall. Some go through an arch. Some find a small opening low to the ground that they must crawl through. A few emerge directly into a landscape. Others find a tunnel that leads them out into their landscape. Still others walk right through the wall. Again, take whatever comes uncritically, and move through the aperture presented by the unconscious.

Take a step out into the landscape when it appears, feeling the new type of ground under your feet. Is it soft or hard, grassy or rocky? What is around you? What is the scene like? Let all these impressions come to you, and let them solidify. What seems to be in the distance? What is the weather like? Be there as totally as you can.

Then with your mind, call for an animal to come to you. Let it be an animal you don't know (not a familiar house pet or some other known outer world animal, e.g., your friend's horse, the neighbor's cat, the lamb you had when you were a child), but not a fantasy animal like a unicorn or griffin. Ask the animal to lead you off *to the right* to where your Inner Guide awaits you. Concentrate on following the animal, and try not to anticipate the Guide. If the animal appears to meander or stops, give it permission to take you *directly* to the feet of your Guide. If you lose sight of the animal or the scene, *will* yourself back to that point where you last saw the animal or scene and allow the action to continue from there. The animals that appear come in all varieties. Deer are common, as are squirrels. Sometimes a lion, or a dog or cat will appear. People have even had skunks and anteaters. Again, take whatever animal first comes to you, and trust it to be able to lead you to your Inner Guide.

The animal will lead you to the feet of an unknown male figure—your first Guide. The initial Inner Guide for both men and women is an unknown male figure. This is probably because the horoscopic area which describes his physical being and personality (the ninth house) is associated with three masculine or *yang* energies: an odd-numbered house, the ninth; the sign Sagittarius, the natural sign of the ninth house; and the planet Jupiter, the ruler of Sagittarius. In my experience of thousands of initiations, without exception, female figures who appear and claim to be the true first Guide have always turned out to be one of the archetypes—which renders them dangerous to the unprotected ego—or a false guide. You will generally feel an outpouring of love, protection, and total acceptance from the figure. Many people weep at this point.

Start receiving impressions about the figure. Begin with the feet. Are his feet bare or in some kind of footwear? Then slowly work up the body. Allow impressions of what the figure is like to come to you uncritically, again as if you were blank film. What kind of dress or costume is he wearing? What type of body does he have? Is he fat or thin? Is he tall or short? What kind of hair, if any, does he have? If the figure is hooded, ask him to throw back the

Figure 12. The Guides come in all the many varieties that we humans do; they are always *unknown* figures, and tend to wear the clothing they wore when they last lived on the planet. Collage from engravings by Gustave Doré from Coleridge's *The Rime of the Ancient Mariner* in the D.O.M.E. collection.

hood. Is he wearing anything on his head? Is he bearded or clean-shaven? What kind of feeling about him do you get? Is he an active or passive man? Gentle and introverted or extroverted and out-going? Is he dressed in the clothing of any particular occupation, trade or time period; any particular country or region of the world? Does he hold anything in his hands?

Let all these impressions come to you as they will. Don't *try* to see the Guide's face clearly right away unless it presents itself easily. One of the hallmarks of the true Inner Guide is that his face isn't usually clear at first, although a false guide's face almost always is. The true Guide's face will clear and come into focus later on as you work with him in the meditation process — when you stop trying to "make him a face." Be sure to ask the figure if he is your true Guide and if he has the power to protect you in the inner realms. Generally a false guide will answer "no" to this question or will disappear. Then ask the figure to take both of your hands in his. *Feel* the hand contact as much as you can. Feel the texture of his skin. Is his hand warm or cool, moist or dry? Is the skin smooth or rough? Now, with your mind, give him your permission to let you feel his feeling for you. If you don't feel total acceptance and love or caring, you're with a false guide. There is no love from a false guide.

Then ask your Guide to take your right hand in his left, so that you're both facing in the same direction, the Guide at your side. (In left-handed people this usually is reversed, the Guide's right hand taking the left hand.) Ask your Guide then to point to where the *Sun* is in the sky of your inner world. Look to where he points. Is the *Sun* right overhead or off to one side? Are there clouds, or does it shine in a clear sky?

At the point where you ask the Guide to point to the *Sun*, a false or ego guide will generally balk, change the subject, try to divert attention in some way, hedge or will simply vanish. Test for his love again if he remains and your doubts are stirred. If you cannot feel it, stay where you are and look to the right of where the false guide is or was. Another male figure will be there, or at least nearby. Feel where the love energy comes to you from and creates a warmth in your chest, and look in that direction. Go through the earlier process of allowing the Inner Guide to appear clearly to you, and ignore the false guide if he is still hanging about. If you happen

Figure 13. The Inner Guides are always human and do not have the powers or attributes of Gods. Engraving by Gustave Doré from *The Doré Bible Gallery*.

to get a false guide, your true Inner Guide is close by, and if you call for him and give him your permission to come to you, you will probably see him quickly. The false guides might be either male or female.

Don't accept any known person from your outer world as your Inner Guide. Your Guide is a being who *wasn't alive on the planet when you were born*, so if your favorite uncle, or your father, or the current or past president of the United States appears, keep looking past him to the right. And if a famous deceased guru or teacher or luminary from the past should appear, test him, and see if another figure appears beyond him on the right.

The Inner Guides come in all the many varieties that we humans do, and they are always unknown figures and not celebrated spiritual teachers or avatars of the recent or distant past. The Guides tend to wear the clothing they wore when they last lived on the planet (or so they say about themselves), which is perhaps why they seldom appear in contemporary dress. They also say that they are connected to us through love or duty, and that we have shared a life on the planet with them at some time and may well again. And, most important, *the Inner Guides are always human and do not have the powers or attributes of Gods*. If a sea serpent, a fairy, an angel or a winged man claims to be your Guide, move past it to the right until your true Guide is encountered.

After your Guide takes your hand and points out where the *Sun* is and you see it, ask the *Sun* to come down, in human or human-like form, to where you and your Guide are. Accept the first form it takes. It may come as a male or a female. It might be a man with a bird's head or a swirling mass of colors and energy in humanoid form. It may take the form of Christ, or it may be a dwarf. Try not to preconceive what the *Sun*, as it exists in your inner world, is going to look like. Let it be what it will.

The *Sun* is the archetype of the *Center* of the Self—the love-giving, life-sustaining, creative energy that animates each of us and gives life and motion to the other archetypal forces we carry within us. Our true Inner Guide generally delights in the initial solar contact. Even if the *Sun* energy in your particular horoscopic pattern is weak or repressed, the Guide will do all in his power to bring you into contact with this central solar figure so that you can begin the assimilation of this vital energy.

When you and your Inner Guide are together with the *Sun* figure, direct your attention to the *Sun* and ask it to send as much light and love into you as you can physically handle at that particular time. Try to absorb the energy as it comes into you. Try not to resist it. It is at this point that most people realize that something real and unusual is happening to them and that they're not "making it up," because they don't know how to make up such an experience. This experience of light and love from the *Sun* is often overwhelming, generating tears of joy and is the first inner world experience of a non-ego, archetypal force. If, by chance, you don't experience this energy physically, give the *Sun* permission to penetrate any blocks that may be up against its energy so you will be enabled to feel the energy flow within you, making sure that you are in your body. Asking the figure to literally touch you with its hands or with a directed ray will generally penetrate the blockage and allow you to feel the energy flow.

The two questions that I recommend for use when interacting initially with each of the twenty-two tarot archetypes are: 1) *What do you need from me and from my life to work with me and be my friend?* and 2) *What do you have to give me* (in the form of a symbolic object placed into your hand) *that I need from you?* The answer to the first question may be a request for a quality such as *Love* or *Trust* or *Honor*. Or it may be a request such as "Come and visit me daily," or "Start being kinder to others," or "Eat more brown rice." Take the first answer that comes into your mind, even if your ego views it as nonsensical. This answer may come in code form to get past the ego's defenses against hearing this information from within. The Inner Guide, or the archetype itself, may be asked to interpret further or decode its need or request. If you reject the first answer or image that comes to you, ego chatter will follow and confusion will ensue. Try to shut off your normal thinking process and become a receiver. Some of the archetypal forms that, in the psyche, are representative of repressed or suppressed energies may initially appear as negative, evil, or sickly in the form aspect they present, and may request things which are opposed to your moral or ethical values — such as, "Poison your dog," or "Shoot your neighbor." Ask your Guide's advice before agreeing to even seemingly innocent requests, especially if your intuition gives you warning or you "get a funny feeling" about the request. Refuse those requests your Guide advises you to refuse, and continue asking the archetype's need until you elicit an acceptable request, *one which you feel you can and will fulfill in your everyday life.*

Remember, you're in foreign territory. Trust and use your Inner Guide to act both as interpreter and counselor—truly let him guide you. Expect from him what you would from a wise teacher. If you become confused or don't understand what's going on there in the inner world, ask him to explain. The true Inner Guides don't volunteer any information, so don't hesitate to ask questions in order to get explanations and interpretations. Another thing about the true Guides is that they will judge no one, neither you nor anyone else in your world. Nor will they usually make predictions about you or others. They will never invade another's privacy in any way. Should your Guide start agreeing with you that someone in your outer world is a "bad guy" or "evil," you're with a false guide. Another thing to look for is the improvement of outer world conditions as you work with your true Guide. These conditions tend to worsen or fall apart when you're working with a false guide. Watch results, and don't be afraid to test the Guides and the archetypes. The Inner Guide Meditation is not fragile and can withstand much testing.

The second question that I recommend asking each archetypal form during the first encounter with it is: "What do you have to give me that I need from you?" Ask that the archetype respond by placing a symbolic object into your hand. Accept the first object that appears. If it is not clear, ask that the object be brought into focus and made more clear. Again, use your senses. Feel the object. Is it round or square, hollow or solid? What material is it made of? Is it large or small, heavy or light?

When you are clear what the object is, ask the archetypal figure to interpret just what talent, ability or power the object represents. If you regard it as a tool, how do you use it? What effects can it produce in the inner world? In the outer world? How do you utilize it in your everyday life?

These initial gifts from the archetypes represent the talents and abilities you were born with that relate specifically to the energy forms that give them to you. You receive the gift in symbol or code form and must then have it decoded. An archetypal gift may have a very common use: "It will make you more aware of your surroundings," or "It will keep your neck from getting stiff," or "It will help you sleep." Or its use may be associated with the twilight zone of extrasensory perception and magic: "It will begin to open your third eye," or "It is the gift of healing with your hands," or "It will allow you to journey out of the body," or "It will begin the safe arousal of the kundalini." Remember to check with your Inner Guide as to whether or not you should accept what is offered. If he OK's it, be sure that you've asked enough questions so that you understand just what it is you've been given. If you *don't* understand, ask more questions until it is clear to you. Ask both the archetypal giver and your Guide to help you understand the gift and the ways you may use it in both the inner and outer worlds.

When you have really understood the talent or ability, ask the archetype that presented the gift to place it in or on your body at a place where you should absorb or carry it. Feel where the energy form of the object settles within you. This absorption into the body is usually accompanied by unusual physical sensations in one or more parts of the body.

Again, check out all the steps in the process with your Inner Guide. He's there to help you, but *he can't help unless he is asked.* (The Guides will not act spontaneously on their own except when physical, spiritual or psychological danger to the ego is encountered.) Nor can he answer unasked questions.

If you utilize the tarot forms of the archetypal energies, you'll finally have at least twenty-two symbolic gifts or powers in object form scattered throughout your body. A crystal may be in the center of your forehead, an apple in the heart, a stick of green wood in the right hand, pearls around the neck, an iron sphere in the genitals, etc. It is helpful to make an outline of a human body on a sheet of paper and keep it as a record of where each of your symbolic gifts is placed. Experiment with these tools or gifts, and record the results in your journal of meditation experiences, the log of your inner journeys. See if they do what you've been told they'll do. If the *Empress* has given you a copper rod which she explained will do healing, think of a sick plant in your environment, and ask your Inner Guide to bring it to where you and the *Empress* are in the inner realm. Ask her to show you how to heal the plant with the rod, and follow her instructions. Ask how long it will be before the plant will be healed in your outer world. Suppose she says "two weeks." Observe the plant. If you see no improvement in two weeks, have your Guide take you back to the *Empress*, explain to her that the plant doesn't seem to be healed, and ask her what you don't understand about using the healing tool or magical implement you were given. *Don't let negative results lie.* Insist that your magical implements work. Don't rationalize them. Always go to the giver of the ability and challenge the results until your tools work for you. When you've mastered the ability of a certain tool, ask your Guide to take you back to its giver and ask if there is any other power that tool may have that you are unaware of. These tools or abilities are for use in our everyday lives — not just on the inner planes.

The two questions that you ask the archetypal energy images at the first encounter, and the answers, actions, and objects they elicit serve to indicate to you just *where* that energy is within you — whether positive or negative, conscious or unconscious. It also serves to establish an initial balance between the ego and the energy of the form you touch and work with. At the conclusion of each inner working, remember to ask your Guide if all the energies that you've encountered are in balance, or if anything has been left undone. Remember that all *taking from* must be balanced by a *giving to*. To receive from an archetype without giving in return seems to allow that force *carte blanche* to take what it wishes from any area of life as a balancing factor. It's best to know the cost of what you are receiving. The Inner Guide will tell you if all is in balance if you remember to ask him.

I recommend the tarot images as a source of archetypal references because of their correlation to astrology and your natal horoscope. If these images aren't compatible with you, however, use any other symbol keys you like: the pantheon of the Greek Gods, the Christian religious archetypes, the Hindu Gods, the ancient Egyptian *Neters* or God forms, cartoon characters from Disney or comic books, figures from fairy tales, the Norse Gods. For instance, one friend reported that all the archetypal figures that appeared to her looked like biblical characters, the *High Priestess* appearing as the Virgin Mary, the *Sun* as Jesus. Another's looked like characters from King Arthur's time.

Any figures you choose, or that appear initially, will start to evolve and change as you work with them. They will begin to remold and alter your initial target images, going through your memory banks and utilizing symbols, forms, and images that best express *their* particular energy as it exists in you at the time you are working with and experiencing them. You may begin with an image of the *Empress* just as she appears in a tarot deck only to find that her form turns into that of a witch stirring a cauldron, and it remains in that altered form no matter how hard you may try to force it back into the tarot original with your mind. Even as the witch figure changes from "evil-seeming" to "good," as you interact and work with her, she will remain uniquely herself, the *Empress* as she lives in *you*, unlike any outer image or symbol.

On occasion the figures will present themselves as pure symbol—*Justice* appearing as an ice cube or a pair of scales, the *High Priestess* as a crystal ball, the *Lightning-Struck Tower* as a phallus. Take whatever comes, and try to work with it as it first presents itself. Ask why it is presenting itself in that particular form. What is it trying to communicate to you? It will change as you assimilate its force and its message, sometimes in the middle of a conversation. If you have difficulty working with a talking ice cube, ask the image to take a human form and accept the first one that presents itself. Sometimes this request for a human form is ignored or refused—it was two years before the *Wheel of Fortune* energy within me would take a human form, although I requested this at each meeting with this archetype.

The way to assimilate the energies most rapidly into the ego is to get as *involved* in the meditative experience as you can. *Touch the figures.* Utilize all your sensory apparatuses. Voice your disagreements. Complain of their harshness or coldness. Hold onto those who try to leave before the interaction is complete, or call them back or ask your Guide to bring them back if they do depart. For those whose response to your questions is silence, give them permission to answer your questions whether you want to hear their answers or not. Demand that they answer. When an archetype is silent, it generally indicates that the ego doesn't want to hear the information which that archetype has to give. Insist that an answer be given. Give permission that the answer be given in picture form, and then ask your Guide to help you understand and decode it. The acts of insisting and giving permission enable the ego to push through its own resistances and defense systems. Give the archetypal forms in your inner world the same reality you would grant any twenty-two individuals in your outer world, and you'll find the changes in your life both rapid and positive.

The side effects of the Inner Guide Meditation are what amaze the ego the most. Psychic ability may suddenly flower without your having worked specifically on its development. Outer world perceptions become acute, and the world literally becomes *new*. The creation energy wells up from within, and a knowledge of a *Oneness* with all becomes a fact of the being. You find yourself automatically thinking: "Brother George has the flu—I'll have to work inside more," or "I wonder what part of me caused her to do *that* to me," or "I'll have to heal that part of myself." Opposites begin to be perceived as poles of a single unity, and the dance of the archetypal energies becomes a dance in which you are a joyful participant. You find that inner temple within you which has *always* existed to contain and trigger your own personal God experience. And you find yourself *seeing* the beauty and goodness of all the worlds.

The Inner Guide Meditation is a way of working on inner planes that is a direct outgrowth of what is referred to as the Western Mystery Tradition. It is an action-oriented method: you move, you utilize your ego and your senses, you ask questions and challenge, you barter and exchange, you argue, you insist, you explore, you discover, you laugh and you cry. It is the method of the Child in us all—open and direct. And it can be used by anyone, anywhere. Children, from about seven years of age on, love the Inner Guide Meditation and take to it like fish to water. The elderly can use it as easily as the young. The rules are those that you and your Guide establish. They change only as that YOU that goes on from life to life and never dies, gently takes over the reins of your life, and the ego and Self work in unity. There is no need for the outer teacher; you carry your own instructor and spiritual mentor within. *Allow him to teach you.* There is no need to project the Guide onto any outer figure—doctor, priest, astrologer, scientist, channeler, minister or politician, once you have contacted him in your own inner world. The Kingdom of Heaven is *truly* within you, and your Inner Guide will show you *your* way.

Figure 14. The Kingdom of Heaven is truly within you, and your Guide will show you *your* way. Engraving by Gustave Doré from Dante's *Paradise*.

Working With Your Guide

There seem to be seven primary Guides within, corresponding to the different vibrational levels of the inner dimensions. The first Guide is the male figure I have already mentioned. The next two Guides are usually, but not always, men. The fourth Guide is always a woman. The fifth Guide is the same sex as the individual. There is not enough experiential data on the sixth and seventh Guides at this time for me to be able to talk about them with any degree of authority. The Guides work with us sequentially, the second Guide following the first, the third following the second, etc.

I mention this here so that there will be no confusion when your first Guide, who will probably work with you for quite a long time (I was with my first Guide, Aman, for four years), indicates that you will be going on to a new Guide. Different people are directed to the second Inner Guide at different times and in different ways. The first Guide generally initiates the meeting. Sometimes it is spontaneous or occurs in a dream. It may take many years to reach a new Guide for some—few for others. One factor seems to be how quickly the physical system, a part of the ego, is safely able to assimilate the archetypal energies and respond with a change in the mind-body vehicle. Also, the ego must accept the fact that inner energies create it and generate the entire reality it is experiencing, and that the ego alone is *responsible for*, although *not to blame for*, all that is occurring in the outer reality. The individual's psychic aspect (tenanted water signs and houses in the horoscope) and the amount of ego resistance and skepticism to be pushed through are also factors.

If a new Guide appears suddenly without any previous indication of his coming, test the authenticity of the figure with your current Guide. Often when the ego finds itself changing as a result of the inner work, it will unconsciously call forth a false guide to attempt to slow down or to stop the transformation process. These false or ego guides are flatterers and liars and go along with the ego's rationalization process. They will tell the ego whatever it needs to hear to sabotage the spiritual evolutionary process. Whenever you are in a transition from one Guide to the next, check out the new Guide with the Guide you have been working with. This testing process has been found to avoid major detours in the inner work.

There are many ways to work with your Inner Guide. You can just turn yourself over to him as your inner guru or spiritual teacher and ask him to teach you in whatever way is best for you. If you have had a dream or a nightmare that you would like to understand and work with, ask the Guide to set up a screening booth and ask him to re-run the dream for you, treating it like a movie you're watching. Stop the action as you wish, and ask your Guide to interpret the various episodes for you. The Inner Guides are skilled and wise dream interpreters. When you finish with the interpretation of the dream or nightmare, ask your Guide whether or not you and he should go back into the dream and change, fix, complete or heal any portion of it. Follow the same process of working with dream figures as you do with the archetypes. Dream figures that appear as evil, diseased, dying or dead often symbolize those aspects of ourselves which need the most love and attention from our egos. They represent energies repressed or suppressed within us. Should the Guide recommend a healing or a transformation of one of these inner dream figures, ask him to call forth the tarot *Sun* archetype, and ask the *Sun* to send its light-love energy into the image that requires the healing or transformation until it changes or resurrects. Remember that *everything and everyone in your dreams represents some aspect of yourself.* If you dream of a known person from your outer world, that person is one of your projection screens, living out in the outer and inner worlds some aspect of yourself.

Never work in the inner world with known figures from your outer reality! If a known figure appears in a meditation or in a dream (your mother, your brother, the woman-next-door), before you work with the energy the known figure represents, *ask that the image of this person take its true form as it lives in you,* not as he or she appears or has appeared in your outer world reality. Working with a known figure from your outer world in the inner world or trying to force a person from your outer world to do something you wish him to do in the meditation process without that person's *knowledge and ego permission in the outer world* amounts to black magic. This will draw commensurate dues for you to pay, usually in the form of headaches or nausea, but often much more extreme.

"Messing with someone's mind," or with his actions or free will without the person's ego consent, is against Universal Law, and the Law is enforced. Even if you're tempted to do what you consider to be "good" for another, such as healing an illness or helping in your inner world to get the person a job in the outer world, *ask permission first* of the person involved *in the outer world*. And ask your Guide's advice also on such projects. The best way to help someone who is troubled or in pain in your outer world is to ask the image of the individual to take its true form as it lives within you, and then heal or transform that part of yourself which unconsciously participates in the outer individual's "bad trip." But remember, once the image is in its true form, it is a picture of the energy that went out of you and manipulated that person as a character in your movie — it no longer has anything to do with the outer world person. It is now a picture of an energy aspect of yourself, and try to remember that *this* is what you are healing or transforming — a real part of yourself unconnected to anyone else.

Another way to work with the Inner Guides is in terms of the events in your everyday life. If you find yourself in some hassle or painful life situation, ask your Guide to take you to the inner energy image that is causing the outer problem. If you are working with the tarot figures or with your horoscope, resist the temptation to figure out or preconceive what single figure or group of figures may be the culprits. Remember that the tarot images are pictures of energies. These energies can combine and re-combine, and perhaps the figure the Guide takes you to will be one you have never encountered before. It may be composed of two parts *High Priestess* energy, one part *World* and three parts *Chariot*. Accept whatever form the Guide brings or leads you to, and work with that form. Trust your Inner Guide to take you to the composite image of all the forces associated with the particular life situation you are dealing with, and work with whatever he presents. *Try not to guide your Guide* or he becomes ineffectual in his role.

If you want a systematic way to work and don't have a tarot-horoscope equivalent worksheet, you can begin with the tarot images by starting with the *Fool* image and working forward through the Major Arcana with each of the archetypal energies in turn, or you can work backward from the *World* figure. (See the list of archetypes in the Horoscope-Tarot Equivalents section on

Figure 15. Never go into the inner world without your Inner Guide. Engraving by Gustave Doré from Dante's *Inferno*.

page 233.) The figures will not generally appear as they do in the tarot card images, and even if they do at first, they will soon begin to change as you interact with them.

Never go into the inner world without your Inner Guide. It can be dangerous for you and could possibly blow all your circuits, much like a frightening or disintegrating LSD drug experience. There is no such thing as losing your Guide once you've contacted him. If your Guide seems to have disappeared while you are working with him, *just call for him and he'll be there.* Don't look for him. The act of looking is full of ego imposition and is generally unsuccessful in locating the Guide's presence. *Allow* him to be there. He'll be there with you, and *feel* his presence and his love.

Sometimes our ego's resistances will put harmless blocks in our way to the Inner Guide in the form of brick walls, monsters standing in our path, people we know attempting to distract us and lead us in another direction. Ignore them. Give them no energy. Walk through the walls or monsters. Disregard those who appear before you have come to your Guide. There is no danger in the unconscious until you are beyond the place where you meet your Guide. Beyond the meeting place (which you should establish with your Guide during the initial meditation) the Inner Guide is with you as your protector from potential dangers.

Another resistance trick you may experience comes from without. Just as you are about to sit down to meditate, your environment may go crazy; your dog will bark, your telephone will ring, an unexpected visitor will knock on the door, someone will break something in the next room, your cat will get into a fight outside your window, etc. This resistance pattern lasts for about two weeks, if you encounter it at all, and, if you find it happening, try to prepare for it in advance as much as you can to insure a quiet meditation period.

Remember also that the Inner Guides are always human figures. They are not Gods and have no God-like powers of their own (although they may have the ability to fly, float, teleport or walk through walls). They neither judge nor flatter. They may have personality traits which seem at first most un-Guide-like. My first Guide, Aman, always seemed rather spaced–out and absentminded. The qualities they seem to share are their protectiveness and acceptance, their love and concern for you and your spiritual growth, and their guidance toward the realization of your own Center or God-aspect. Everyone loves his or her Inner Guide in a very personal way. In fact you can develop such a strong love and attachment to your initial Guide that when it is time to go on to the next Guide, you may have to overcome your own ego's resistance to the transition — much like having to separate from a much-loved friend in your outer world.

Drugs of any kind (alcohol, marijuana, heroin, opium, cocaine, hashish, barbituates, PCP, amphetamines and the like) will interfere with or block the Guide contact and sabotage the meditation. Try not to have any alcohol on the day you are to first contact your Guide, if you are being initiated by a D.O.M.E. Inner Guide Initiator, or for at least two weeks if you are working alone. Marijuana tends to stay in the body as a blockage from eight to fourteen days or longer, and it takes about a year to clear from the body entirely. The other drugs in use in our culture vary in their blockage effects. For a clear initial contact with your Inner Guide, try to have your body and nervous system as pure as possible. The natural organic drugs have a tendency to stay in the body and cause blockage effects for a longer period of time than the chemical drugs, so allow sufficient time for your body to expel them if you are using drugs.

Insist on the availability of all your senses when working with the Inner Guide Meditation, and *always use them* — especially seeing and hearing. There are many speakers within. Be sure you are seeing the speaker. Keep the meditation experience fully sensory. For example, the *High Priestess* may be giving you important information and may sound as though she is in good shape within you, but without your vision you would not see that she is weeping as she speaks.

Many people ask if they should study the tarot figures before they attempt the Inner Guide Meditation and the working with the inner images and energies that the tarot represents. I would generally advise people not to study the tarot until they have *experienced* each of the tarot energy forms at least once. It becomes impressive to a skeptical ego to read about what they *should* be like *after* the initial experiences with them. The tarot archetypes are *living* energies. As our horoscopes demonstrate — by accurately describing our individual realities — these archetypes are creating and sustaining us, not vice versa. We seem to have learned everything exactly backwards about the way reality-generating energies actually flow. The archetypes always *are* as they *should be*. There is no other choice for them. They are first, we are second, and the rest of reality is third.

It is also impressive after the experiences with the archetypes to have an astrologer explain directly from your own natal horoscopic pattern *why* the *Last Judgement* figure appeared to you as a jackal, why it gave you a butterfly, and why the figure placed the symbol into your genitals. It is just as if you had studied all the tarot-astrology symbolism beforehand, expressing it directly according to astrological theory and symbolism.

We live in a culture that teaches us that we should know about things in advance, but this seems to interfere with the Inner Guide Meditation. We are already programmed with enough "shoulds." Going inside with ego information about how the archetypes should be, should look and should act will often interfere with how they *are*, how they *do* look, how they *do* act, as they present themselves in the individual psyche. If you can take it on faith in the beginning, even if you think "I'm making this all up," or "This is silly," and can really trust your Guide, you will be more impressed later on with the information you receive. Working without preconceptions is somewhat difficult, especially for us in Western civilization, but it is the most rewarding way in the long run.

If an inner voice tests you by whispering, "You're making this all up," respond with, "Making it all up from *where*?" The images, the feelings, the thoughts that come, can only arise from your own psycho-spiritual system. Continue "making it up," if you think that's what you're doing, and you'll find the results and changes in your outer world astonishing—as if circles of healing light were touching and changing everyone and everything around you, affecting your whole environment. Remember—it's the movie that *your* energies are creating that you think of as reality.

The Inner Guide Meditation doesn't seem to interfere with any other way of meditating or "working inside." Nor does it seem to be incompatible with any religious system except for the most dogmatic and insecure. It gives you a safe and direct access to your own unconscious. If you are a Christian, it deepens your understanding of Christ. If you are into Yoga, the Guide smooths your way;

the Jew becomes a better Jew; the humanist, more humane; and the atheist or agnostic experiences the spiritual, perhaps for the first time.

The Inner Guide Meditation places spiritual authority back *within* the individual — its true and holy place. Your Guide exists to teach you *your* spiritual path, *your* way to God, not someone else's.

Kundalini

Kundalini is a Sanskrit word meaning "that which is coiled." It is also translated as the "Serpent Power" or the "Serpent Fire." It is the Supreme Spiritual Power in the human body and lies coiled and sleeping at the base of the spine until awakened, when it rises and pierces the six internal energy centers or *chakras* along the spine, finally fountaining out through the seventh chakra at the crown of the head and causing the experience called *Enlightenment*. The kundalini is associated in the lower centers with the clitoris and the glans penis.

In the American Indian Mayan scripture, *Popul Vuh*, kundalini is called *hurakan* or "lightning," and the spinal centers are depicted by animal glyphs. The African Zulus call it "the fire of the Gods." Knowledge of kundalini is found in the secret teachings of all spiritual communities throughout the world.

I bring up the kundalini at this point, because it awakens as a "side effect" of most meditation practices, and awakens rapidly as a result of regular Inner Guide Meditation, especially meditations involving sexual unions with the archetypes. It can also awaken accidentally as the result of a fall or be triggered by drugs, especially LSD and the hallucinogens, and by alcohol.

When the ascending kundalini rises and pierces the Crown Center located four fingers above the top of the head, intense white light is usually perceived, as of a thousand white suns. Here the male/female energies unite, producing the union of opposites or Nirvana for the Buddhists, Samadhi for the Yogis, or Christ Consciousness for the Christian mystics. Here at the Crown, the kundalini reaches its apex, having pierced and opened the six lower centers, and a "rupture of the planes" occurs along with the phenomena of transcendence and "emergence from time." The energy then descends over the face or head, down through the throat, into the solar plexus, and back down to the root, where it again begins to rise and continues its flow pattern. The experience of the fully awakened kundalini remains forever an unforgettable spiritual event, often feeling like "having sex with God," and it changes your life and your values dramatically and permanently.

When the kundalini force starts to awaken, it starts moving up an esoteric, non-physical nerve channel, which the Mayans call an "air tube," from the base of the spine to the top of the head. There are two additional nerve channels called the "two-fold air tubes" by the Mayans. Energy flows through them, crisscrossing between the six interior spinal centers all the way up to the crown of the head. It has the form of the symbol called the Caduceus of Mercury/Hermes (used as the symbol of medicine and healing by physicians, who often are unaware of its meaning), the wings being the two rays experienced in the throat center, the staff being the central air tube, and the two snakes representing the kundalini rising in the two channels on either side of the spine, with the pine cone at the top representing the pineal gland. When the energy flows only through the side channels, a person does not transform spiritually. Only when the kundalini journeys up through the central tube does spiritual transformation occur.

Another aspect of the kundalini is called "the Descent of Grace" in Western tradition. This descending aspect travels down from the crown of the head, over the face (or over the entire head, if the head is shaved), continuing with lightning-like speed down through the larynx, and going further down into the solar plexus. From here it descends all the way down to the root of the spine, where it triggers the ascending aspect of the kundalini into awakening. This seems a less noted occurrence than the ascending aspect, although both streams must be flowing for circulation of the kundalini energy in the four-body system to be both balanced and complete. The ancient Egyptians pictured these two aspects of the kundalini in the headdress of the pharaoh, the rising aspect shown as a cobra and the descending aspect as a vulture. In Meso-

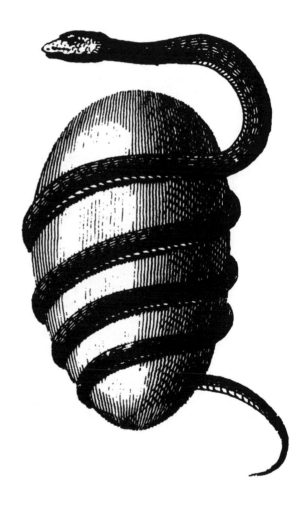

Figure 16. The Orphic Egg is a symbol of initiation and shows the kundalini energy in its ascending aspect flowing around the auric egg. Illustration from Jacob Bryant's *A New System, or, An Analysis of Ancient Mythology*, London, 1774.

American tradition, the two aspects were combined in the symbol of the "Feathered Serpent." The ascending, or emotional aspect, of the kundalini energy is associated with the planet Pluto and the sign Scorpio and with the water or astral body in balance with the physical or earth body. The descending or electrical aspect is associated with the planet Uranus and the sign Aquarius and with the air or mental body in balance with the fire or spiritual body.

For the kundalini to be experienced safely, the physical, mental, emotional and spiritual bodies must all be in balance. As the force awakens and travels up the central tube, it encounters and must penetrate each of the interior centers. If any of these have blockages of any kind (marijuana is one of the greatest culprits in chakra blockage) symptoms occur in one of the four bodies as the kundalini seeks to dissolve the blockages. Most of the heart attacks, skin problems, muscle spasms, nervous disorders, strokes, mental diseases, flus and epidemics are the results of kundalini awakening in imbalanced systems. In a person who is totally blocked, rigid and full of fear, paranoia and negative judgment, the accidental arousal of kundalini can produce the phenomenon called "spontaneous human combustion," a peculiar kind of fire which can totally consume a human body, leaving only ashes, but leaving the clothing the person was wearing unsinged. This is the most extreme, and most rare, of all kundalini effects.

The most common physical experience of the kundalini is a throbbing, a tingling, or a sensation of heat, cold, or electricity at the base of the spine, or in the feet, head or hands. Sometimes in an acute awakening, the nail of the left great toe turns black and falls off. The general metabolism might be affected. There might be experiences of hot flashes or of extreme cold. Sometimes there are spontaneous body movements, such as twitching or violent shaking. Night sweats are common. Physical illness may suddenly increase, or peculiar subjective states, such as weightlessness or the feeling of movement of one of the limbs when the actual limb is motionless, may be experienced. Dreams may suddenly increase, or lights may be seen in the head or sounds heard which have no physical world causes. Sensations of pain or numbness may be experienced in the back, head or limbs.

Emotionally, the kundalini may cause abrupt changes. You might suddenly decide to become celibate or give up alcohol or

Figure 17. Death or rebirth is associated with the astrological sign Scorpio and the ascending aspect of the kundalini energy. The kundalini awakens as a "side effect" of most meditation practices, and awakens rapidly as a result of regular Inner Guide Meditation, especially meditations involving sexual unions with the archetypes. Tarot trump of *Death*, or *La Mort*, from an original drawing by Leigh McCloskey, ©1986. Used by permission.

begin a macrobiotic diet. You might sell all your possessions to travel or to seek your "spiritual home." Old values may become meaningless. Total transformation on all levels of reality is a major part of the kundalini awakening.

When these symptoms appear, the person experiencing them usually has no idea of what is happening, becomes frightened and seeks medical help. Because most physicians, psychiatrists and psychologists are ignorant of the kundalini and its symptom patterns, the conditions are labeled "anxiety attack," "psychotic episode" and the like, or the person is told that "nothing is wrong." If the symptoms are treated with medications, the symptoms tend to "freeze" until the medication is discontinued.

If kundalini energy is awakening in you and you are experiencing pain or discomfort, sometimes a warm bath with a cup or two of baking soda in the water is helpful. This tends to draw the energy out and balance it. Keeping busy and active helps—swimming, washing dishes, all water activities, gardening and other work with the earth, all activities which might serve to ground you.

A balancing diet is highly recommended. At D.O.M.E. Center we have found that eating macrobiotically serves best to balance the kundalini, because whole foods have a grounding and balancing effect on the four-body system. At least try to let go of sugar, red meat and processed foods. Alcohol can also be dangerous to the awakening kundalini force, as it tends to release the energy wildly in the bodies, causing much pain and havoc.

But the most important thing to do when the kundalini starts to awaken is to work with your Inner Guide! He is the one who intimately knows your design, both inner and outer, and who can teach you how best to cooperate with the energy as it does its transformational work in your four-body system. In a sense, you are being "raised an octave," and your Guide can teach you how to go through the transition in the most peaceful and comfortable way for you.

Kundalini is the source of our sexual energy. Like sexual energy it is alchemical. You can expect changes to occur in your sex life when kundalini begins to activate, because the energy changes who you are. If you are having sexual encounters with many people, remember that each of these produces a different energy effect on you and may serve to keep you off balance. If your sexual activity is confined to only one partner, it is somewhat easier to stay in balance. But whatever your mode, it will probably change as the kundalini changes you. You may suddenly want a whole different kind of sexual expression or no sex at all.

If you are celibate, or if celibacy is one of the results of the kundalini rising, you might find it easier to stay in balance because of the containment of the energy. But whatever the changes that occur, be patient with the process. Kundalini awakening can be traumatic in the life and hard on the four-body system. Don't make demands on yourself or others. Let the process take its course, and work with your Inner Guide throughout the awakening. You can't control the energy, but he can. My first Guide, Aman, promised me that I'd never experience a major kundalini event unless I were at home in my own bed or meditation space, and that's the only time they come.

My first kundalini experience was almost more than I could assimilate. It erupted spontaneously and lasted for eight hours. I suddenly became God's Phallus and was creating EVERYTHING—stars, English villages, Model-T Fords, dinosaurs, galaxies, cultures, individuals, atoms, black holes, crystals, herds of buffalo, other universes, continents—everything that is, was, or will be. The experience coincided with eight hours of continuous physical orgasm. I know this is "impossible," but it happened. I, the ego, kept dissolving into the experience. I thought I'd never come back to any kind of normal ego state where I was "Ed" and could think. It was like no experience I had ever had or heard of ever before. It enormously changed how I viewed my sexual energy. This energy suddenly became like money in the bank: "How do I want to spend this?" I didn't want to do anything that would jeopardize my having the experience again. It felt to me that I was in total spiritual and sexual union with God. Human sexual experience pales by comparison.

Other people's awakenings are often quite different. A friend of mine had her kundalini awakened by one of the major gurus from India at his ashram. When I asked her what it was like for her, she replied, "It was just like being raped." She had been given no preparation for the experience and no help afterward, except for permission to wander the ashram unattended. And at that time she was not in contact with her Inner Guide. It was months before she was able to function in the world once more.

Awakening kundalini in those unprepared to handle it seems to me irresponsible and dangerous. Too often we hear of people having true psychotic breaks in groups working to activate this potent energy.

Descriptions of personal accounts of additional individual kundalini experiences are given below. I have included these personal narratives so that the reader will begin to understand and appreciate the variety of ways the kundalini is individually experienced, and also so that individuals who have such awakenings will have some information about how this phenomenon has occurred in others.

Maggie Bott of Ojai, California, did the following collection of personal experiences of people whose kundalini was activating and wrote them up in an article for D.O.M.E. Center's journal, *Aquarian Changes*:

"I have such a pain in my tailbone I can't sit down."

"My big toe on my left foot begins to throb and throb and won't stop."

"My hands tingle all the time. Sometimes they look red and blotchy. It isn't a normal tingling, like when your foot falls asleep. It is physical and at the same time not physical."

"My heart will suddenly start beating very rapidly — or it *feels* that way, but my pulse is normal!"

"My heart started thumping, and I could feel it in every cell of my body.'

"I feel like I am being rocked slowly, turned sideways . . . I lose my sense of gravity, and I feel a tingling sensation in my body, especially in my hands and feet. It feels like hot champagne."

"I'm awake all night, first real hot and then real cold, back and forth. When my Guide tells me it's kundalini flashes, I sleep — but I wake up with burns on my fingers under my two gold rings."

"I think I'm having a heart attack. My heart is beating so hard and so fast I can hardly breathe, and there's a terrible pain in my chest. I go to the hospital, and they hook me up to an EKG machine, and my heart beat is normal! They can't find anything the matter with me."

"I get heart palpitations at work that are so severe an ambulance takes me to the hospital. They think I'm hyperventilating, but my oxygen count is normal. They don't know what it is, so they send me home."

"For about a week my feet up to the shins were cold and wouldn't warm up. No matter how covered they were, it was like there was a cold breeze blowing on them. My Guide told me it was the kundalini and not to worry."

"It feels like my body is transmuting poisons. It's hard to explain. I get a warm rush and then funny sensations in parts of my body – I guess where the energy is blocked. But the rush of warmth makes stuff start to move. Sometimes it's a little painful, but not so much if I relax and let it flow. It feels like I'm changing poisons to something else. Sometimes it happens from *outside*: people around me will get hurt or angry, and I'll get that sensation in my body, that I'm changing it to something else. I guess since it's all One, it doesn't matter if the message comes from the outside or the inside – it's all your own poison."

"I woke up and felt hot, uncoolable. It felt like a huge disk was emanating from my back, right over my womb in the back, with rays extending to the top of my head and bottoms of my feet. It was heat, but not sweat, fever, stove heat or red heat. It was like warm Perrier water, but not as carbonated – but it was like warm *water*. I was so hot I opened the door. It must have been cold out, because the floor was cold under my feet, but I was too hot to cover up at all. Finally, I began to cool down. The first place to cool was the back of my neck. Next the soles of my feet. Next over my heart in the back. It felt like cold spots in these places that would then cool the surrounding areas. The last place to cool was the disk over my womb (it felt like a slightly convex piece of metal two or three inches in diameter, an unknown metal). The heat was like the heat of atomics: fusion or fission, neither cold nor hot."

"When the kundalini action started, it was a physical sensation that isn't the same as indigestion or the flu, though sometimes it feels similar. It feels more like it's happening *between* the bodies, what I've heard called an "alpha state," where both the inner and outer realities are the same, of equal strength to the perception. The next day there was a vibrating, thumping sensation in my midsection, as if sonic waves were trying to rise in my body. It felt like the waves were getting stuck just below the heart center and building there, and then would suddenly break through and rise to the top of my head with such force I'd feel dizzy."

"I was at work, and I felt the whole building shake. As I looked around me, it looked like everything was moving. When it stopped, I asked the girl in the next office if we'd just had an earthquake. She said she hadn't felt a thing. Since she knew about kundalini, we joked that I must have just had an experience. To me there is no other explanation of what it could have been."

"It feels like something hot is climbing up through me filling my chest and expanding it with heat and light. Everywhere it touches expands with heat and light. It fills my head with a blissful feeling, and I feel like I'm made of light."

"I was meditating. It felt like there was a small flame in my belly, and then somebody turned up the gas. The flame shot through me, filling me with heat and light, burning a hole in the top of my head and shooting out. It made me tingle all over. My Guide said it was kundalini and not to be afraid."

"I am filled with a slow wave motion, like the spume from a wave breaking on rocks."

"I meditate and the kundalini rises. I am filled with wonder, with the Oneness of all things, with bliss, with warmth filling my heart, my chest, my head. It is so energizing I can't sleep, but the next day I'm not tired. Another time I get a rush unexpectedly, and it makes me feel in a terrible hurry, like there isn't possibly enough time left in this life to get it all done, to finish my karma and become One before I die."

"It starts with a tingling in the body that suddenly intensifies, and everything gets very clear. It works like LSD: it intensifies almost beyond bearing (and sometimes beyond) whatever you happen to be making in your reality right then. A way to balance it is to see the assimilation of the energy on the cellular level, each cell absorbing the change."

"I began to get intense kundalini rushes. My Guide told me to burn candles: that the bouncing flame would be an indication of whether tomorrow would be another kundalini day for me or not."

"At night before going to sleep, it was red all over. I wasn't seeing red. It *felt* red all around me. I had this blissful feeling, mentally, and I heard voices singing about the glories of the Spirit. I had heart palpitations and wondered if I were having a heart attack. But it was really as if my heart would burst with the wonder of it all, with the love of humanity and the love of all life."[1]

• • •

From his articles, "Kunda-What"? in *Aquarian Changes*, Andrew Varela of Los Angeles shares the following:

I felt the bed (I was resting on my back) start to slowly rock from side to side. I smiled and opened my eyes to see who was trying to get my attention. I must have been sitting up staring blankly around the room for some time after I realized no one else was in the house. I know I lost track of time for the rest of the afternoon. Every time I'd go back to the meditation, those power-

---

[1]Maggie Bott, "Kundalini," from *Aquarian Changes*, vol. 5, no. 1, January, 1983, pp. 12–15. Used by permission.

ful waves of energy would rock me gently again, first from side to side, then up and down my spine, then all over. I decided that I had definitely found a substitute for sex when all else failed.

Everything I read had scare stories about how the kundalini energy had nearly killed its practitioners, yet my experience was just the opposite. For a time . . . the kundalini was the only energy I had. It has always been gentle, reassuring and somehow loving for me.

I witnessed a huge, nuclear-type explosion. I've never had a closed-eye vision as vivid as this one. Directly in front of me I experienced what looked like stars exploding in space (à la *Star Wars*). A body other than my own familiar physical one was vibrating much faster than the slow rate that I had become accustomed to. The light was red and yellow, and more brilliant than any I have ever seen, but didn't seem harmful to watch. When the explosion cleared, I found myself awake, viewing stars more clearly than ever, from a position out in space. I know what you're thinking, but I also know when I am this sure about what I see.

Episodes of kundalini experience end in many ways for me now, but most commonly leave me feeling weightless for a short duration. Sometimes I go out of body (not yet in a wakeful state though), and sometimes I'm just left with a desire not to let it go. It can be painful at times to "return" to an environment so excruciatingly slow and inefficient—that we must walk or drive lumbering, noisy automobiles to get around. Sometimes I am left feeling as if that gap were easily bridgeable, and that with one small nudge we could all be in that new place.

The experiences come regularly; about once a week. It always starts with the vibrations, beginning with the slow kind of waves that are almost always present in my waking life, and increasing to about the same frequency as the wall current in your house. It finally speeds up to a rate that makes it impossible to feel individual waves.[2]

---

[2]Andrew Varela, "Kunda-What?" from *Aquarian Changes*, vol. 6, no. 1, Spring, 1984, pp. 20–21; and "Kunda-What? II," from *Aquarian Changes*, vol. 6, no. 2, Summer, 1984, pp. 11–12. Selections used by permission.

Marsha Lane of Livermore, California, shares her experience in a letter to D.O.M.E. Center:

> This sensation felt like a menopause flash with the difference that the former had a loving feeling that the menopause flash does not have, and also it generates energy which the menopause flash does not do. I wasn't sure, then, if this was Kundalini energy, but from the beginning of this month . . . these kinds of "flashes of energy" became stronger but just as wonderful; they were overwhelming and useful. I began to count on them. . . . Sure enough, after awhile this beautiful, warm energy would come up and permeate my whole body and I would get up . . . so refreshed and rested that sometimes I would then sit at my desk and write for two hours before going to bed. Furthermore, my sleep would be very sound, and I would get up in the morning ready to start another heavy day.
>
> I don't have any doubts now that what I am experiencing is a Kundalini surge, and I want to share with you that it wasn't an uncomfortable or painful experience but a wonderful blessing, and I must say I attribute this to the fact that I have been meditating all along.[3]

• • •

David Benge of D.O.M.E. shares: "In meditation I got a helluva buzz. I was working with the archetypes of the *Tower* and the *Fool*, red and electric blue respectively, and the Pluto energy (the *Last Judgement* in tarot), which came as a gold pterodactyl splitting the air with its screams and the razor edges of its wings. The wind was howling so hard I could hardly stand up. The *Tower* and the *Fool* each had a sword, the tips of which were touching, and they bid me touch the point of Excalibur, which I held in my hands, to the tips of their swords. I did so and got a shock of electricity passing through my entire body. My Guide told me to withdraw Excalibur, and the *Empress* came and put her arms around me for healing and protection."

---

[3]Marsha Lane, "Letters . . .," from *Aquarian Changes*, vol. 7, no. 1, Winter, 1985, pp. 18–19. Used by permission.

"I dreamed I had pyramids at my feet emanating green energy, and I couldn't figure it out. Then later in waking life I had sensations going up my legs, like having the flu, but I had a great appetite. I felt my body *was* undergoing changes. In meditation I got that I was undergoing changes. The pain changed into emotional feelings of bliss. It was strange energy coming up my legs from my feet: the energy was 'organized,' like braided hair or fingers moving up my body. I had thoughts of sex—it felt like sex, but I had the mental realization that we really misuse sexuality. It's an incredible energy. The potential for sexuality hasn't been tapped yet by humanity."

• • •

Skye Atman of Culver City, California, shared the following in the pages of *Aquarian Changes*. (She was not practicing any form of meditation during or previous to these experiences.)

. . . My head touched the pillow and the entire bed began to shake violently. In a few seconds I realized it was not the Great California Earthquake. The bed wasn't shaking. I was. My whole body was rapidly vibrating as though a jackhammer were pulsing through me. I was shocked and scared. A powerful wave of energy gathered in the pit of my stomach and rapidly churned upward, forcing my mouth wide open. I felt as though a helium balloon had blown up inside me and now it was trying to come out. The balloon burst upward with an explosive force, hovered overhead, and then slowly settled back inside me. When it was over, I felt immensely peaceful, full of wonder, and elated. Without moving a muscle, I fell asleep.

This great feeling lasted about twenty-four hours, during which I told everyone about my strange experience. Reactions were mixed. No one knew what it might mean. However, the wonderful sensations soon faded and were replaced by unexplainable physical and emotional pain and agony.

Over the next eighteen months, in roughly chronological order, I had the following symptoms, each lasting for weeks: itchy feet, heat waves coursing up and down my body, tingling sensations all over, stomach cramps, nausea, a huge lump in my throat, sharp pains in the solar plexus, burning hands, sudden gagging, dizziness, insomnia, a feeling of bugs crawling all over me, fears of having epilepsy or brain damage. I was frightened and prone to conclude I was dying.

I thought I had brain cancer (dizziness and disorientation), throat cancer (the lump that wouldn't go away), stomach cancer (pains in my abdomen). I invented a cancer to match every physical symptom. I dreamt about dying, decided the whole thing was repressed sexuality, and so on.

Always the vibration, nearly every night. Something was trying to get out of me, and I wanted to stop it. But at the same time, I desired the new feelings and experiences. I wanted to protect the integrity of my body and mind, which equaled "me" as far as I knew, but it seemed that forces stronger than I were winning the battle.

. . . As I read and questioned, I realized that modern Western science didn't officially recognize OOBE's [out of body experiences]. However, I found such experiences have been consistently reported, but primarily from an Eastern spiritual viewpoint. For me, this presented a problem, since I had no religion and few opinions or beliefs about the eternal. I was quite confused.

. . . Occasionally, something tremendous would happen, and I'd take another step forward in acceptance, if not understanding. Once I was forcibly pulled out of my body through the crown of my head and taken on a fantastic trip through space, past planets, stars, huge white faces looking up at me. There was no light. The travel speed was terrifying, and the wind was roaring past my ears. I heard my voice say, "Cold!" My speed rapidly decelerated and my rpm's audibly diminished. The next thing I remembered was trying to reach for a pencil to record every detail. I couldn't move. I was paralyzed for several minutes. As feeling gradually came back, I realized my body was burning hot, and I was perspiring. For several days after I had enhanced hearing and could pick up overtones and nuances in music that I hadn't heard before.

Once I was lying down listening to a tape of myself playing the piano, when I felt the "rising hands." My physical hands were lying at my sides, and I distinctly felt another set of hands rising up into the air. Another time I was thinking about what my piano teacher had told me about an area of tension in my left side that inhibited performance. Suddenly, I felt a laser beam of energy boring hard into my scapula, right at the point of constriction. The force of the energy was so powerful it pushed me over onto my side. Now I either play better with my left hand, or I think I do.

. . . I knew that something was going to happen. I had "funny feelings." When I lay down for a rest in the afternoon, I made up my mind to try confrontation. When the vibrations started, I asked, "Who is Aga?" (In 1980 I had a significant dream about a person in a long orangish brown robe whose name was revealed to me as Aga, a spiritual figure or Guide.) Immediately a powerful force zoomed up my backbone. It seemed to singe the barrette in my hair, shot past my head and literally moved me around on the bed. Each vertebra felt as though it were being massaged and invigorated. The impact was astonishing. It felt like a new kind of orgasm.

After this I called on Aga many times, as he is clearly an important force . . .

. . . From all the reading, talking, feeling and experiencing, I've reached some conclusions at this time, although everything is, of course, subject to change.

1. The physical symptoms are indicative of basic physiological changes taking place inside me. I believe that new pathways are forming in my brain and nervous system that allow me to receive more input from the universe. Some would say the chakras are opening up.

2. The vibrating energy inside me is quite simply life energy that can be released in many ways — sexually, creatively, physically, and through OOBE's. I feel the OOBE's encourage and stimulate my renewed dedication to music and playing the piano.

3. The energy forces that permeate my physical body are real. I'm not hallucinating or imagining them. I don't know by what name they should be called — higher consciousness, astral souls, aspects of God. Of course, I have my own Aga, and I feel his energy is healing and protective.

4. We are all more than just a physical body. I know now that I'm not tied to my body or brain. Instead, "I" am the consciousness that animates my body. I am a spirit or soul that exists within and without my body. I'm not afraid to die, for it has been made clear to me there is much more to come.

5. As my mantra concludes, "Nothing bad can happen to me." All the aches and pains eventually go away. I always come back to my body. I'm not crazy or sick. I still function in the "real" world, knowing that it is far bigger and more exciting than I ever imagined.[4]

• • •

Stephen P. Connors of D.O.M.E. reports: "In a dream a friend and I were searching around a house for a light switch. He found it and switched it on. I was waiting for the light to come on so that I could investigate the source of two strange lights I had seen at my feet. When it did, two ten-inch snakes darted out toward the doorway behind me. I raced out after them, and there was my Guide standing off to the side. I felt excitement at discovering these two beautiful snakes, but also a fear. I have become used to my Guide appearing in my dreams, so his presence there didn't surprise me. He told me to pick up the snakes. With some hesitation I bent down to do so, and to my astonishment they literally leapt into my hands.

"In my right hand I now held an iridescent blue-green snake which was cool to the touch. In my left was a sort of opalescent snake emitting a warmth that went into my hand and up my arm. It felt like warmth was flowing in from my left hand and out through my right.

"The snakes began to grow and vibrate in my hands. I felt a tingling as if electricity were flowing through me. Now approximately three feet in length, each coiled around my arms as I held their heads between my thumbs and forefingers.

"Suddenly they opened their mouths and let out the shrillest, high-pitched scream I've ever heard. It felt like it went right through me, and my body began to shake.

---

[4]Skye Atman, "Of OOBE's and Aga," from *Aquarian Changes*, vol. 7, no. 1, Winter, 1985, pp. 15–17. Used by permission.

"This woke me up. I found myself sweating from the heat and shivering from the cold. I immediately closed my eyes, went into meditation and found myself with my Guide. He pointed out that the snakes were still coiled on either arm. Each was now purring like a kitten, and this felt very soothing to me."

• • •

Gwen Gilliland of Los Angeles gives this account: "While meditating, I had quite a strong kundalini experience. As I sat with the *Magician*, my mind began to drift. Suddenly, the *Magician* raised his wand and cracked it down hard on the table. A white light, similar to lightning, shot through my body. This blinding explosion sent hot energy from my head to my toes in one bright flash. Following the experience I felt tingly and acutely perceptive."

• • •

Kundalini is an energy that can be transferred from one person to another through a touch or through some organic material, such as a peacock feather. The Eastern gurus who awaken kundalini in others use this method. However, this can create problems. First, an outer teacher cannot know a person's unique interior design as well as the Inner Guide does, so he or she cannot always gauge what another person can handle. And second, if another person raises your kundalini, you think that that person, not you, is the source, and a spiritual dependence is fostered.

Let the kundalini awaken in you naturally, as you are ready, with your Inner Guide as teacher. This way your power is your own and can't be used to enhance the material plane or inner plane power of another.

Part 3

QUESTIONS AND ANSWERS

Questions and Answers

1) Q. What is the best way to approach the Inner Guide Meditation?

A. Let each meditation be new, fresh, unexpected. Try not to compare your meditations one to the other or to anyone else's meditations. Try not to anticipate what will happen. Let it flow by itself under your Guide's direction. Most importantly, *don't guide your Guide*. Allow him to teach you as he does, and try not to pre-program how he is to teach you.

2) Q. Is the Inner Guide always a positive figure?

A. Yes. I've talked to some people who have initially had a disapproving ego reaction to some aspect of the Guide, but even these people end up loving their Guides. Everyone loves and is loved by the true Guide. It's the essential part of the relationship. The most crucial factor determining whether we have a positive or negative reaction to the Guide at first seems to be the degree to which we project the Guide outside of ourselves onto others.

3) Q. Is the Inner Guide Meditation just common sense?

A. Common sense has little to do with it. Because we are still ignorant of the physics involved in the relationships between the inner and outer realities, the archetypes frequently make requests or suggest actions that may seem irrational. For instance, an archetype might tell you that to plant flowers or to re-position your bed will solve a certain health problem; and it does. These energies exhibit a multi-dimensional symbol physics we don't yet understand.

Figure 18. The *Twins* in tarot, and Gemini in astrology, are associated with the mind and its dualistic function which allows us to see differences in things—to make choices. The *Twins* as archetypal figures are the question askers and complement the Sagittarius teacher function. Trump of the *Twins* from an unpublished D.O.M.E. tarot deck ©1987 the D.O.M.E. Center.

4) Q. Why do you emphasize the *Sun*, *Fool* and *High Priestess* of tarot as being so important in terms of the inner work?

A. Although all the tarot forces or archetypes are ways of perceiving aspects of the God energy, the *Fool* and *Sun* represent the Center pole. Both are aspects of love energy. The *Sun* is our life-giving essence — the Center of the Self, the Prime Mover within. The *Fool* represents freedom, friendship and altruistic love — the love of all humanity without discrimination. And the *High Priestess* represents an aspect of the inner mother, the loving, caring, nurturing part of oneself. The more you work with these particular energies, the more you will find that your base transfers itself from ego to Center. That's why I consider it important to concentrate on the *Sun, Fool* and *High Priestess* in inner work. Their combined love energies will heal and transform the most negative-appearing energy forms.

5) Q. Is the Inner Guide Meditation essentially a spiritual discipline or does it have materialistic uses?

A. The Inner Guide Meditation is a spiritual discipline and technology, but I've worked with people whose primary current ego interest was making money or finding a partner. The Guides accept us however we operate, whatever our current values may be, wherever we are in our spiritual evolution, and they help us work toward an understanding of our lives and goals. What I usually find is that the Guides subtly direct us toward our own inner spiritual goals as we continue to work with them whether we are initially conscious of this or not.

6) Q. Does the Inner Guide Meditation have any influence over physical disease?

A. It seems to work dramatically with physical diseases, but much further research will have to be done in this area. People have reported all sorts of "miraculous" healings, such as the absorption of tumors, the remission of cancer, bones mending overnight, ulcers disappearing, nerves regenerating and the like. I had an expe-

Figure 19. The *Wheel of Fortune* has to do with the planet Jupiter in astrology, the archetype of the teacher or way-shower, and with the energy connected to the Inner Guides and meditation. Trump of the *Wheel of Fortune* from tarot deck in *Seed*, published by Crown Publishers, New York, 1969. Used by permission.

rience with an abscessed tooth that had swollen my right jaw and was painfully throbbing. When I worked on it in meditation, the Guide first had me literally separate the pain from my physical body by moving it two feet away from myself. When I was able to do this, the tarot *Sun* form came and healed it. The problem was gone within half an hour. X-rays I had months afterwards showed no evidence that there had ever been an abscess in that area or any cause for one. Usually healings happen as side effects of the meditation, rather than anything as dramatic as the previously mentioned experience. However, physical problems that we are taught to think of as permanent or incurable or terminal often disappear, remit or heal as we work with our Guides and the archetypes, especially as we resolve conflicts between those archetypes that have been fighting since we were born.

David Benge of D.O.M.E. Center reports: "The Inner Guide Meditation worked dramatically for me in healing some physical problems I had developed. I had done years of unbalanced eating, which had created a slightly expanded heart, a minor prostate problem, liver trouble (from the over-use of alcohol, analgesics and sugar), and, worst of all, chronic constipation.

"I put the meditation to a real test, determined to heal this physical degeneration. My Guide had me work with the archetype the *Last Judgement* (Pluto in astrology), which appeared as a tall woman bathed in golden light. After working several times with this figure, I began to open to her, to feel tremendous love between us. She sent iridescent light into the areas of my body that needed healing. I received a 'new' colon made of meadow-green iridescent light. This new organ just came out of her and moved toward me and entered my body at the location of my intestines. The light making up this intestinal shape was not just color alone. It was as if it were charged with emotional-spiritual love energy, alive with the essence of the universe. She did the same for my heart (iridescent magenta), liver (gold iridescence with a bright blue aura), and prostate (silver iridescence).

"In addition to this healing from the *Last Judgement*, I got valuable information from the *High Priestess* about how to adjust my macrobiotic diet to augment the healing. I worked two or three times a week on this. The constipation and prostate problems were healed in four weeks, and the heart expansion cleared up in two months. The liver problem is much better and well on its way to regeneration. I believe that if we take total responsibility for our physical problems and ignore most 'facts' of the medical establishment (like obediently dying from so-called 'terminal' illnesses), we can heal them with diet and the meditation. In my opinion, we should heal the problem first, then, if we need to, go to a doctor for verification that 'the problem is gone. It's only a matter of un-creating what our energies have created in the first place. Our Guides can show us how to do this."

7) Q. Are there any other physical results from working with this meditation?

A. As you work with the energies through the Inner Guide Meditation, you will find yourself changing physically. You will start craving foods that you disliked before or lose your taste for foods that you liked. This dietary change is one of the first things you'll notice when you're working with the archetypes and your Guide. I had been meditating for about six months when red meat "went away." This wasn't the result of any philosophical decision or insight. I would order a steak or a hamburger out of habit, then find that I couldn't eat it. Chicken and fish soon followed as I sort of involuntarily became a vegetarian. Later my taste for all milk products left, but white fish returned to my diet along with a desire to eat only organically grown foods and to avoid all processed foods and stimulants. Finally, I discovered that eating macrobiotically suited me best.

8) Q. Why does dietary change occur as a result of the Inner Guide Meditation?

A. I suspect that the sensations, often unusual or intense, experienced in the physical body as the archetypal energies touch us and we interact with them result in real changes in our cells and their needs. The cells develop new nourishment requirements, needs for new minerals and nutrients, new balances. *Spiritual change is physical change.* To project a new reality or to change the current hologram, the projection unit itself, i.e. the four-body system, including the physical body, must be changed. As the cells call out for new foods, we respond by seeking them out and losing interest in the old.

9) Q. I'm able to see my Guide and the archetypes outside of me, projected around me into my environment. Is it all right to work with them in this way?

A. This is much like laying out the tarot cards and reading them. When the forces are projected outside of us, our egos are able to filter and control them too easily. *The Secret of the Golden Flower* tells why it is necessary to focus inwardly. This secret is that we must learn to make the *light* flow backward, to follow the energy that projects out of us *back toward its source*—to face *toward* the sources of the archetypal energies. In this manner the ego is able to filter and control less, and we receive truer information and more unexpected insights. *Always work inside.*

10) Q. Why do you say it is important to record Inner Guide Meditations and dreams?

A. Writing down meditations and dreams helps to bring the inner energies out into daily life—to *earth* them. It also prevents the trickster, the human mind under the ego's control, from juggling, forgetting, or editing our inner experiences (both dreams and meditations). Recording this inner material furthers the interchange between the inner and outer worlds. This interchange can be likened to an infinity sign, one loop being the inner world, the other, the outer. A written record serves as good eye evidence of this interplay.

11) Q. Sometimes I receive images of grains or vegetables from the archetypes. What does this mean?

A. This often indicates a dietary need. Ask the Guide and the archetype that gives the grain or vegetable if this is what is being indicated. For instance, people with strong Uranian or Aquarian elements in their patterns are often given apples. Apples and apple

Figure 20. In astrological/tarot terms, the ego is akin to Aries/*Emperor*, the sense of "I am" and the difference from You or Other. It is one half of the whole of the ego/Shadow polarity, the two halves sharing a common center. Trump of the *Emperor* from Aleister Crowley's Thoth Tarot Deck. Published by Samuel Weiser, Inc., York Beach, ME, and U.S. Games Systems, Inc., Stamford, CT. Used by permission.

juice seem to calm the electrical system, under the rulership of Aquarius (the *Star*) and Uranus (the *Fool*).

12) Q. How would you define "ego," "mind," and "Self?"

A. I see the ego as who you see yourself to be, the person you see in the mirror. The Self is that deathless central part of each of us, the heart *Center,* and represents the primary purpose in life. The ego is the vehicle the Self inhabits and gives life to. The mind is the archetype of consciousness and discrimination—the witness to both ego and Self. Too many of our words say "self" when it is the ego that is actually being referred to, e.g. self-esteem, self-interest. In astrological-tarot terms, the ego is akin to Aries/*Emperor*, the Self to Sun/*Sun* and the mind to Gemini/*Twins* or *Lovers*.

13) Q. Can two people work together with the Inner Guide Meditation?

A. Yes, definitely. This works well with someone who knows what you want to work with, the questions you want to ask, and the kinds of things you want to accomplish. Have the other person record for you when you meditate, and you record when he or she meditates.

People working in tandem this way seem to experience an accelerated growth. When someone is writing down the experience for you, you can get into the experience more fully without having to consciously attempt to remember all the details. The experience of the inner planes is much like the experience of a dream. When you come back, details tend to fall back into unconsciousness just as they do with dreams. Another problem this solves is that of getting so involved with one experience that you forget the other things you wanted to do in meditation.

If you are working with someone personally involved with you, your husband or wife, for instance, be aware that there will be a tendency to try to maintain each other's projected role relationships. The person recording might try to guide your Guide in accordance with the wishes of his or her own ego, conscious or unconscious. This will be less of a problem if both persons are aware of this tendency and verbalize it. Though the Guides will usually take care of such outside interference, always trust your Inner Guide over any outer figure acting as a guide or counselor.

14)   Q. I'm working with a psychologist who is against my utilizing the Inner Guide Meditation. How should I deal with this?

A. The Inner Guide Meditation can be threatening not only to psychiatrists and psychological counselors in general, but also to astrologers and leaders of spiritual groups. If you work with your Guide regularly, there is usually little need to continue with an outer guide for long, unless you need the additional ego support, want to accelerate the inner process, or wish to develop more rapidly some latent talent or ability. If you have an accurately calculated horoscope and can translate it yourself or get it translated into tarot terms, you have the road map of your essential structure, inner and outer. The Guide can do the rest. He is your teacher. The Inner Guide Meditation can also represent an economic threat to many of us in the counseling professions.

As with any new idea, the Inner Guide Meditation meets with resistance in established quarters. Some psychologists incorrectly equate the Inner Guide Meditation with Jungian "active imagination," a potentially dangerous method. The Guides, however, prevent these dangers by their protective presence and knowledgeable guidance.

Ask your Guide why your psychologist objects and what energy within you is causing his or her objection.

15)   Q. Does the Inner Guide Meditation lower one's resistance to "the powers of darkness" or "the lower astral"?

A. No. The contrary seems to be true. Working with your Guide, and especially those tarot archetypes associated with light, such as the *Sun*, the *Fool*, the *Star* and *Strength*, in a truth-seeking manner, seems to attract fewer and fewer negative elements into your life. I've never known a true Guide to advise or encourage anyone on a power trip, especially of the "black magic" variety.

The Guides will not interfere with us, nor will they aid or direct us toward dark paths or ways of unconsciousness. They will let us set up unconscious situations if we don't ask their advice, and they will not interfere in these situations unasked unless there is a possibility of physical death or irreparable harm to the ego. Good teachers will often let their charges fall flat on their faces when they're not asked for assistance or instruction.

16)   Q. Why don't I get life results that others claim to get? The results I get sometimes seem negative to me.

A. Perhaps this is due to ego resistance or to working with a false or ego guide. If you aren't getting results in the form of positive life changes from the Inner Guide Meditation — and usually they are quite rapid, positive and dramatic — and, if you've been meditating regularly, ask your Guide to take you to that part of you that is preventing the life changes from happening or to those parts of you that are not being heard or accepted.

Also, the ego is not always the best judge of results in the long run. Sometimes people tell me: "I began working with my Guide, and my whole world fell apart." Though this may be quite true, in a few cases, the world that fell apart generally turns out to have been a frozen reality that prevented the individual's growth and evolution, while the world coming in and replacing the old is an open-ended one with an infinity of possibilities, both material and spiritual. Often what the ego holds onto most desperately is exactly what is preventing its own growth and change.

Challenge your Guide for explanations of outer life changes, especially if they seem negative to you. If you ask why, he'll explain.

Outer physical reality corresponds *exactly* to the inner energy structures — to the inner reality. If negative results occur in your outer life, demand to confront their sources within.

17)   Q. I find myself skeptical of the Inner Guide Meditation itself and the results other people tell me about. How can I overcome this?

A. Skepticism, fear, doubt and judgement are generally caused by the forces which are called in the tarot the *World,* and *Old Pan* or the *Devil* (the Saturn and Capricorn energies in astrol-

Figure 21. Saturn (the *World*) is the ruler of the sign Capricorn (*Old Pan*). The Saturn and Capricorn energies we all carry are part of our safety systems. They are the energies that test our egos and our realities. Their job is to maintain our limits and our structures, on all levels, until we are experienced enough to change or go beyond them. The illustration of the *World* from an original drawing by Leigh McCloskey, ©1987. Used by permission.

ogy). If you meet and interact with these energy forms on the inner planes and do what they need so that they can become more conscious in you, you should find that your skepticism abates.

The Saturn and Capricorn energies we all carry are part of our safety systems. They are the energies that test our egos and our realities. Their job is to maintain our limits and our structures, on all levels, until we are experienced enough and strong enough to change or go beyond them. They want to make sure we miss no steps. We often think of them as the "bad guys" within, but in fact, they function in their ways as protectors. These two energies project out of us onto father, boss, the policeman, the establishment, career, reputation and the law. They represent the living bone of our reality structures. The only proof that Saturn and Capricorn accept is that of living experience in our everyday lives.

So if you're skeptical of others' results, try the meditation yourself over a period of time and see what happens. "The fruit of the tree" is the only real proof of any spiritual system.

18)   Q. How can I be sure that my Guide and the contact with him and the archetypes are real?

A. In lieu of the horoscope, which describes the appearance and personality of your Guide, accept the Guide figure that presents himself and go by your feelings. If you really feel love, acceptance and protection coming from him, work with him. Have him take you to the archetypes within. See what happens in your outer world as you work with him. The test of the real Guide is what happens in your daily life, what happens around you.

After reading many horoscopes and initiating thousands of people into the Inner Guide Meditation, I'm beginning to see that we *can't* make anything up, even though the ego may tell us we can. The ego takes credit for everything. In initiation after initiation, people often think they are "making up the whole thing," but, in fact, what they see, hear, feel and report about their inner experience corresponds exactly to their personal horoscopic symbolism, usually without prior knowledge of astrology or the tarot as it applies to them. An uncomfortable fact seems to be that if an astrologer can accurately read a horoscope and describe a person and that person's reality, then these archetypal energies are primary, the person is second, and the rest of reality is third in the flow of creation. We're not making them up—they're making us up!

A technique I recommend to firm up your Guide contact is to ask your Guide to take *both* of your hands into his, and then to give him permission to let you *feel* his feelings for you. With the true Guide, you will *always* sense his love, protection and care. You will not sense this with a false guide.

19) Q. "Forward, left, then right" seems too pat a formula. How do you explain it?

A. I arrived at this "movement of the mind" through experimentation with many different directional approaches. Through this trial and error method, I found that this is the one sequence of movement that always works, pragmatically, in contacting the initial true Guide. I don't know why it works.

20) Q. My main difficulty is inertia—making myself do the meditation. How can I overcome this?

A. I discovered this tendency in myself during one period of Inner Guide work. I corrected it with the device of setting daily appointments with myself at specific times to meditate. This structuring of time *utilizes* the same force that *causes* resistance, Saturn, the *World*. Saturn cannot stand to waste time. If you allot a certain daily time span, you'll find that you won't just sit and do nothing— you'll meditate. Another way is to work with someone else, again, on a definite schedule where you record for the person and he or she records for you. The commitment to another seems to help many who otherwise procrastinate.

21) Q. What is the relation between my archetypes and those of other people?

A. The archetypes are universal. Although we speak about "my *High Priestess*" and "your *High Priestess*," there is only one energy principle in the universe that the *High Priestess* stands for as symbol. That energy exists in and flows through all creation, as do the energies of all the other archetypes. If we picture the unconscious as an ocean containing all the archetypal forces, and each of us as wave peaks on that ocean receiving the archetypal images in our individual ways, we can begin to get a clearer understanding of how we perceive these energies. There is only one energy corresponding to each of the tarot symbol forms. Our personal patterns, illustrated by our individual horoscopes, determine how each archetype manifests itself to our personal ego views, e.g., the form that a *High Priestess* of a person with the Moon in Capricorn in the eighth house takes will be different than the form of the *High Priestess* for a person with Moon in Aquarius in the third house, although the *High Priestess* archetypal energy in both is the same. You might think of it as light of one color coming through two different colored filters.

22)   Q. When an archetype places a symbolic gift into the body, does it make a difference whether it is placed on the right or left side?

A. The gifts that are placed into the left side of the body seem to be abilities, aptitudes, or powers that function automatically, like our breathing or heart action. Those that are placed into the right side of the body seem to require an act of will to make them function. Those that are centrally located seem to partake of both the unconscious and ego-conscious qualities. This may be reversed in left-handed people, but I haven't studied a sufficient amount of data on left-handed people to determine whether this is true or not. Information on this point would be greatly appreciated.

23)   Q. Define the ego more specifically.

A. The ego is a process — *current ego* would be a more accurate term. It is like a two-dimensional body-mind membrane that energies flow through and affect. I understand it best in terms of the cusp of the first house or point of the Ascendant (also called the rising sign) in the individual horoscope. It is our physical vehicle and includes our *persona*, the mask worn in life through which we

Figure 22. The animal that leads you to your Inner Guide seems to be related to the power animals of shamanism. Engraving by Gustave Doré from La Fontaine's *Fables*.

relate to others. It is who we see when we look in a mirror, our idea of who we are and what we look like. It has a certain material continuity, but it adapts and changes according to which forces are flowing through and affecting it. The ego at noon is not the same as the ego at midnight. At different times it experiences thoughts, feelings, emotions and outer reality differently. It is a reactive part of the Self. Its material manifestation allows it to perceive and experience the flow of reality in an orderly manner. It contains our point of view and acts as a filter through which we perceive external and internal realities, the kind of colored glasses through which we look.

24) Q. When and how often should I do the Inner Guide Meditation?

A. Meditation requires concentration. If there is a tendency to become sleepy or to lack the necessary concentration early in the morning or late at night, I would advise meditating for twenty or thirty minutes during the part of the day when you are most alert. Your Guide can advise you further on this.

Regular meditation, once or twice daily, or as often as prescribed by your Guide, is important. Getting into a meditation rhythm — like a healthy heart beat — helps to develop inner concentration and the ability to focus easily.

25) Q. Can I continue working with the animal that first took me to the Inner Guide?

A. The animals that lead us to our Guides were a suggestion from a psychiatrist in Santa Fe, New Mexico, who presented the paper, *The Inner Guide to the Archetypes*, to the Annual Conference of the Society of Jungian Analysts of Northern and Southern California in March, 1972. He and I had both been having difficulty in getting people to move from the point where they leave the cave and enter the landscape to the point where they meet their Guides. He came up with the idea of calling an animal (a symbol for the instincts or the feeling nature) to lead the way.

The animal that leads you to your Inner Guide is not a Guide, but it seems to be related to the *power animals* of shamanism and can be used as such with the OK of your Guide. (Michael Harner's *The Way of the Shaman*, Harper & Row, New York, 1980, discusses this at length.)

Since the introduction of the animal into the meditation technique, there has been greater ease in getting people to their Guides. If you should lose contact while the animal is taking you to your Guide, remember to go back and recreate the scene *where you last saw the animal*. If you wander aimlessly, give the animal *permission* to take you *directly* to your Guide, permission to penetrate any unconscious blockage that is being created, and then try to see *where* in the landscape the animal seems to be leading you.

If asked, your Inner Guide can tell you whether or not you should continue to use the animal in your meditation practice. He can also give you additional advice concerning the most efficient method of contacting him. Setting up a specific *meeting place* in the inner landscape to meet your Guide each time you meditate seems to be helpful in reestablishing contact for future meditations.

26)   Q. My main difficulty is in seeing the figures. What can I do about this?

A. I find that if you are with your Guide and a figure that is very nebulous presents itself, it will usually cooperate if you ask it to appear more clearly or give it permission to do so. This will generally be a figure that represents a repressed or suppressed energy. If this phenomenon occurs with all the figures, just persevere in the meditation, and they will become clearer. Through practice, you will get used to the inner world. You will develop the senses that operate there.

There seem to be two ways of *seeing* on the inner planes. Some people have a highly developed visual sense and see as clearly within as they do in a dream or in outer reality. Others, more commonly, don't have this acute visual ability at first, but they are still capable of describing minute details of the scene or figure they are experiencing. They describe their way of seeing as "imagining," "knowing," "getting a mental picture," or "seeing with the mind's eye." Accept whatever you see in the meditation, however you see it. Don't compare your meditations or visual experiences with others. You are unique. See as *you* see. Often, as you meditate for a length of time, clear and colorful visual images will appear and fade. Let them come and go as they will. Take what you get. Remember to *receive* the images as if you were blank film receiving impressions. Don't look — receive; and learn to accept the *first image that comes.*

Sometimes it helps to concentrate on one of your other senses at first — touch, smell, hearing or taste. This tends to also draw in and open up the visual ability.

Mars and Aries (the *Tower* and *Emperor* in tarot) are the archetypes associated with sight, as is the sign on your Ascendant (first house cusp). Work with them to enhance your visual ability.

27) Q. How can I get a clear answer from my Inner Guide and the archetypes?

A. Give them permission to tell you the answer to your question *whether you want to hear the answer or not.* Frequently, our own resistance to the information that our Guides, our Shadows or one of our archetypes holds for us causes the apparent lack of an answer. Insisting that you want to know and pushing through your own ego resistance for the answer will almost always bring it forth.

You can also ask them to write the answer or make words appear in the air before you — or ask for a picture or a symbol that represents the answer, then let your Guide decipher it for you. When I have been unable to get a clear answer in myself or others because of resistance to the psychic material being dealt with, I have asked that a home movie screen be set up in the inner world and images (that can then be decoded by the Guide if necessary) be flashed upon it, or that a movie be shown representing the answer to the question that was asked. Accept the *first* thought or answer that comes to you after asking the question, even if you judge it to make no sense or to be otherwise inappropriate. It may well be the answer in code. You can then work on decoding it.

28) Q. How do I deal with someone in my life who is always very negative to me?

A. Ask your Guide to take you to the image of that person in the inner world. Then ask that image to take its true form *as it exists as an energy form in you.* Accept whatever form appears. If it turns into a green frog, work with the green frog. Ask what it needs from you to be healed *as an energy within you* (having nothing to do with the outer world person). Ask what it may have to give you that you're not receiving or accepting from it. Ask what part of you it represents. This "true form" will represent the force that is projecting out of you onto that outer person and causing him or her to act negatively toward you. You will find that the outer person will either change or go out of your life when you heal the unconscious form you project on him or her. You will change the role need of the energy.

Say, for instance, that your neighbor is trying to poison your dog. Ask your Guide to take you to or bring you the image of that neighbor as you know him to be in the outer world. Then give that image permission to take its true form as it lives in you. Say that it turns into Dracula. The Dracula image is a picture of the energy in you that projects out from you onto your neighbor and gets him to try to poison your dog. Call on the *Sun, Fool* and *High Priestess.* Ask them to send their love into the figure to heal and transform it so that it reaches its highest possible form in you at this time. After they do this, say that the Dracula figure has turned into a King. Dracula and the King are the *same energy,* the King being its higher, more conscious form. Ask the King what *you* have to do new in thought, action, or behavior (having nothing to do with your neighbor), so that the energy the King represents in you will remain constant and not sink back into unconsciousness and its Dracula form. When you have received this information, give the King energy form permission to enter your body. Feel what part of your body this energy lives in and where it radiates from. If the transformation is successful and you have really changed this part of yourself, the neighbor will either change dramatically or go out of your life immediately. Because you have changed your role needs and no longer need a dog poisoner in your reality, the neighbor's choices are to change as a role player for you or leave your reality.

Never work with images of known people from the outer world in the inner world. It tends to sustain rather than release negative unconscious projections. Always ask the image of the known outer world person that your Inner Guide brings to take its true form *as it lives as an energy within you.* This insures that you are, in fact, working on an aspect of yourself. You can go to images of everyone you know and ask each of these outer world figures to take its true form as it lives in you. Here you will get the images of what you are projecting on each of them. It's both fascinating and revealing to do this and to discover just what we are projecting on those people we love best or least.

Healings of outer world people may not be done on the inner planes without their conscious ego consent. Interference, no matter how well intentioned, with the life or free will of another *without that person's permission given verbally on the outer planes* is against Universal Law. Healing, all too often, turns into an ego power trip, so be sure to call or write the person to be healed for their permission for a healing from you. The only things we are allowed to send another without his or her permission are love and light.

Finally, let people be new. Allow them to change in your mind, in your thinking about them. Know that a person who was negative to you ten years ago has also been growing and evolving. Then the part of you which they represent won't be stuck and can change and grow. Always let everything be new.

29) Q. Money is a constant problem in my life. Which archetype would I see to work on this and make this area more conscious?

A. This would have to do, in terms of the horoscope, with factors relating to the second house (the sign on the cusp, a planet or planets in the house, the planet ruling the house, or the so-called "hard angles" to any of these) and the archetypes of the *High Priest* or *Hierophant* (Taurus) and the *Empress* (Venus).

Problems in the money area are always connected to problems in three other areas of life: love, sex and life goals. If there is a problem in the second house (money, resources, oral needs, income, food, supply), look also to the fifth house (the personal love area, relations to children, self-expression, art, creativity, hobbies), the eighth house (sex, regeneration, death, debt, metamorphosis, taxes, rebirth, astral projection, transformation, levitation, kundalini), and to the eleventh house (life goals measured by one's personal death, impersonal love, altruism, humanitarianism,

Figure 23. The *High Priest* or *Hierophant* (Taurus in astrology) is the arche-type concerned with all manifestation and building—especially with income, money, resources, food and talents. Trump of the *Priest* from the Servants of Light Tarot Deck, Jersey, Channel Islands. Used by permission.

friendship, groups you belong to — or don't belong to). A change in one will foster a change in all. Let your Inner Guide advise you where to focus.

The eleventh house is one of the least understood areas of the horoscope. It is the key to all manifestation. I recommend getting a blank book that you title, *The Things I Want To Have Done Before I Die*, and write everything you can think of in the book, whether you judge them to be possible, impossible, personal or transpersonal. Some might be: "I want to have no starvation on the planet by the time I die," or "I want to levitate twenty-five feet before I die," or "I want to travel to the Moon and back before I die." Whatever. Write them all down. But then pick out the top five, giving yourself the option to change your mind tomorrow. But keep the top five prioritized. This lets your manifestation energies know what your current priorities are. Within weeks they'll begin bringing you the first steps toward those end goals. Otherwise they don't know what you want, and nothing happens. And by having your end goals clear to yourself, all the other things you're doing in life will become more clear. Nothing furnishes a better measuring stick for everything else you're doing in life than goals measured by personal death.

30) Q. Will meditation help my lower back pain?

A. Lower back pain is the classic symptom of a partnership problem. It has to do with the natural Libra area or seventh house of the horoscope, which rules the lumbar region and the kidneys. It also has to do with the individual's Shadow — the *other half* or *alter ego* which is always projected onto and manipulates the marriage or business partner, the roommate, one's third sibling and one's second child. The Shadow figure exists within you as a constant partner and is always of the same sex as yourself. As the ego separated itself from the Great All between birth and seven years of age, the Shadow simultaneously formed on the inner planes to balance the ego and keep it from dissolving. As the ego became the "I," the Shadow formed itself from the "not-I" elements — everything the ego thought it was not or did not possess as negative or positive aspects of itself. The Shadow is both partner and balance to the ego. It must be confronted and made a conscious friend and ally before the ego can achieve stability with the Center and the other aspects of Self. *You and your Shadow are the two halves of one whole.*

I recommend asking your Guide to present your Shadow to you as one of the first steps in the Inner Guide Meditation. Ask the Shadow figure what it needs from you to start functioning as friend and conscious *equal* partner. Ask, if you were to give it part of one day of every week to do what it needs to do for its expression through you in your life, what would it like to do, where would it like to go? Give your other half expression compatible to you both. As you deal with your Shadow, lower back pain and all other seventh house problems will begin to clear up.

31)   Q. I ask the archetypes to have certain things happen in the outer world. They say they will, but then the things don't happen. I feel that I'm putting myself on with the meditation. Why don't the promises of the archetypes come true?

A. You're experiencing what is called the "magic mirror effect." When the ego is heavily invested in the results of outer world situations, it will only accept answers that coincide with its desires. (Think of the Wicked Queen and her magic mirror in *Snow White*.) We always encounter this effect when we try to change outer reality without focusing on changing and becoming more conscious ourselves. If you approach the meditation asking for things, the "magic mirror" will operate until the ego understands that all outer changes result from changes on deep inner levels. As you meditate more and allow the process to flow, you will find that your needs are filled without your having to ask.

A technique for helping to overcome the "magic mirror effect" that we have developed here at D.O.M.E. is to ask your Inner Guide to flash a *red light* if you are not getting truth and a *green light* if you are. It seems to be easier for us to create and manipulate words than it is to create or manipulate colors or images.

Perhaps instead of asking for certain things to occur, you might ask your Guide to take you to those parts of you that *prevent* things from changing or flowing in your outer life. You can then remove the blockages in your life flow and learn to co-create with the reality-generating energies.

32) Q. If you were to recommend only *one* question to ask and work on with the Inner Guide, what would that question be?

A. "How do I wake up and become *all* of myself?"

33) Q. When I describe the Inner Guide Meditation, friends and acquaintances say that I am dabbling in black magic and the occult, or put the meditation down in some way. What can I do about this?

A. Your friends and acquaintances are living out your own unconscious doubts and fears. Ask your Guide to take you to the figure or figures that are causing these doubts and fears. Work with them to bring them into conscious and useful forms, and you will find that your friends and acquaintances will change their attitudes or go out of your life. No amount of words will convince people of the truth of any spiritual practice. Only the example of your own life and being will demonstrate the validity of your path. The fruit of the tree is the proof of the tree.

Remember, our Saturn and Capricorn energies (the *World* and *Old Pan* or the *Devil*) test us every inch of the way to make certain that we don't miss a step in our personal spiritual evolutions.

34) Q. As I go along from meditation to meditation, my results seem to be less dramatic, less certain, less precise, slower. Why does this happen?

A. This could indicate that you're approaching an *ego death*, a period when the current ego will be assimilating a major energy which heretofore has been repressed or suppressed, triggering a transformation of the ego. Often an ego death is preceded by a depression or by the symptoms you mention. Fear and resistance to change are what cause the experiences you have described. If you really discipline yourself at this point to meditate more, to give more permissions, to receive instructions on how to ease and facilitate the transition, to really *listen* and *be receptive* on the inner planes, you will find that the entire meditative experience becomes more clear and that the contact deepens with both your Guide and the archetypal energy forms.

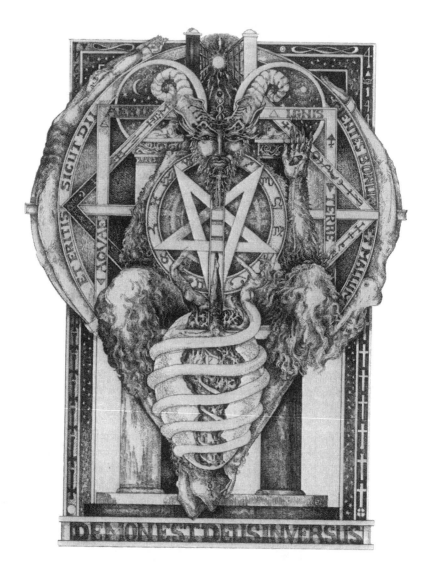

Figure 24. Our Saturn and Capricorn energies (the *World* and *Old Pan* or the *Devil*) test us every inch of the way to make certain that we don't miss a step in our personal spiritual evolution. Trump of *Old Pan* from an original drawing by Leigh McCloskey, ©1987. Used by permission.

35)   Q. What does the Inner Guide Meditation have to do with God?

A. As you work with and feel the inner forces you carry in their various forms, you will discover your connection to and understanding of what God (or The Great Spirit or All That Is or The Source of All or whatever words you personally use) is all about in a very direct and individual way. The spiritual experiences that occur in the inner worlds are intense and personal. Realization that God exists and is not just a theoretical concept is overwhelming to most, especially to those whose reality is based on materialistic concepts and beliefs. The twenty-two energies that the tarot images symbolize are twenty-two different aspects of the God force. We are unable to experience the totality of God in one step — *Enoch walked with God and was not.* But as we experience these energies one by one, we begin to evolve our own realization of God. This is probably why the first apparent results of the Inner Guide Meditation tend to be a dramatic change in the personal value system and a deepening of personal spirituality.

It may be that your God Center or the Solar Center figure within, which represents your *primary purpose*, what you've come in to do this life, will encourage a different spiritual path for you than the one you were born to or the one you are currently following. Go with it, if your Guide approves. It's OK not to be Christian, or Jewish, or Hindu, or atheist, or agnostic — or whatever form you have come from. Be who YOU are. Take your own spiritual path, your own path to God. It may well not coincide with any outer path.

Many of the old religious structures that we in the West held to so strongly for so long a time have broken down, as the second phase of the Piscean Age establishes itself more strongly into the collective unconsciousness of humanity. It may be that a new pantheon of Gods and Goddesses is pushing into human consciousness, new forms to contain the many facets of Spirit. Greet them with joy. Allow them to help in the healing of ourselves and our planet.

36)   Q. Do the Inner Guides ever function if you don't plug into them through meditation?

A. Yes. The Guides function from birth. Many people experience the Guide when they are children or in mortal danger, before a possible car accident, for instance. They might hear a voice from out of nowhere say, "Stop!" "Turn to the right," or "Take your hands off the steering wheel." The answers that we receive when we pray for help come through our Guides, who act as mediators between ourselves and Deity. The Guide is the inner teacher who seems to have the job of trying to keep us alive on the planet so that we can accomplish what we came here to do. He leads us toward whatever personal realization of God we can accept. One of the characteristics of the Guide is that he doesn't judge or flatter or volunteer anything. He's just *there*. The only times I've heard of Guides interfering within the meditation context or out in life were in cases of physical danger or when there was danger of the psyche being overwhelmed by the archetypal energies. In these latter situations your Guide will act spontaneously to pull you beyond the influence of the energy.

37)   Q. Are the Inner Guides ever known figures from this life?

A. No. Never accept as your Guide a figure, either living or dead, that you have known or known of previously in life. The Guide is not a person who was alive when you took your first breath on the planet.

You might find that people whose rising sign corresponds to the sign on the cusp of the ninth house in your horoscope or whose Sun is in the sign that is on your ninth house cusp will automatically take the projection of your Guide's energy. But that outer person is *not* your Guide. If a known person does appear, look past him to your right and your inner world Guide will be there. The Guides are always within us during our lifetime, not outside of us.

38)   Q. I have heard you say: "To know how you are doing, just look around you." What do you mean by this?

A. Forces that are being projected *through* each individual create the reality or holographic universe that each individual experiences. This is the process that a horoscope describes. Thus, *what-*

ever is in your world is not there by accident. *There are no chance happenings or coincidences. Your* energies are completely responsible for *everything* that is going on around you. If this weren't so, it would be impossible to read a horoscope. If you see two people suddenly get into an argument in a restaurant, though it may appear to have nothing to do with you, an inspection of your horoscope would reveal that a Mars vibration is being activated in your particular pattern. It's in the nature of a warning to you, the ego, to work on the developing problem before it moves closer. Many people think that taking responsibility for the total environment means that they are to *blame* for that reality, but this is not so. We are truly responsible for the outer dream, but not to blame for it any more than we are to blame for the inner dream. We develop only as rapidly as we can accomplish the necessary psychological and physical changes. But, if you accept responsibility for what is happening in your world, then you can do something to change it in yourself. You don't have to be a victim. If you separate from something in your reality experience by thinking of it as unconnected to you, then *there is nothing you can do* to improve it.

If a negative event is occurring anywhere in your world, ask your Guide to take you to that part of you that is either causing it or connected to it. Accept as correct whichever figure your Guide presents to you. It may not be one of the tarot archetypes. It may be composed of energy aspects of many different archetypes, e.g., one part *Tower*, two parts *World*, five parts *Strength*, and appear as a figure you've never encountered before. Find out what the figure needs from you to heal the negative situation in your outer world. Also, ask what it might be trying to communicate to you that the ego is not accepting.

The ego takes credit for everything. Taking either credit or blame for outer world situations is equally arrogant, because we usually don't really know what we're doing, and we rationalize after the fact.

39) Q. Where am I when I'm working with the Inner Guide?

A. It seems that meditating with your Guide is a way of altering the level of consciousness so that you are *awake* on the reality level immediately adjacent to and primary to your own, the level where dreams take place. That's why meditations have the tendency of slipping back into the unconscious if not written down, in the same way that dreams often do. Fifteen minutes after returning from contact with your Guide and the inner world forms, you might begin to lose details. An hour later, you may lose the entire experience, unless you write it down in your journal. The reality level on which you work with your Guide seems to be *primary* to the outer world reality level. It *produces* the experience that is called reality; therefore, changes made on the inner level rapidly change your outer world. We seem to have been taught everything exactly backwards. That which our culture calls "just the imagination" actually is the level that creates our outer experience. As Einstein said, "Imagination is more important than knowledge." We get lost in the outer world *symptoms* and ignore their *causes* on the inner planes, closer to the Source of All.

"I don't have time to meditate," or "I'm too busy to meditate," are thoughts that keep us locked at the symptom level and powerless to effect change until the pain of our unconsciousness prods us in some way.

40) Q. How do you regard pain?

A. Pain is a warning. Whenever we are feeling pain on *any* level — physical, emotional, mental or spiritual — it is an indication that we are out of, or moving away from, our own Centers. There is no pain when you are moving *toward* the Self. Pain is one of our safety sensations that tells us that something major is wrong. Sometimes it's the only way the Self can get us to stop and listen.

41) Q. How can I know which archetypes to work with?

A. The easiest way to determine which archetypes to work with is to have your horoscope calculated with an Astrology-Tarot Equivalent Worksheet that translates the horoscope into tarot image terms. This presents the *bones* of your reality–generating energy system. This worksheet may be obtained from D.O.M.E. Center (see back of book). In lieu of this, just trust your Guide. He knows the inner worlds, their laws and the archetypes and entities which inhabit them.

42) Q. I find that the tarot pictures bring forth an immediate identification with fortune telling, black magic and the like. I find them not relevant to me. They seem to impede my progress with my Guide.

A. If you have this difficulty, don't use them. Trust your Inner Guide. Your own unconscious will present these archetypal energies in the forms they take within you. I utilize the tarot images because they are the most convenient and accessible forms for translating a horoscopic pattern into images that an individual can use immediately. The archetypes, as they are encountered on the inner planes, seldom resemble the images on the tarot cards. *Old Pan*, for instance, may present itself as a man in a business suit; the *High Priestess* might be a grandmother figure. At any rate, they will change and evolve no matter what forms they initially take or what images you initially choose to use.

43) Q. What are the dangers of working inside?

A. There is no danger as long as you're with your true Inner Guide, but it can be extremely dangerous to work with the archetypes without your Guide. The archetypes are aspects of God. The energies of God are dangerous to us mere mortals. Your Guide will not allow you to touch more of the inner energies than you are able to physically and psychologically absorb. Because of my enthusiasm when I first discovered my Guide, I would ask to work with ten or twelve of the archetypes in one meditation. My Guide would seem to go along with this, but then, after we worked with three or four of the figures, he would say, "That's enough for now," and would return me to our meeting place. Your Guide is the one to trust in knowing whether or not you are interacting with the archetypes too much and overloading with energy. If such is the case, he may suggest just sitting and talking with him or resting and getting calm on the inner plane.

Many people also say that, on occasion, they lose their Guides. This generally happens when one resists the inner process. The person goes *looking* for the Guide to no avail. In this instance it is better just to *call* him. He will be there. Once you've touched your Guide, you will find it difficult to lose him. He's with you for life and possibly thereafter. You may feel his presence often during the course of your daily life.

Don't forget how dangerous it can be to work in the unconscious without your true Guide. The archetypes are your reality makers. They are extremely powerful energies. They can literally blow your circuits or cause death if your Guide isn't there to serve as both buffer and gauge of their energies. For example, about three years after I had begun working with my Guide, my cat developed an abscess behind one of her eyes. Since, in my particular horoscopic pattern, the *Empress* has to do with pets and with healing, I asked my Guide to take me to the *Empress* form and asked her what I had to give in return for healing the cat. I was told what I had to do, my Guide OKed it, and I agreed to do what she asked. The *Empress* agreed to heal the cat. I completed the requested task, but after two days, I could see no change in my pet's condition. This time in meditation I went directly to the *Empress* without calling my Guide (rationalizing that I had already worked on this problem while he was present and not wanting to "bother" him about it again). The *Empress* said, "She's healing." I pointed out that, since I had immediately kept my part of the bargain, I thought it only fair that the cat be healed by the next morning. The *Empress* replied that she would do this, and I returned from the meditation satisfied.

However, I awoke during the night perspiring so profusely that I had lost what seemed like gallons of water from my system and was continuing to lose more. The mattress was soaked. The next morning I found that the cat's abscess had broken and healed, but I was so weak that I thought I was going to die. I immediately went to my Guide. He said that I had been foolish to work with energies I didn't really understand without his presence. Without his being there to set up safeguards, the experience could have caused me serious damage if my cat had been a little more ill. He said the healing energy of the *Empress* had to go through me, the physical vehicle, to heal the cat. That was the last time I worked in the inner world without my Guide.

Various kinds of spiritual emergencies are becoming common now with so many people using so many different techniques to explore inner dimensions without a true understanding of the inherent dangers. Christina and Stanislav Grof of the Esalen Institute in

Big Sur, California, have outlined six major forms of these emergencies: 1) Awakening of the serpent power (kundalini); 2) Shamanic journey (a death-rebirth experience); 3) Psychological renewal through activation of the central archetype, the Solar *Center;* 4) Psychic opening—unexpected and usually unsought; 5) Emergence of a karmic pattern—invasion by past life material; and 6) Possession state—possession by an archetype. These are presented in their paper, "Spiritual Emergency: Understanding and Treatment of Transpersonal Crisis."[1]

The safety record for the Inner Guide Meditation is truly amazing. I share it with great pride and joy. We have been working in meditation on the archetypal level with the Inner Guides since 1969 without a "freak out" or psychotic break. The Guides have dealt safely and easily with all six of the above spiritual emergencies. I doubt that any psychologist using Jung's active imagination technique as a therapeutic tool or anyone teaching "guided visualization" or that any group teaching equally powerful meditation practices or working with the kundalini can make this claim. If done as designed, the Inner Guide Meditation is safe enough for children to use, despite its power.

44) Q. Do you regard yourself as higher or spiritually better than other people because you are working with your Inner Guide?

A. When, through practice, you understand the philosophical and spiritual implications underlying the Inner Guide Meditation, you will see that everyone you experience is a projection of a combination of your own energies. Since you have all possibilities within you, those you experience are aspects of yourself. This is a humbling and unifying realization. You won't be able to put yourself on by looking in the mirror and saying, "Boy, have I got it together," when your Uncle Jim's health is breaking down, for instance. Uncle Jim is an aspect of you, a reflection of your internal energies. Thus, if he is in bad shape, so is some inner part of you that he corresponds to. All the people in our lives correspond

---

[1] For a copy, write to Spiritual Emergency Network (SEN), 250 Oak Grove Avenue, Menlo Park, CA 94025.

in this way to inner aspects of ourselves. In a Universe of Oneness, who can be higher or better than any other? We just have different jobs to do.

45) Q. Do you think you have come up with "the" spiritual answer for contemporary Western woman and man?

A. I've spent my lifetime looking for tools for evolving spiritual consciousness. This one continually works, bringing positive results and life changes. It is not a fragile method and can endure the skeptical testing of Western man and woman. It is an active method involving doing, image-making, question asking. It begins with an emphasis on the use of the senses and on stabilizing the physical plane, and it progresses according to each individual's needs. Any path that moves one toward his or her own experience and realization of God or Spirit holds "the" spiritual answer for the person utilizing it.

46) Q. Are you against Eastern spiritual practices?

A. I feel that Western methods work best for Westerners, and that we are born in a certain geographical place for good karmic reasons. But, of course, the test of any spiritual practice is in the life results it produces. If you see the members of your family and those around you getting healthier and more conscious coincident to your spiritual practice, you will know that the practice is working both inside and out. If you don't see these changes happening in your life, you might seriously question your current spiritual path.

Three years in the Orient demonstrated to me the need of the West to get its spiritual tools back, tools hidden, lost, or destroyed because of the severe suppression practiced for centuries by the Western Christian religious establishment. The tools of the East are useful and beautiful, but we need to get the rust off of our own and to rediscover those we had.

However, I'm for any method that will enable us to get to God. Whichever spiritual path works for you is the one you should be on. But *stick to it*. Most delays and detours in one's spiritual evolution are the results of "trip tasting" — bouncing from one spiritual trip to the next and gaining the rewards of none of them.

47) Q. How important is the horoscope in terms of the Inner Guide Meditation?

A. I find it invaluable because the horoscope tells which energies are in conflict (or polarized) and which forces can be utilized to help resolve the problems. Working in terms of a horoscope that has been translated into tarot imagery gives you a way to re-wire yourself, in a sense. You can zero in on problems that may have remained hidden for years in a psychiatric context. Many psychiatrists and psychologists, especially the Jungians and the younger therapists, use astrology as a time-saving tool. By working with your own archetypal energy patterns you are working at the *core* of your reality-creating, reality-sustaining mechanism.

48) Q. What can I do when I can't stop blaming someone for something they've done to me? My mind is willing to stop, but my feelings won't.

A. What I recommend in this instance is changing the thought from "Look what they've done to me," to "Look at what *my* energies have made them do to me." If you make this change in your thinking pattern, you should notice a corresponding change in your feelings. Seek out the energy form within yourself that manipulates the outer person or persons, and heal it within yourself.

49) Q. Why do you use the word "parts" to refer to the people in our lives?

A. A part is a piece of a whole. I use the word "part" to remind myself and others that any person or thing that appears to be separate from ourselves is actually an aspect of the greater whole. Oneness is a fact.

50) Q. Dark menacing figures block the exit from the cave into the landscape when I attempt the Inner Guide Meditation. What should I do?

A. Occasionally an ego's resistance to change will put blocks in the way to the Guide in the forms of walls, snakes, a beast

Figure 25. If you have ever been out-of-body or have had a temporary death experience, you already know that death is not an ending. Finally, if the experience isn't beautiful, you haven't died! Trump of *Death* from the D.O.M.E. Meditation Cards, ©1978 by Sheila Ross. Used by permission.

standing in our way, or known or unknown figures attempting to distract us from the goal of contacting the Guide. IGNORE THESE. Walk through the things in your path, and you will find they dissolve. Disregard the people or entities who try to distract you from meeting your Inner Guide. There is no possible danger until you are beyond the place where you first meet your Guide. Just follow the animal to your Guide. Beyond the meeting place, the Guide remains with you as a teacher, friend and protector.

51) Q. With your world philosophy, do you take responsibility for the actions of the President of the country?

A. Yes. This has to do with what I call the "seven circles of movement." Our reality tends to give us messages that move toward us through a sequence of seven circles. First, we read a newspaper account of an event happening in a foreign country. Then we hear about its happening in our country. Then, we hear about its happening in our state, then in our city, then to an acquaintance and then to a friend or family member. If we're not getting the message by this time, something will happen to the ego itself.

When a problem is healed or transformed within, it moves away in these same seven circles, but as a succession of *resolved* problems that you hear about in various ways. This means that the President of the country does give us a message of what's happening inside of ourselves. We can go to the force within that corresponds to the outer world President. If we keep that part of ourselves healed, it will help him (or remove him) in the outer world.

52) Q. What do you think about death?

A. We are just becoming aware that more than one "body" constitutes a human being. Acupuncture makes us aware of this second body, as does Kirlian photography, and medicine is starting to recognize that there are two bodies, not one, to be dealt with. It may soon recognize that there are more than two.

More and more out-of-body experiences (OOBE's) are being acknowledged and reported. People are beginning to discuss more openly these astral projection experiences. If you have projected astrally, you already know what death is like. It is just like astral projection, but without the ability to re-enter the physical body.

Because our materialistic society has lost its spiritual base, we are ignorant of what death is and what it does. As we become more aware of who we are and what we carry, the experience of death and our fears about it will change dramatically. If you have ever been out-of-body or have had a temporary death experience, you already know that death is not an ending. Finally, if the experience isn't beautiful, you haven't died!

I would refer anyone interested in this subject to the book by Dr. Raymond A. Moody, Jr., *Life After Life*, and the work of Dr. Elisabeth Kübler-Ross, the "death and dying lady."[2]

53) Q. My Inner Guide has approved when archetypes have requested behavior that is highly frowned upon by society or my family, friends and peers. Why is this?

A. The true Guide will encourage *whatever* is necessary or useful for an individual's spiritual growth and evolution, often despite current social values. Of course, this can be painful for the ego until it adjusts to a new view of society and its structures and rules. I've never known a true Guide to encourage or approve of anything that would harm another person in any way or interfere with another's freedom or evolution. Nor have I heard of a Guide encouraging anything that would be destructive to the individual's spiritual growth. Remember that society's values are ephemeral and often conflict with eternal truths.

54) Q. How do I know that results from the Inner Guide Meditation aren't just coincidence?

A. At first, when the Inner Guide Meditation moves beyond theory into experience, the results may seem coincidental. After a while, however, they go beyond coincidence, because the number of coincidences becomes too overwhelming. We then begin to experience the fact that changes in our environments correspond

---

[2]Raymond Moody, Jr. *Life After Life* (New York: Bantam, 1986).

directly to our inner work. Each of us carries the power of God! All the power in the universe is available to each of us. This is often shocking to the rational system of the ego, because it must develop a new view of how reality works, one which supersedes the established materialistic view. We get the evidence that the energies we carry are creating our individual realities as fast as the ego can handle it.

55) Q. Why don't I *want* to meditate?

A. When large-scale changes in a personality occur, it is frequently threatening to the current ego. We become habituated to certain opinions and types of behavior. Just as conservative factions develop out in the world to slow down social, political and spiritual changes, so do elements of the ego with vested interests in a certain manner of being try to prevent changes in these areas. Even when we eventually learn that the changes are beneficial, we unconsciously and automatically do this. For most, it is frightening to move into the unknown.

Defenses against changes that develop take the form of being "too busy to meditate," feeling that "this doesn't work for me," or taking a "Who cares?" attitude about inner work.

Interestingly enough, it's when the changes and growth *do* start that many people say, "This doesn't work," and go off to find another spiritual path which they remain on until *that* path begins to change them, and so on, *ad infinitum*, or until they become aware of the game they are playing with themselves, and choose to end it.

56) Q. What about the third house guide? Is it always "bad" or "evil?"

A. Not at all. It seems that the third house guide serves to maintain the ego's stability. This guide seems to represent the rationalization system of the mind. Some people work with the ninth and the third house entities together. This seems to work fine as long as the ninth house Guide's primacy is not usurped.

The third house guides have no ability to protect us in the inner worlds, nor do we feel the quality of love and acceptance we feel from a true Inner Guide. However, if a male or female third house guide shows up, trust your true Guide to advise you on how to relate to the figure. The third house guides are entities or constructs that communicate through people who "channel" information from the inner dimensions. They often seem clever, entertaining and informative, but little they say aids in the individual spiritual quest.

57) Q. I get very strange physical sensations when I work with some of the archetypes, especially when I ask my Guide to bring two or more together to touch each other and me, or when I make a circle of hands with a group of them and my Guide. What causes this?

A. Remember that the energy forms you are interacting with are those potent energies that create and sustain your personal reality. What I call "the Alice Phenomena" (from *Alice in Wonderland*) are common experiences in the Inner Guide Meditation. These are feelings of shrinking, falling, expanding physically and of extreme weight or weightlessness that usually take place in the presence of the archetypal energy forms.

Activation of the kundalini energy or serpent power which "sleeps" at the base of the spine, with its attendant sensation of heat, cold or electricity shooting up the spine or up from the feet, is also a side effect of this meditation and necessitates the presence and supervision of the Inner Guide to insure the safety of the experience.

58) Q. I'm afraid of my psychic ability. I see accidents and other negative events before they occur, and then they happen. How do I shut off this ability?

A. Instead of trying to shut off your talent, you might begin using it in a new way. If you are picking up a future event, you are somehow connected to the event. Ask your Guide to take you to the figure that connects you to the event. Ask the figure what it needs from you to change the manifestation of the energy so that something better, more positive and harmonious than that which you foresaw can happen. The energy has to express, but it can express in many different ways. Your talent equips you to practice psychic preventive medicine, so to speak. Nothing is "written" or fated. We can always get energy to flow along another route.

What you are picking up is a probability pattern — what will probably happen if nothing is done to alter it. By going within and redirecting the energy, the negative event can be prevented.

59)   Q. I've heard you use the term "metasexuals." What do you mean by it?

A. The metasexuals include celibates, virgins, gays, lesbians, those individuals who have been changed by a full kundalini arousal, and some bi-sexuals — the group whose sexuality is *other* than the sexual norm and who seem designed and equipped to function in unique ways to help the evolution of greater humanity. They are akin to the *bote* of the Crow Indians of North American — "notMan/notWoman but Other," and they usually have one or more of the "Alien" patterns in their natal horoscopes. (In our culture metasexuality is often still inaccurately regarded as a breakdown in the developmental process.) I suspect it is from them that the priests and priestesses, the shamans, magic makers, seers, artisans, mediators and innovators of the new spiritual forms will emerge, and I honor them in their uniqueness.

60)   Q. Why do our Guides communicate with us?

A. From what many Inner Guides have said, I gather that their help and teaching is part of their own further evolution. For a more specific answer to this question, ask your Guide.

61)   Q. Now when I begin to meditate, as soon as I close my eyes I find myself with my Guide on the archetypal level. Is it all right to not go through the procedure of cave, landscape, animal, etc.?

A. This phenomenon occurs in most people after they have been meditating for a while. It seems to indicate that the ego has learned to instantaneously transfer itself to the level where the Guide and the archetypes live without need for the previous structure. If your Guide approves, it's all right.

62)   Q. What does it mean when archetypes change form dramatically, especially after months or years of being in the same form?

A. This usually indicates a major breakthrough in the area that archetype has to do with in outer and inner life. It is generally verified by people in your outer world commenting that you have "changed" in some respect, or you yourself noticing that an entire area of your reality experience has altered.

63)   Q. I see people in my outer world who seem to have it all together but who don't have any interest in spiritual or inner work. They seem happy and have good jobs and family lives. Why can't I get it together as easily as they do?

A. We can never be sure what is going on in another person's reality experience or look through their eyes. All we can know is what we experience of our own energies projected onto the screens of others. What you see in those people are those parts of yourself that *are* together within you. As you come more into Center, you will find more "together" people in the world around you.

64)   Q. A friend of mine has been working with the Inner Guide Meditation for only a month, and she is already working with her fourth Guide. How can I get to my other Guides faster?

A. Because of the slowness of the physical body in changing, I would suspect that your friend may be experiencing a procession of false guides. We reach the second Guide only after the physical vehicle has changed enough to handle more intense vibrational energy. This often takes years. Observe what your friend reports about her outer life, what fruit the tree of her life has truly produced. At any rate, spiritual progress is not a foot race. *Which* Guide one is working with has little to do with one's spiritual progress or evolution. Someone working with the third Guide might well be further from their Center than someone working with the first. There is no hurry. We have all the time we need for our own evolution. When we miss steps, we often get a severe message from our own lives or from the lives of those close to us that this is the case. See what her life's events have been trying to tell your friend.

65) Q. My Guide predicted the death of a friend, but it didn't happen. Why?

A. True Guides do not make predictions, especially about other people and their lives.

66) Q. I asked my Inner Guide the date of my death and could not get a clear answer. Doesn't he know?

A. A death date could only be given based on the assumption that you would stay exactly where you are in your evolution without further change or awareness. It's like the idea of fate and implies continued unconsciousness. The very fact you are working with your Guide in the inner dimensions will change the state of your consciousness to a marked degree, thus changing everything in your reality somewhat. We are only predictable if nothing in our interior systems changes.

Astrologically we go through many death cycles during the course of one lifetime. The horoscopic factors that indicate a physical death and a spiritual rebirth are the same. We die physically when the ego no longer is able to serve the Center—the Self which represents the primary purpose of the life—and the Center withdraws. According to the horoscope, death or rebirth usually correspond to the simultaneous activation of the first, fourth and eighth houses of the individual's natal pattern, or the second, seventh and tenth houses of the partner's natal pattern.

67) Q. What tarot cards correspond to the planets beyond Pluto or within Mercury's orbit? I'm referring to the planets Vulcan, Trans-Pluto, Psyche, Lilith and other invisible planets I have heard astrologers refer to.

A. Until these "planets" appear on the physical plane of our universe, I recommend ignoring them. I have *never* found any event which was not explained by the action of one of the eight known planets or the Sun or Moon. These "invisible planets" (or "moons") only have the power you invest them with in your thinking until they become manifest in the universe, as Pluto, our most recently discovered planet, did in 1930. Discuss this question with your Inner Guide and ask his opinion.

68) Q. You use the term "Alien" in describing some horoscopes. What do you mean by this, where do Aliens come from, and what is the responsibility of an Alien this lifetime?

A. The teaching about the Aliens (which I received in a dream, November 8, 1974) is explained in a later section: How to Translate a Horoscope into Tarot Terms for a Worksheet. As to *where* an Alien comes from, I don't know, nor do I regard it as important. I use the term to describe the subjective feelings that the possessors of certain horoscopic patterns experience. An Alien pattern contains highly specialized talents and abilities, usually of an ESP or other paranormal variety—the kind of talent or ability which would get one burned as a witch or a warlock by the Christian establishment some centuries back. The responsibility of an Alien is the same as for anyone: to awaken to himself and bring his gifts into consciousness for the service of humanity. (All the Aliens seem to have begun "waking up" since November 21, 1974, when the planet Uranus went into the sign of Scorpio, and the awakening process has accelerated since August 27, 1984, when Pluto stabilized in Scorpio.)

The Aliens are people who are born different in "kind" rather than in "degree" from their fellow human beings. It's like being born an apple in a world of oranges. There seems to be a consistent pattern in life which all the Aliens experience. Their powers are accepted and taken for granted by themselves (although not necessarily by their families) until they first encounter their peer group at about seven years of age. They frighten their peers or are thought of and reacted to as strange, weird or different, and their peers reject them. Aliens usually react with "there must be something wrong with me," and begins to regard their talents as "bad" aspects of the self. The suppression of these talents begins as they learn to "fake it" out in the world, to appear "like everybody else," to pass for "normal" in human society. (The first seven years of an Alien's life are generally locked away from memory.) This "faking it" process is usually successful, but the sense of alienation or *otherness* remains acute. There is often a period of extreme depression or of suicidal feelings or attempts in the late teens or early twenties, and we lose many Aliens during this time if the Alien is not recognized and helped by another Alien or someone with insight into the actual problem. Most metasexuals have one or more of the Alien patterns in their natal horoscopes.

The awakening, which began in 1974 and got stronger in 1984, has not been easy. When a person has been suppressing something since seven years of age, he doesn't rush to re-embrace it. A number of steps are necessary. The Inner Guides ease the re-acceptance of the Alien components and allow their re-assimilation into the life in as non-jarring a way as possible.

69)   Q. Because of the connection to astrology and the tarot, is the Inner Guide Meditation anti-Christian?

A. Jesus taught: "In my Father's house are many mansions." Ask your Guide to take you to meet and talk with Jesus about this and any other questions you have about his role and the teachings of the bible and of the Christian churches. Many priests, brothers and ministers are beginning to utilize the Inner Guide Meditation for themselves and others. Love and truth are never threats to true spiritual practice.

The Magi or Wise Men from the East in the biblical story of Jesus were astrologers. As the late Moby Dick, an astrologer from Honolulu, Hawaii, put it, "Wise men follow the stars."

70)   Q. My wife and I both have Worksheets with the astrological factors translated into tarot terms. Should we also have our horoscopes compared to see how they affect one another?

A. To me, horoscope comparison (comparing the astrological factors in one horoscope to the astrological factors in another, or making a "composite chart") does little to decrease unconscious

Figure 26. The Shadow in the horoscope is associated with the astrological sign Libra, the seventh house, and with the *Justice* figure in the tarot. Based on the trump of *Justice* shown here from *Seed*, published by Crown Publishers, New York, 1969. Used by permission.

projection between two people. In fact, it seems to do the reverse. Your wife's role in your reality experience is *totally* described in *your* horoscopic pattern. She lives out *your* Shadow side. The comparison of your charts would further increase the illusion of separation.

71) Q. Is the Inner Guide an aspect of my ego?

A. No. The Guides do not cater to our ego whims and fancies. They say and do what is needed, not wanted. They know our limits and our inadequacies and allow exposure to unconscious materials which the ego itself would never choose to deal with. The Guide's personality is seldom similar to that of the person he guides.

72) Q. Why is it easy for some people to contact the Inner Guide and difficult for others?

A. The individual make-up determines the ease or difficulty of the contact, as does the ego's motivation to change, grow and expand beyond current limits. Feeling based, non-cerebral individuals seem to have the easiest time with the Guide contact, as do creative artists and those with a strong psychic or mystic bent.

73) Q. Is my Shadow described in my horoscope?

A. Yes. The horoscope of your Shadow side is *your horoscope upside-down*. The Descendant of your horoscope (the cusp or beginning of the seventh house) is your Shadow's Ascendant or rising sign. The Shadow contains all the astrological energies that the ego represses and thinks it does not possess, both positive and negative. Our Shadow figures are always of the same sex as we are, a male having a male Shadow.

74) Q. What is the difference between how I use my imagination in day-dreaming and how it is used in the Inner Guide Meditation?

A. Dr. Carl Jung answers this question in his book, *Psychological Types*, written in 1921:

Figure 27. "Active fantasy is one of the highest forms of psychic activity. For here the conscious mind and the unconscious personality of the subject flow together into a common product in which both are united."— Carl Jung. The *Wheel of Fortune* and the *Sun* as a child as they might appear and relate in an Inner Guide Meditation, a practice that springs from Jung's active imagination or active fantasy ideas, but adds the Inner Guide. Engraving by Gustave Doré from La Fontaine's *Fables*.

We can distinguish between *active* and *passive* fantasy. *Active* fantasies are the product of intuition; i.e., they are evoked by an attitude directed to the perception of unconscious contents, as a result of which the libido immediately invests all the elements emerging from the unconscious and, by association with parallel material, brings them into clear focus in visual form.

Passive fantasies always have their origin in an unconscious process that is antithetical to consciousness, but invested with approximately the same amount of energy as the conscious attitude, and therefore capable of breaking through the latter's resistance. Active fantasies, on the other hand, owe their existence not so much to this unconscious process as to a conscious propensity to assimilate hints or fragments of lightly-toned elements, to elaborate them in clearly visual form. It is not necessarily a question of a dissociated psychic state, but rather of a positive participation of consciousness.

Active fantasy is one of the highest forms of psychic activity. For here the conscious mind and the unconscious personality of the subject flow together into a common product in which both are united.[3]

75) Q. How do I change my outer world more quickly? I keep working with my Guide to change things, but the negative people in my life seem to never change.

A. The first step toward reality change is *acceptance*, without judgment, of the way things are—the way *you* are. The goal of the Inner Guide Meditation is not to change other people or to change the outer world. It is to evolve oneself spiritually through increased awareness of oneself and the energies one carries. To focus on outer change is to block our flow through involvement

[3]*The Collected Works of C. G. Jung*, ed. Herbert Read, Michael Fordham, Gerhard Adler, William McGuire; trans. R. F. C. Hull. Bollingen Series XX, vol. 6, *Psychological Types*, © 1971 by Princeton University Press, p. 428, reprinted by permission.

with *symptoms* instead of *causes*. The "negative people" are there to show you *your* resistance to change. To keep focused on negativity *feeds* that negativity. Don't worry about those other people. Focus on yourself. They'll change when your creation energies no longer require them to show you certain aspects of your own unconsciousness.

76) Q. You speak of the "Law of No." Would you explain this?

A. What we say "No" to in life literally structures our realities, both inside and out. The *absolute* No's, "Thou shalt not," "Under no circumstances would I ever," give form to the walls, floors and ceilings of our reality boxes. The *qualified* No's, "Usually I wouldn't do this, but," and our "Maybe's," are the doors and windows of our reality boxes. A Yes is non-structural. It's just space, inside and out. To change an absolute No to a qualified No, a qualified No to a Yes, or to invent a new absolute or qualified No, literally changes one's inner and outer realities.

To discover what the current No's are in your life, start making two lists of the things you say "No" to; one list of the absolute No's, the other of the qualified No's. Every time you feel anxious, guilty, depressed, paranoid, uptight or a "should" comes into your mind, one of your No's is being activated. Try to find out just what it is you're saying "No" to, and whose No pattern you're obeying or reacting to.

The No's of the physical body, for instance, are the bones and the skin. They are useful to the body by giving it form and limit, so that it doesn't spill out as a boundless amoeba.

Measure your No's by their *usefulness* to your spiritual life, growth and evolution, not by whether they are "right" or "wrong," "good or bad." Perhaps you've outgrown some of your No's. Perhaps you don't have enough No's for structure in your life, and chaos reigns. "No" serves to give form and structure, but it becomes destructive when it begins to box in or strait-jacket life. Examine your pattern of No's honestly, and see if they truly serve *all* of you.

When we change one of our No's or invent a new No, we experience a testing process from outer life. You've probably experienced this if you've ever gone on a diet or tried to break a long-standing habit. It seems that suddenly everyone around you is conspiring to get you to eat something that's not on your diet or to fall back into the old habit in some way. This represents your own testing energies (the Moon, Saturn, Cancer and Capricorn in astrology) *making sure that you really mean it.* It's their job to maintain a stable structural reality for you, so, when they hear of a change in your present structure or rule system, they bring to you those individuals or situations in your outer reality which will function as your testers.

77) Q. I don't get the magical results in my life that others report. Why is this?

A. Much would depend on how you define "magical." Two hundred years ago flicking a switch and having electric lights come on would have been regarded as magic. We now understand this as physics.

A friend and astrological colleague of mine, John Woodsmall of Denver, Colorado, reported that one of the people he worked with had this same complaint. She had worked on a stubborn health problem and complained that she had gotten no results on this from her inner work. My friend asked her how the condition of her health was. She replied that she had "accidentally" run into a doctor at a party who knew exactly what was causing the problem, and that he had it cured in a week.

Because so-called results happen in our everyday worlds in everyday ways without rays coming down from heaven and thunder booming, we tend to think of them as coincidence and do not relate them to our inner work. There is no predicting how "results" will occur. I, the current ego, may think of six or seven ways a problem in my life might be solved. The energies within have infinite ways to cause things to happen. If we see, in truth, that our whole reality is magical, the surrender to our own Centers becomes easier, and all life becomes richer and more awesome.

Another cause of lack of results from meditation is a lack of emotional involvement during the meditation process itself. Try to *feel* as much as you can while interacting with the archetypal fig-

Figure 28. Trump of the *Hanged Man* from the tarot deck in *Seed*, published by Crown Publishers, New York, 1969. Used by permission.

ures. Yell at them if you're angry. Weep if you're sad. Scream if you feel you're about to explode from frustration. Throw things. And remember to use your five senses to help involve yourself in a feeling way in the inner reality. It seems that the more emotion is felt during meditation, the faster outer results occur. Being too detached and mental can give you information, but very little result in your everyday outer life. Have *all* of yourself there when you're with your Guide, not just your intellect.

78) Q. What exactly is depression?

A. As I see it, it is much the same as a depression in the ground. Something within the earth causes soil to sink in or down. We, too, are pulled in or down by a depression, but, generally, we don't think to turn around and face its cause within ourselves. We look to the outer world for reasons and solutions. Current psychological thought regards depression as either anger turned inward or as low self-esteem from an identification of the ego with the internal "bad me." Sometimes either one of these is the reason. Sometimes the reason is something else entirely. If you ask your Guide to take you to the cause of a depression, a figure or thing you can interact with, you can find both cause and cure quite rapidly. The cause is *never* outside, only the symptoms are.

In tarot, the *World* and *Old Pan* (Saturn and Capricorn in astrology) are the energies generally associated with depression, guilt, low self-esteem and worry.

79) Q. What is a good cure for "spaciness?"

A. Neptune, the *Hanged Man*, and Pisces, the *Moon*, in the tarot are the archetypal energies having to do with spaciness. Working with these energies in meditation is one good way to deal with the problem. A walking-around-in-life cure seems to be to feel *all* of yourself in your feet. Feel what the ground feels like under your feet. Feel what your shoes feel like, what the bones in your feet feel like. Feel your weight on your feet. Center yourself in your solar plexus. This exercise seems to bring all four of the bodies together and ends the feeling of spaciness by insistence that your thoughts and feelings plug into your physical body.

80)   Q. What tarot archetypes are involved in the life crisis that often occurs after someone begins meditating and moving towards his or her Center?

A. The tarot *Tower* and the tarot *Old Pan* (Mars and Capricorn in astrology) are pictures of the energies involved. The crisis involves an ego experience of great isolation, often coinciding with outer life trauma or extreme change on the physical, emotional, mental and/or spiritual planes, a "Dark Night of the Soul." This crisis is produced by any spiritual system that is designed to unite one with one's Center, rather than just producing a pleasant, harmonious life plateau.

If the crisis is passed successfully, the individual is then able to function in *vertical polarity* with his (or her) spiritual forces and in *horizontal polarity* with outer world relations. If he fails this spiritual passage or point of crisis, he usually stops pushing further into spiritual work for the time being. He then returns rapidly to the psychological condition he was in prior to working with the Guide on the inner planes. Because of the moth–to–flame pull of our spiritual natures, many of us face the crisis point again and again until a breakthrough is finally achieved. The biblical story of Job is a good example of the process.

81)   Q. When I am with a person of the opposite sex with whom I am in love, just *who* is that person in my movie? What aspect of myself is he, and what role am I playing?

A. Generally, in this situation, you, the woman, will be living out your own feminine energies (akin to Jung's concept of the *anima*), and the man you are in love with will be acting out, through projection, your unconscious masculine energies (akin to Jung's concept of the *animus*). The "I" we speak of is almost always the current ego, in this case allowing certain energies to flow *into* it, projecting others *through* itself onto the man.

82)   Q. Doesn't meditation encourage passivity to real world problems and actions?

A. I find that the contrary is true. Meditation during part of your day doesn't cause withdrawal from the rest of life's activities. It isn't a retreat from or a running away from life. The archetypal energies frequently make recommendations concerning outer world actions and encourage outer world involvement. Also, meditation resolves the hang-ups and attachments to the outer world that prevent you from becoming yourself freely and fully. This enables you to cope much more effectively with the outer world and the problems you encounter in it.

The Inner Guide Meditation does not encourage passivity to the problems of the outer world at large, but rather suggests that an individual is responsible for dealing with all the inner problems of which these outer problems and reactions are symptomatic. Working on these problems within tends to heal these outer world situations without the fruitless strife caused by isolating certain people, groups or political units outside of oneself. Labeling them as the "bad guys" or fighting them directly tends to make them stronger and more unconscious.

83) Q. Sometimes I seem to go into a trance when I'm working with the Inner Guide and the archetypes. Is this all right?

A. No. It seems that, at present, inner plane vibrations are too intense for trance or mediumistic states to be safe for us (if they ever were). The Inner Guide Meditation requires full ego consciousness and participation. Ask your Guide to take you to the archetypal energy form that is causing this problem, and resolve it. Meditation is not a trance or hypnotic state. It is absolutely imperative that you, the ego, stay totally awake and self-aware in the meditation state.

84) Q. Are we in the Aquarian Age?

A. No. According to Robert Hand's book, *Essays on Astrology*,[4] we're still in the Piscean Age, which began in 111 B.C. and which doesn't end until 2813 A.D. But the constellation Pisces

[4]Robert Hand, *Essays on Astrology*, (Gloucester, MA: Para Research, 1982).

consists of *two* fish, and we left the first or Eastern fish and entered the second or Western fish in 1817 A.D. The symbol of Christianity is *one* fish, not two. I feel that this latter date established the beginning of the Post-Christian Spiritual Era, the time we are now in. Pisces is a dual sign, as are Gemini and Sagittarius. Where the first fish moves away from the plane of the earth (symbolizing the whole denial aspect of Christianity), the second swims parallel to it. If the fish represents the Higher Self or Solar Center, then the job now is to bring spirit into the everyday world—to spiritualize the material. The choice we face is either gross materialism or the bringing of energy in from inner dimensions to enlighten and transform the material plane as we know it.

In his two books, *Beneath the Moon and Under the Sun* and *Lord of the Dawn, Quetzacoatl*,[5] Tony Shearer gives a date for the beginning of a new cycle to which I had a gut level *"That's it!"* response: August 17, 1987, the day that the so-called "Aztec Calendar" ended. It's the date that the American Indian Medicine Lodges say that "the medicine wheels" (chakras, or energy centers along the spine) began to turn. Perhaps the kundalini energy latent at the base of everyone's spine is more easily able to rise in each person on the planet since that time. That would certainly fill the bill for the world ending in fire—the Holy Fire of Kundalini, the Serpent Power of God.

Kundalini activation has already begun in many receptive people, especially those doing the Inner Guide Meditation, and the awakening of this energy on a larger scale will probably be occurring dramatically from the August 17, 1987 date through the 1990's and early 2000's. It is the energy that will push humans into their next evolutionary step as transformed beings, ready or not. It is also coincident with the kundalini planet, Pluto (*Last Judgement*), being in the kundalini sign of Scorpio (tarot trump *Death*) from 1983 to 1995.

This might be explained symbolically by another astrological event which occurred in 1943, the year World War II began to resolve and the Atomic Age began—the year that war ceased to work as a way of resolving conflicts and disagreements between

---

[5]Tony Shearer, *Beneath the Moon and Under the Sun* (Albuquerque, NM: Sun Books, 1977); *Lord of the Dawn: Quetzalcoatl* (Happy Camp, CA: Naturegraph, 1971).

nations. Usually we pay attention only to what the Vernal Equinox point does as it precesses or moves backward through the constellations. But there are three other points which may also be considered: the Summer and Winter Solstice points and the Autumnal Equinox. Both Robert Hand and Ray Mardyks of Santa Monica, California, are doing research on these points. Of these three, the Winter Solstice point is most interesting, because it is the time when the West celebrates its most important religious holidays and begins a New Year. In 1943 the Solstice point entered the constellation of Ophiuchus, "The Man Struggling with the Serpent." The serpent is the kundalini power in humankind. Perhaps the August 17, 1987, date mentioned has to do with the acceleration of this cosmic cycle.

85) Q. In brief, can you define what the tarot trumps are?

A. I consider them as twenty-two aspects of the energy I call God. They represent a way to experience individual aspects of Deity without blowing all the circuits. Remember, "Enoch walked with God and was not." The tarot archetypes are a way to begin touching intense spiritual energies — a way to develop spiritual muscle, so to speak.

One way I like to think about it is to imagine God as a twenty-two-faceted jewel. The *Emperor*, then, can be thought of as a red facet, the *Empress* as a green facet, etc. Each of us sees only a partial grouping of facets, those facing us. But we're still all talking about the same thing, the One.

86) Q. Can you give a one-sentence definition of a horoscope?

A. A horoscope is a symbolic diagram which describes one person's entire universe from that person's point of view.

87) Q. I know that the symbol for the Piscean Age is the two fishes. What is the symbol for the Aquarian Age?

A. The fixed air sign Aquarius has for its symbol Ganymede, the cup-bearer of Zeus. (Originally, the constellation Aquar-

Figure 29. Zeus disguised himself in the form of an eagle and abducted Ganymede, carrying him off to Mount Olympus. Engraving by Gustave Doré from Dante's *Purgatory*.

ius was identified with the hermaphrodite Egyptian God (or *Neter*) Hapi, who presides over the source of the Nile and whose being is shrouded in mystery because of the peculiar sacredness always ascribed to him.) Ganymede is usually depicted as a nude young man in a trojan cap with a mantle thrown back over his shoulder. He was the most beautiful of all mortal youths. Zeus was smitten by Ganymede's extraordinary beauty and desired him as his bed-fellow and favorite. Zeus disguised himself in the form of an eagle and abducted Ganymede, carrying him off to Mount Olympus.

Ganymede's father, King Tros of Phrygia, was possessed by incurable grief at the disappearance of his son and lamented continually day after day. Zeus finally took pity on him and gave Tros the magnificent steeds, "swift as the storm," that bore the Gods, a golden grapevine (the work of Hephaestus), as well as the promise of immortality for his son, setting Ganymede's image among the stars as the constellation Aquarius. When Ganymede's father heard this message from Zeus, he rejoiced in his heart and lamented no more.

Ganymede then replaced Hera's daughter, Hebe, as Zeus' cup-bearer. He brings joy to the eyes of all the Gods by his great beauty. Ganymede functions on Olympus as Zeus' lover and the server of the red nectar and ambrosia from the golden mixing bowl of Zeus and the other Gods. His symbol is the cock, a love gift from Zeus.

The word *Ganymede* comes from the two Greek words *ganues-thai* and *medea*, which translate as, "rejoicing in virility."

Ganymede is comparable to the Vedic Soma who, like the Trojan youth, was ravished by Indra and changed into a sparrow-hawk.

During this time of AIDS, it is interesting to meditate on why the symbol for our next Great Age is a metasexual youth.

88) Q. What sign is ruled by the newly discovered planet Chiron?

A. I regard Chiron as a planetoid with much the same influences as the asteroids and without zodiacal sign rulership.

89) Q. Why do you call marriage "Shadow-Dancing," and would you talk more about this?

Figure 30. Marriage is the unconscious agreement on the part of two individuals to accept each other's Shadow projections and live them out. Engraving by Gustave Doré from Milton's *Paradise Lost*.

A. Shadow-Dancing has to do with the physics of partnership. The unconscious interaction between the two people involved produces psychic and physical movements which to me seem like dancing — each having to respond or react quickly to the projection coming from the other when they are in the same physical space, each taking as perfectly as possible the unconscious role needs of the other.

Shadow-Dancing occurs at its most unconscious when you marry or legalize a living together relationship with marriage; but it also takes place between roommates and business partners. At the moment of marriage (a contractual partnership) it really seems like the other is separate from you — that you have very little or nothing to do with his or her behavior as you observe and experience it. However, this is not the case.

We seem to have lost consciousness of what marriage is or could be about. We're ignorant of what it's for or how to best use this particular institution. From my point of view, marriage is an agreement between two people (regardless of gender) to come together, to remain together willingly, to help each other achieve consciousness and to remain sexually faithful to one another. We understand very little about sexuality, what sexual energy does or can do. We don't realize that marriage forms a container, a pressure cooker if you like, around the two people involved. Sex outside of this partnership vessel literally makes leaks in the transformation vessel called marriage. If you've got leaks, neither of the partners is going to be able to change, to transform. That's what marriage is supposed to be about, where two people come together and agree to help each other through the rebirth process — where both achieve spiritual transformation. Until this process is completed, both must take the responsibility for understanding that what partner "B" is doing is what partner "A's" unconscious energies are making him or her do and vice versa.

Marriage is the unconscious agreement on the part of two individuals to accept each other's Shadow projections and live them out. The Shadow is the *alter ego* or *other half of the whole* of each of us. It comes into being between birth and seven years of age as you develop an ego.

When you were born, when you popped out of mother's womb, you were dissolved in the All. There was no difference between you and the sky and the house and mother—it was all one thing. You then went through a sorting process between birth and age seven of: "This is me. This isn't me." At about the age of seven a stable ego had formed which you could recognize in the mirror. (Astrologically, the ego is formed when the planet Saturn, by transit, squares the natal Saturn for the first time—around seven years of age.) To maintain this ego and prevent it from dissolving back into the All or the unconscious, an entity of the same sex as yourself develops on the inner planes. It contains everything you have repressed or separated from, positive or negative, good or bad, yin or yang. This is your Shadow. A man has a male Shadow, a woman, a female Shadow. This Shadow side of yourself projects onto anyone you marry or partner with and onto all strangers. It then communicates to you through them. This projection onto a marriage partner disguises the Shadow even more than it innately is, because it is a male Shadow communicating through the wife, and a female Shadow, through the husband. It is often useful to occasionally ask your Shadow to reverse its sex to acquaint yourself with the opposite polarity of your Shadow side and to see more clearly what you project onto your mate, if you are married or living with someone.

One way to illustrate this is through astrology. A horoscope demonstrates that a person's partner is living out the person's Shadow side. By turning the horoscope upside-down, an astrologer can read what a person's partner is doing in life and how he or she is behaving, all from the person's own horoscope, without looking at or having knowledge of the partner's horoscope.

Until you get to know and come to terms with this Shadow side of yourself—literally the other half of the whole of you—there is no way to really see or understand your partner. When your Shadow is unconscious to you, you're just interacting with that part of yourself that your partner is mirroring for you—and you for your partner—because projection of the Shadows is always a two-way street.

Each of you lives out for your partner what your partner doesn't know or accept about himself or herself, positive or negative. Your Shadow projectee may well be living out your best qualities. You may keep thinking, "I'm the unconscious one with all the hang-ups, and I have this marvelous conscious being for a partner."

That's your own best stuff you're seeing in your partner, that your partner is showing you. You can put it back into your own life by becoming conscious of and caring for the Shadow entity within you — learning what it needs from you and your life so that it gets some conscious expression and can work with you as friend and conscious equal partner from within. This would let the Shadow-Dancing relationship — your outer partnership — become that much more joyous and rewarding for both you and your outer partner.

The only way I know to get your Shadow into consciousness is by meeting and working with the Shadow figure in meditation. It is helpful to first intellectually understand just what the Shadow is and how it operates. Initially, we must know what it is we're projecting onto our partners despite the unconsciousness of the process. Your Inner Guide will bring your Shadow figure to you if you ask him to. You can then get to know that other half of yourself that projects onto and manipulates your partner.

Pragmatically, in marriage, the place to begin is by accepting that your partner is doing exactly what your energies, unconscious though they may be, are manipulating the partner into doing or saying. And you have to take the *full* responsibility of this without saying, "Well, hey — Come on. He's doing something too." What he's doing in *his* movie, in his reality experience, doesn't make any difference. It's what he's doing in *your* movie that carries the message from your Shadow. You have to begin by taking 100 percent responsibility for that — not 50 percent or half and half — or the insight will never come. Only when you do take full responsibility (without any blame) for your partner's behavior, for your partner's speech and actions, only then are you in the place of power where you can begin to experience the manipulation of your partner by your Shadow side. You can then begin to bring this energy back to live comfortably in your own life. Then it no longer has to manipulate your partner into getting its messages to you or doing whatever it is that may be causing the problems between you, causing the barriers or the feelings of separation.

If you truly achieve this and can help each other through the transformation process (which is set into motion by the coming to terms with and giving personal expression to each of your Shadow sides), you've completed what the Shadow-Dancing relationship called marriage is really about. Then you are free to choose to stay together or go your own ways as best of friends. If *both* partners do not achieve this transformation, I believe they should stay together (till death do them part if necessary), because *both* are unconsciously dragging their feet despite the fact that one will look like the "good guy."

Even if you're not married, you have people who live out your Shadow role, people who take your Shadow projection and live it out for you. The mechanics of astrology furnish us with other examples. If you are living with someone on a shared responsibility basis, a roommate or housemate, they will show you what your Shadow side is like. Anyone you've fathered a child with, or conceived a child by (regardless of whether the child was born, stillborn, miscarried or aborted), lives out your Shadow side. The child of your second pregnancy or the second child you've fathered shows you your Shadow, and your Shadow communicates to you through that child. (If you want to know how someone's marriage is doing, just look at how their second pregnancy child is doing. That's how the marriage is doing. That's the child that usually receives both parents' Shadow projections, unless one of the parents had children, pregnancies or abortions prior to the current marriage. It's the hardest slot to get born into in a family, because both parents are projecting onto that child — and onto each other — what they're not accepting in themselves.) Your third sibling (brother or sister) — technically, the child of your mother's third pregnancy not counting you — also functions as a Shadow barometer for you, as well as the partner of your marriage partner's or roommate's third brother or sister. Any business partner also lives out your Shadow side as long as the partnership contract is in effect, and all strangers (people you haven't "role slotted") also take your Shadow projection, as well as your peers.

On the extremely negative side, the burglar, the mugger, the rapist, the kidnapper and the murderer are Shadow sides of their victims. In these cases the Shadows will be seen to contain deeply unconscious archetypal material which has never had any assimilation and has received no expression in the victims' lives.

If you've ever tried to change a partner, you already know the impossibility of doing this. Your partner can't change as long as you continue projecting a consistent Shadow energy onto him or her. But if you've ever gone on a real "I'm going to get my own act together and change" program and have accomplished this change in yourself, you find that your partner automatically changes too. In fact, your partner or Shadow barometer can be on the East Coast and you can be on the West Coast and your partner will still change coincident to your change and new consciousness. Projection has no spatial limitations. You can be in the same house or one of you can be in China. In either instance the projection ability remains the same. So the only way to make a change in the Shadow projectee or projectees is to make a change in yourself.

Also, divorce doesn't work so far as the Shadow projection is concerned. No matter how many ex-partners you may have, each of them lives out your Shadow side — you are Shadow-Dancing with each and every one of them, even if your ego doesn't know where they are on the planet. And when you have a current partner and one or more ex-partners, it usually works out that the current partner lives out the more positive aspects of your Shadow side and the ex-partner or partners, the more negative aspects.

Try to remember that your partner or anyone who lives out your Shadow side shows you your own hidden qualities, those elements which are unconscious in you. If you take the responsibility for this, treat it as message from the other half of you and act on it, soon you will become conscious of what you're projecting onto your Shadow projectee. You will then find that Shadow-Dancing becomes a dance of joy, not of misery and aggravation.

90) Q. You say that "God doesn't take sides." Then how do we act and make responsible choices in the world if *not* taking sides becomes the model?

A. By examining and meditating on the two aspects of any polarity you must choose between, and then choosing that aspect which best serves your spiritual evolution at that particular time, or finding that third element which resolves and harmonizes the polarity.

91) Q. How can I become a pure vehicle for the God-force?

A. Perhaps by remembering that purity is not a matter of morality, but a matter of vibration.

92)   Q. The background and landscape where I usually meet my Inner Guide has suddenly changed. Is this a common experience?

A. Changes such as you mention are not uncommon. They generally go along with a new aspect in the relationship with the Guide and the archetypes. Often the landscape evolves and changes along with the individual. All changes in the structural aspects of the meditation are meaningful. Your Guide would be the one who could best explain the significance of the change.

93)   Q. I seem to be stuck in my spiritual growth, and, whenever I work on this with my Inner Guide, he takes me to the figure of *Death*, who talks about making payments on a loan I took out long ago. What does this have to do with my spirituality?

A. *Death*, the Scorpio energy, has to do with both transformation and financial indebtedness. One sure way to paralyze your spiritual transformation — and your own personal income — is not to pay your debts on the physical plane. Even a small regular payment on a very large debt keeps the Scorpio area flowing. This is probably what *Death* is trying to say.

94)   Q. Are what you call the "Aliens" and what you call the "Adepts" the same?

A. I don't think so. The Adepts have expertise in specific reality areas, as do the Aliens, but they don't always experience the alienation and rejection common to the Aliens.

95)   Q. When you use the term "Alien" to describe a person, do you mean that the person is from another planet?

A. No. I mean it is *as if* the person were. The so-called Alien individuals perceive and are perceived by others much as if they were non-humans from Mars or Arcturus. They often make others "nervous," until they accept and assimilate their Alien abilities into consciousness.

96) Q. I never have enough time to accomplish what I want to do in my life, including meditation. What can I do about this?

A. Time, as it is perceived in our outer worlds, has to do with the archetypal energy forms of the *World* and *Old Pan*, Saturn and Capricorn. If one or both of these energy factors is pronounced in your particular horoscope pattern, learning the control of time is one of your lessons in this life. The secret of expanding time seems to be to schedule it, from when you wake up in the morning to when you go to bed at night. When time is structured, it expands. When time is not structured, it shrinks. Remember to include free time, play time and meditation time in your schedule, otherwise Capricorn and Saturn tend to forget about these uses of time. Don't let your schedule become a straitjacket. Try it out for a while. Then evaluate whether or not it is useful for you and your growth. If it is stultifying in any way, chuck it and make a new schedule for yourself. When you achieve the schedule that *works for you, not you for it*, you will solve your problem with time.

97) Q. What do you mean by "separation?"

A. Inner Guide Meditators use this word often, as in, "I caught myself separating ten times today," or "We're separating again." I use the word to remind myself that what each of us perceives is another aspect of ourselves, not something separate. The *illusion* of separation, of separateness, is provided by the *Old Pan* archetype. It is his job to maintain this illusion until we are psychologically and spiritually prepared to begin the penetration of the illusion. This learning not to separate takes constant, conscious PRACTICE. It is a new way of thinking and feeling about the world, by experiencing the *unity* instead of the separation.

98) Q. Why is it important for me to ask the archetypes what they need if you say that they will express themselves anyway?

A. If you don't know the needs of your archetypal energies and they remain in the darkness, what they take for their expression may well be what you, the ego, will least like to give. The expressions of an archetype you are working with in meditation and one that is pushed into deep unconsciousness and ignored are quite different, the ego generally labeling the former "good" or "positive," and the latter "bad" or "negative."

99) Q. I am severely affected by violent movies and TV programs that I chance to see, and the negative emotion holds on in me for days. How can I work with this?

A. In your meditation, treat the movie or TV program in exactly the same way you would treat one of your dreams. Heal or transform that which needs it. Question the characters as to what aspects of yourself they are showing you. *The outer world is literally all message* — from you, to you. Question your Guide. Some of my most potent, transformative meditations have been based on such violent films.

100) Q. When I gave up some of my bad habits, my partner seemed to take them over. Why did this happen, and what can I do about it?

A. This occurs when you, the ego, instead of transforming the energies that have to do with the habits, suppress or push against them. The desires are still there — only now they are unconscious to you. And in a "Shadow-dancing" relationship these energies are projected onto the partner for him or her to live out until you truly change them in yourself. The need in the ego/Shadow balance is to raise the middle, that point of balance and equilibrium between you and your inner Shadow. This allows consciousness to increase for both you and your Shadow projectee.

101) Q. Can you suggest other uses for the dream/meditation journal that you recommend keeping?

A. I use the right hand pages of my journal to record dreams and meditations and the left hand pages to record *I Ching's* and ego conscious thoughts and ideas. One meditator suggests a monthly *written* evaluation of growth on all levels. Let your Guide and your Shadow man or woman help you with this evaluation on the inner planes.

102) Q. I sometimes get a headache after I meditate. What can I do about this?

A. There seem to be two kinds of headaches people get from meditating. The first results from forgetting to ask the Guide whether all has been left in balance in the inner world or by returning to the body too fast (suddenly opening your eyes instead of allowing time to get all four of your "bodies" back together in one place). A second type of headache seems to have to do with what the ego judges to be an overload of new information from the inner worlds. It makes the head feel over-expanded. Discussion with your Guide about either type of headache is the recommendation.

103) Q. Do you use the Inner Guide to go back into previous lives?

A. Yes. When a continuing problem in this life has its origin in an earlier one, this is most useful and can produce dramatic results. Often it is difficult to work with, say, a fear that seems to have its origin in this life. The experience has impressed itself on the body, and cellular memory won't let go of it. If you learn from your Guide that the fear's actual origin is in an earlier life, you can go back into that life and transform the fear energy into something more conscious and useful, and this is generally quite easily done. This is because you now have no cellular memory from that life (that body is dust from this life's point of view), so the resistance isn't there.

Stephen Connors of D.O.M.E. Center has developed techniques for working with the Inner Guides on past lives. The following is one example. Ask your Guide to take you to the "life of origin" of a particular problem or situation you wish to heal or change. When you're shown the life where the problem originated, ask your Guide to take you to the "choice point," that point in time immediately before you performed some action which created the

Figure 31. A change made in one life changes all your lives. "Tombstones appear, tombstones disappear." Trump of *Death* from Aleister Crowley's Thoth Tarot Deck, published by Samuel Weiser, Inc., York Beach, ME, and U.S. Games Systems, Inc., Stamford, CT. Used by permission.

problem in all subsequent lives. Ask your Guide to "freeze" time, and ask him to bring the figures of the *Sun*, the *Fool* and the *High Priestess*. Ask the three archetypal figures to please send their love and light into the person you were in that life. When they do this, thank them, let them go and ask your Guide to release time once again. Watch what the new choice and new action are. Let this "new" life continue until its death. It's like re-recording over a cassette tape. Then ask your Guide to release the changes into all your lives. At this point you will probably feel strange sensations in your body, which I call "the ripples of time."

A change made in one life changes all your lives. "Tombstones appear, tombstones disappear," to quote my Guide's comment upon returning from healing and changing one of my past lives. All lives are happening simultaneously.

104)   Q. I understand you were once diagnosed as clinically dead and then you came back to life. What was death like?

A. In April, 1953, I experienced my own accidental physical death for seven minutes. This occurred under clinical conditions (my heart was being monitored on an EKG) at the Army Medical Research Laboratory in Fort Knox, Kentucky. I had been drafted into the U.S. Army as a conscientious objector and had "volunteered" as a human guinea pig for environmental cold research. The entire experience happened in full consciousness. I went into shock from the pain of one of the experiments, but I didn't lose consciousness, even though my heart stopped. There was no break in my awareness between the time my heart stopped beating and when it spontaneously started up again seven minutes later. For a skeptic like me, it was one of the most important experiences of my life. I found myself in a pearly grey iridescent space which was filled with total love. Understanding was crystalline and complete — I was able to understand *everything*. It was a state of complete freedom and happiness. I knew I was "dead" and that I had the choice of continuing on from where I was or returning to my body and to life. I learned that no one judges us but ourselves, because I *experienced* the result of every thought, word and deed of my life, how I made others feel, my effect on the planet and all of life. Death ended all my previous formal Christian religious beliefs, and it verified for me that there was no hell. I also learned that "if it isn't beautiful, you're not dead." This certain knowledge removed forever my fears of death and replaced them with understanding and compassion.

105) Q. If your heart stopped for seven minutes, why didn't you get brain damage?

A. The experience took place at 40° below zero. I was refrigerated.

106) Q. What about children? Do abused children, children with horrible diseases and mentally ill children create what is happening to them?

A. No. Like the rest of us, their archetypal energies — pictured in their birth patterns — create the realities they experience. When a child takes its first breath, its pattern is "set." Then, as the child breathes out, the archetypes carried by the child immediately begin creating the reality experiences of that child, including illnesses and other negative experiences which may be promised in the child's horoscope. These negative experiences are the result of archetypes that are repressed when the child is born.

There is no choice for anyone until the ego is sufficiently formed to begin the process of becoming conscious. Many people cling to and rationalize unconsciousness throughout an entire lifetime. We see examples of this around us everyday. They have no more ego consciousness than a child does.

But difficulties and painful experiences a child may have will also appear in the parents' horoscopes. Therefore, if the parents take responsibility and meditate — heightening their degree of consciousness and removing their unconscious archetypal participation in the child's problems — the difficulties can fall away in the child's life.

107) Q. For years now it has seemed that time has speeded up. What accounts for this?

A. The planet Pluto is the generation marker and has to do with the illusion of things changing around us. Pluto usually takes thirty years to go through a sign of the zodiac, but since the mid-sixties Pluto has been speeding up and now it is about to go through a sign in eleven years. It doesn't slow down again and go back to thirty year generations until the early 21st century. In a sense we're moving toward getting almost three days in one, and things appear to be changing more rapidly around us.

108) Q. What do you mean by "you get what you attend to?"

A. Energy follows attention. There is at every moment a 100 percent positive or a 100 percent negative universe available to each of us. Our energy goes to where our attention is focused and feeds what it is focused on. If we go through the evening newspaper and focus on all the negative, destructive news, we are in effect increasing the probability of negative events occurring in our lives. If we can learn to focus on the "positives" in our lives, those are thereby fed and will increase.

109) Q. I have trouble meditating when it is daylight or the room is bright. What can I do about this?

A. People with prominent Neptune, Pisces or twelfth house factors in their charts (Sun, Moon or Ascendant in conjunction with Neptune; Sun, Moon or Ascendant in Pisces; or with the Sun or Moon in the twelfth house) are extremely light-sensitive. A sleeping mask, called a "hoodwink," will generally take care of this problem.

110) Q. I find that many things irritate me. How can I deal with this?

A. Irritants show us where we are being vague about our rules or structures. If possible, learn to say "No" to the things that irritate you, or to compromise if the irritant has to do with another. In either case, use the irritants as messages about what you do allow and what you don't allow in your life and just where you are being vague about these areas. Irritation and anger are associated with the planet Mars and the astrological sign Aries—the *Tower* and *Emperor* in tarot.

111)   Q. I have an aversion to snakes, flies and spiders. What do they represent in my unconscious?

A. Snakes are related to the *Death* archetype, flies, to the *Old Pan* or *Devil* archetype, and spiders, to the *High Priestess.* You will generally attract flies when one of your "shoulds" or "shouldn'ts" is activated, and spiders when your security system is being rattled. Snakes have to do with sexuality, the kundalini energy, and change. Ask *Death, Old Pan* or the *High Priestess* why their messengers were sent and what the message is that you're not hearing or listening to.

112)   Q. When I am extremely ego involved in something and I can't get a clear answer from my Guide or the archetypes, how can I resolve this?

A. You might try asking your Guide, before you go to sleep, to send a dream that will answer your question. When you receive the dream, your Guide can then help you decipher it. In this way material from your unconscious can get past your ego defenses.

113)   Q. You speak of certain archetypes as being associated with specific parts of the body. Is the Inner Guide associated with any part of the body?

A. Yes. The Guide is associated with the solar plexus, the Jupiter chakra (or energy center) in the body. Our gut feelings are often messages from our Inner Guides.

114)   Q. What is your opinion of circumcision?

A. Prejudice against circumcision arises from metaphysical ignorance. Marc Edmund Jones in his book, *Occult Philosophy,* gives the following information:

Circumcision is the excision of the male prepuce . . . which as a religious ceremony dramatizes the necessity of self-preparation for the enjoyment of social values through a conscious redirection of control of physical sensation. It is the preparatory rite for MATRIMONY primarily, and for the ALCHEMICAL MARRIAGE ultimately. The ALCHEMICAL MARRIAGE of the esoteric tradition presents a divine self-unification as the supreme goal of all initiation. This is marked, physiologically, by the development of an actual nerve tract [as the result of the circumcision] composed of white nerve tissue which links the brain areas containing the pineal and pituitary glands, respectively, and facilitates the exalted immediacies of high illumination [or the awakened kundalini].[6]

The rite of circumcision comes to us from the ancient Egyptians, and it facilitates the spiritual awakening or enlightenment experience. I recommend it for any man undertaking his own spiritual quest, especially if he wants to move through a shaman role to one of priest.

115)   Q. If you were to think up a New Age motto, what would it be?

A. "How can I help?" would be my nomination. If each of us could keep consciously in mind at all times, *How can I help?*, the transition from the old consciousness to the new could take place much more harmoniously. How can I help the person who is doing what I can't do? How can I help, and on what level? — the spiritual? — the mental? — the emotional? — the material? How am I best equipped to help? What do I have that others need? How can I best share what I have?

If we can first establish what it is that we have in order to help and then the direction in which we would like to see that help move, the necessary actions will become self-evident. Perhaps I can help by giving a tithe or some other kind of material support to a person or a group that I believe is doing something important for spiritual consciousness. Perhaps I can help by calling on those in emotional turmoil, lending an ear to those who have no listeners. Perhaps I can help by sending the book or the idea which might be the neces-

[6]Marc Edmund Jones, *Occult Philosophy* (Stanwood, WA: Sabian Publishing, 1971), pp. 298-333. Used by permission.

sary key or catalyst for someone. Perhaps I can help by sending love consciously to those in need. There are many ways each of us can find to help, to share in this great spiritual adventure.

When you find how you can help — ACT ON IT! Don't procrastinate. NOW is when the help is needed. As the old saying goes, "The road to hell is paved with good intentions."

116) Q. If I'm gay, would my Inner Guide ask me to change or give up my sexual orientation in order to be able to unite with my God-Center?

A. The Inner Guides judge no one for his or her sexual orientation. But the requirements of one's God-Center are another matter. The ego, that person you see in the mirror and call yourself, must be willing to let go of or take on *any role* or anything else required by its God-Center. Maybe your Center will ask that you be celibate or heterosexual. Maybe, if you were now heterosexual, your Center would ask for same-sex expression or no sexual expression at all. If you were married, you might be asked to put the marriage aside. If you were unmarried, your Center might ask you to marry.

One never knows what the requirements of one's own God-Center are going to be. But try not to worry about it. Our Centers generally ask for ego role changes when the ego is prepared for and willing to make them.

But if your will to unite with God, your seeking of enlightenment or permanent kundalini arousal and balance is phrased in your mind along the lines of "I'll do anything my God-Center asks me to do *except for . . .*," forget it! The one thing you are unwilling to do or don't want to do will block all the rest of your spiritual work until you overcome such resistance to the will of your Center. On the spiritual path your sexual orientation is totally irrelevant, and sometimes being gay (which I included among the metasexuals) has certain advantages on the spiritual path. Love will never separate you from God, no matter what its variety.

117) Q. When I do my daily meditations, I find that the information and experiences I receive from the archetypes are things that

have already been in my mind. How can I achieve deeper levels with the Inner Guide Meditation?

A. At D.O.M.E. Center we schedule meditations together daily. We also discovered that what you are experiencing was happening in some of us. What we now do is a series of three meditations on the same subject.

For instance, if we are meditating on the Love-Creation energy form (often experienced as a solar figure) and the Moon or Mother archetypes, we will first have our Inner Guides bring these two figures together with us and ask what they need from each other and from us in our daily lives to work in harmony as energies within us. It is during this initial meditation that those thoughts that have already been in our minds become more specific and those rationalizations provided by our minds in terms of these two archetypal energy forms come into clear form. But generally during this first meditation, nothing new comes forth, nothing that will change the ego in any way in terms of its thoughts, actions or behaviors. We record this initial meditation.

We then go back with our Guides and encounter the same two energy forms once again. We note our ego's resistance during this second encounter, as the mind has already given all it contained in terms of rationalization and logic during the first meditation. But as we remain in the presence of the two figures with our Guides, new information and insights, new symbols present themselves with a life quality not experienced in the first meditation, and the group experiences the new life quality and freshness in itself among its members. We record this second meditation in our journals.

We then meditate a third time on the same energy forms, and it is during this third meditation that the deep level information and energy come forth and affect our ego personalities, causing a deeper unity between ourselves and our inner and outer worlds.

It is best to do these three meditations in the same time period, one following the next, rather than, for instance, one in the morning, one in the afternoon, and one in the evening, or on three consecutive days.

118) Q. What is it that you consider you are doing when you are interacting with the archetypal energy forms? For instance, if you

are using the tarot images, such as the *Fool* or the *Hanged Man*, just what does your mind judge is going on?

A. I consider myself to be making friends with and assimilating different aspects of myself and of the Oneness.

119) Q. You speak of the necessity of a person having three absolute No's. Why?

A. In a three-dimensional reality it seems that three absolute No's are necessary for reality stability. Less than three make reality too wobbly, and more than three make it too rigid. Earlier in this book, I speak of the "Law of No," which I would suggest reviewing.

Your "No's" are most useful if they are not imbued with morality. Try to keep the concepts of Good and Evil, Right and Wrong, Good and Bad, out of your thinking mechanism, and replace them with the thoughts, "This is *useful* for my spiritual evolution," and, "This is *not useful* for my spiritual evolution."

If you have labeled something "Good" and three or four years go by and it becomes destructive to you, it is difficult to let go of it because of the label of "Good." The label makes whatever is labeled Good "sticky" and hard to let go of. But if you had labeled the same thing "useful to my spiritual evolution," it would be easy to let it go when you discover it has become no longer of any use to you or to your growth.

The three absolute No's do not necessarily have to have anything to do with moral or ethical issues or considerations. Perhaps the only absolute No's you can discover that you have currently are, "I will not kill anyone under any circumstances," and "I will never smoke marijuana." In terms of usefulness, the No: "I will never wear the color orange until I make the conscious decision to change this absolute No to another," will suffice as the third.

No's are structural. Our absolute No's make the walls, floors and ceilings of our reality boxes, as I have mentioned previously, and the qualified No's—the Maybe's—are the doors and windows. Yes is not structural. It is space, inside and out. When you change a No to a Maybe, a Maybe to a Yes, or invent a new absolute No, you literally change the structure of both your inner and outer realities.

120) Q. You speak of a four-body system. What are the four bodies?

A. The most apparent of our four bodies is the physical or earth body. It's our anchor to the material plane. Without it our three inner bodies would have no transformation vehicle, no "pot to cook in" for the spiritual, alchemical change. Next there's the mental or air body. Every thought we think or idea we have occurs in that body. Next is the astral or water body—the emotional body. Every feeling we have, every sensation we feel, with the exception of sight, takes place in that body. It has the same form as the physical and is the body we perceive in an out-of-the-body experience or upon death. The fourth body and the least dense is our spiritual or fire body—the love body. The ability to give love, to create, to see, occurs from that body. It is the body we experience when we feel the quality of life, the sense that "I am." The three upper bodies interpenetrate each other, and all penetrate the physical body giving us our life and animation.

When we begin to see auras—the colored light around people—it is the inner three bodies' radiance that is being seen. People look like great, glowing Easter eggs, each one unique and full of light and color.

You might ask your Inner Guide to bring figures that represent each of the four bodies. See what they look like. Ask each if they are in balance with the others. If not, ask what you can do to get them in balance. Ask also what each one needs from each of the other three. Once the four bodies are in balance, it is safe for the kundalini energy to begin to rise. When your four-body system is in balance, you are "centered."

121) Q. I began working with my Inner Guide, and he introduced me to one of the archetypal figures who said he wouldn't interact with me or give me any information until I got a job and a permanent place to live. Then I met several other of the archetypes who said the same thing. Are these just reflections of my old materialistic hang-ups getting in the way of my spiritual growth through the "magic mirror effect" or could this be true?

A. To separate the material from the spiritual is false in my opinion. If everything is One, what isn't holy? Spiritual growth can

Figure 32. To handle highly intense spiritual energy—the energy of the archetypes—a strong material base is necessary. Taurus, a fixed earth sign (the *High Priest* or *Hierophant* in tarot), is the astrological symbol associated with such a base. Trump of the *Hierophant* shown here is from an original drawing by Leigh McCloskey ©1987. Used by permission.

often be compared to a pyramid. The bottom of the pyramid is the physical plane. If this isn't solid, there is no base for spirit. This may be why you are getting the messages about a job and a home from the archetypes. Without this firm earth plane base the changes brought from archetypal interaction would create too much turmoil in your life.

It is common for archetypes initially to request a stabilization of the earth plane. Sometimes it takes the form of dietary requests, sometimes, getting a health problem taken care of, and often, requesting much the same things requested of you. To handle highly intense spiritual energy — the energy of the archetypes — a strong material base is necessary.

122)   Q. How can I learn to visualize color more strongly in my meditations?

A. David Benge of D.O.M.E. Center has come up with a useful technique that seems to help some people see color in meditation: "Get a 75 to 100 watt incandescent light bulb and lamp. Set it up on a stand and look directly at it for thirty to forty-five seconds. Then cover your eyes with your palms, being careful not to touch the eyelids themselves. (The bright light will not harm your eyes. In fact this is a method used in the Bates Method of eye exercises.) The optic nerve will "see," with your eyes closed, a series of colors in the same shape and outline as the bulb.

"When I do this exercise, I see orange, followed by meadow green, then magenta, then violet, and finally deep purple. Your brain will remember and record this color experience, and you will be able to apply these colors to your meditative life. Becoming adept in using the Inner Guide Meditation has a lot to do with retraining yourself to bring together mental and emotional aspects within yourself. This color exercise does much to develop the mental application of color to your meditations."

It is also useful to visualize the inner colors as iridescent. Iridescence seems to be strongly connected with spirit. Practice by looking at sea shells, iridescent butterfly wings, iridescent insects and the iridescence found in the feathers of birds. Seeing the inner colors as iridescent brings much power into the meditative experience.

123)   Q. How can I work with my Inner Guide to allow energy to flow more easily in my physical body? I have a lot of problems with stiffness and aches and pains in certain parts of my body.

A. In meditation call on the *Sun*, and ask the *Sun* to radiate those specific areas of your body corresponding to the horoscopic house Saturn is in, the sign Saturn is in and the house of the horoscope that has Capricorn on its cusp. For instance, if you have Saturn in Sagittarius in the fifth house, you would ask the *Sun* to radiate and create energy flow in the liver, buttocks, hips and thighs to just above the knees (Sagittarius), the heart (fifth house) and the intestines (sixth house, the house with Capricorn on its cusp). Our bodies tend to block energy in these specific areas, and giving them this conscious attention removes not only physical problems, but also out-in-the-world problems the Saturn/Capricorn energies may be causing.

124)   Q. Why are you so against the "transference" encouraged by most psychologists and psychiatrists?

A. Transference creates a dependence on the outer counselor or therapist, a loss of your Center, and a projection of your authority and Inner Guide outside of yourself onto an outer world person. It limits the function of your Inner Guide to teach and protect, or sets up the outer world person as mother or father. It is the old guru trick and seems to exist more for the counselor's needs than for his or her patient's.

Also, therapists often have a hard time with counter-transference, because if a patient makes a transference onto the therapist, a counter-transference onto the patient necessarily develops in turn. Projection remains always a two-way street. Therapists wish they could just make it go away. In my experience most therapists seem to believe it's inevitable, that it's unconscious projection and that it's the only way to untangle the projective patterns. If the Inner Guide would be incorporated into the therapy situation, the transference/counter–transference dilemma wouldn't occur. Then the problems that brought the patient into therapy could be resolved rapidly without further complicating the process with new problems.

125) Q. Why is lying destructive?

A. Lying to yourself or to others confuses the archetypes which are creating and sustaining your reality. When they register your perceived outer reality in one way and then you define this same reality in an entirely different way by lying, two separate sets of instructions are received by them—two contradictory suggestions are made as to how to create your reality experience. These contradictions create imbalance, first in yourself, then in your outer reality, and imbalance generally brings with it pain or disease.

126) Q. How would you use the Jungian concepts of anima and animus in your work, the anima being a personification of feminine psychological tendencies in a man's psyche and the animus being the same in a woman's?

A. The Jungian terms anima and animus are necessarily general and contain many different specific archetypes, some of which may be antagonistic to one another. For instance, a man might have the relationship of Moon opposite or polarized with Venus in his horoscope. This implies a tug of war or conflict between two aspects of his feminine side, in tarot terms, the *High Priestess* and the *Empress*. To incorporate these two archetypal energies into one anima figure can blur the relationship between them and create confusion.

But if the person intellectually understands that the anima or animus figure—or better, the figure Mitch Walker in his book *Visionary Love* calls the *Anim*—may well contain these contradictions, it can be most valuable as an inner world figure, because it is the source of the sexual opposite in the person.

127) Q. I am a lesbian, and the thought of working with a male guide is abhorrent to me. Isn't it possible to work with a woman as the first of the guides?

A. Lesbian women I have worked with generally have gotten guides that seemed androgynous, but they were clearly not female. If you could try to put aside your prejudice and remember that both the masculine and the feminine reside in each of us, your

Inner Guide's unconditional love and acceptance might allow you to make an exception about working with men in his case.

128) Q. My husband is a scientist and disparages astrology and meditation. How can I deal with this?

A. Ask your Shadow woman what she's trying to communicate to you by manipulating your husband to have this attitude. Perhaps it's an unconscious "fundamentalist" part of yourself. Superstition and hysteria about tarot and astrology seem prevalent among the fundamentalists in our society, whether of science or religion. If scientists would use the scientific method and study before judging, new information sources would open up to them along with a new understanding of multi-dimensional physics.

129) Q. What do you mean when you use the word "conscious?"

A. By conscious I mean that of which the ego is aware, whether internal or external, inner or outer. I use the word "consciousness" to mean maximum ego awareness infused with knowledge and experience of spirit.

130) Q. Why do I feel horny all the time, and what can I do about it with the Inner Guide Meditation? It makes me do irrational things and interferes in my life in a major way.

A. A strong sexual drive is often an indication that one inner archetype is seeking unification with another or with the ego. Many of my friends and people I work with tell me of positive results they've gotten from uniting sexually with the archetypes — sacred sex, as it were. This can be done systematically, working with each one of the twenty-two tarot archetypes in succession — *Fool* through the *World* — and having each archetype relate sexually with you in both its masculine and feminine forms. Let each archetype design the experience and the interaction. Truly let each teach you. Initially, use the gender normally pictured on its tarot key for each of the first twenty-two experiences. Next, go through the sequence again, asking each of the tarot figures to reverse the sex it was at first. Finally, repeat the forty-four experiences with you reversing your sex.

These eighty-eight sexual interactions with the archetypes will give you the full spectrum of experiential information about spirit, sex and the kundalini as they operate on all levels of reality. Of course, both the permission of and supervision by your Inner Guide are *vital* in these meditations because of the incredible power of these experiences, for they often awaken the kundalini force which your Guide can control, but which you, the ego, can't.

131) Q. Did the ancient Egyptians know about archetypes?

A. Yes. In ancient Egypt the archetypes were called *Neters* and were understood with a depth and sophistication that make our current understanding seem naive. Isha Schwaller de Lubicz speaks of them in her two books: *Her-Bak, "Chick Pea," The Living Face of Ancient Egypt,* and *Her-Bak, Egyptian Initiate.* Throughout the following quotations from her books I equate archetypes for *Neters.*

> The Neters are the causal Powers — primary causes and secondary causes — of everything that manifests itself in the Universe; they are the principles, agents and functions of these manifestations.[7]

> Neters are . . . ideas immanent or virtually contained in nature which give substance form throughout the phases of continuous creation and all genesis. . . .
> The Neters are the functional principles of nature. . . . Our sense and cerebral intelligence can't grasp them in the abstract; but sense and cerebral intelligence can study the evidence of their essential quality throughout the scale of creatures. . . . Power originates action. . . . It is therefore immanent in the Neter-nature. But it comprises two elements, natural force and its potential, which can be modified by other Neter-powers and conditioned by the creature, thing or situation in which it is active. . . .

---

[7]Isha Schwaller de Lubicz, *Her-Bak: The Living Face of Ancient Egypt* (Rochester, VT: Inner Traditions, 1978), p. 340. Used by permission.

But it is difficult for human intelligence to grasp the idea of
unity in the creative source and the multiplicity evident in
nature. The Neters are spiritual powers, qualities of divine
Force, potentially all that will appear, work, develop in crea-
tures. They are states of a consciousness which is not to be
confused with the consciousness that results from existence.
Their consciousness is a quality that enters into relations with
things in a character that is invariable and doesn't change, as
for example the quality "warmth," whereas the creature
changes constantly in the growth of its consciousness, which is
the road to liberation from its corporal state. . . .

We know that Neter is before man, idea before thing. We
know that the same function, in the same circumstances, will
give similar results: it is sensible to note the characters of
function and circumstances that produced such and such a
phenomenon. Isn't a Neter a manifest quality? One ascends
from nature to Neter, through whose symbols one may get to
know nature. . . .

A Neter is a principle or an agent of a cosmic law or function. It acts and manifests itself by virtue of its own determin-
ism, which is a law of "necessity" independent of the subjects
that submit to it. A Neter acts according to its function
whether it is unknown or known to human beings; it is indifferent to the names that are attributed to it. . . .

In order to understand the meaning of the Neters, they must
be regarded . . . in their own domain of action, nature. We
have nature incessantly before us, imposing her laws upon us
and *manifesting* the development of a being through all its
transformations. Whatever . . . names are given to the forces
that rule nature they always relate to principles that can be
known through their effects—that is, through natural phenomena. These principles are the Neters, or cosmic
functions. . . .

When a man has liberated his [personal] Neter [the Self], he
becomes an "emitter" . . . and does the work of "those who are
in their caves." That is, he shares the work of cosmic powers
with the acquired consciousness of cosmic Man. . . .

We must note . . . what differentiates Neters from human
beings relative to the microcosm: A Neter is not the micro-

cosm, but an aspect or a principial function of it. A human being is the microcosm; he synthesizes the Neters. . . .

Going deep into Egyptian theology, beyond the three principles of creator, animator, and redeemer and the universal feminine principle, one finds that the *Neters are of nature* (by "nature" is meant all states that are transitory and relative in relation to the eternal state of the spirit of origin and to the spiritual consciousness acquired throughout nature).[8]

132)   Q. Is there another test question to ask the Inner Guide?

A. One that has been suggested is, "Is your existence dedicated to the cause of total truthfulness?"

133)   Q. What is your stand on abortion?

A. In abortion questions, each case must be considered individually. Although the incoming soul is certainly "around" the mother during her pregnancy, it generally doesn't enter the infant body permanently until just before the birth.

I have worked with pregnant women whose Guides have advised that an abortion be performed, and others whose Guides recommended the child be born. One woman I worked with discussed her pregnancy with her Guide, *High Priestess* and Center figure. They all decided that the pregnancy would be harmful to both her and to what she was to do this life. The next day she had a spontaneous abortion. So many circumstances must be taken into consideration that only the Guides of the parents would have the right and the correct perspective to advise in such a matter.

There is a terrible problem with guilt, usually, once an abortion has been done. Long ago I worked with a woman in her late sixties who was in an acute state of depressive melancholia and facing possible electric shock therapy to attempt to break the state. Somehow she found me, and I initiated her. Her Guide told her that her state was due to an abortion she had had in her early teens,

---

[8]Isha Schwaller de Lubicz, *Her-Bak: Egyptian Initiate* (Rochester, VT: Inner Traditions, 1978), pp. 90–91, 148–149, 157, 225, 310, 326. Selections used by permission.

which she no longer even thought about! He advised her to make something creative – a painting, a poem, a quilt, anything out of her own personal creativity, allowing her loving feelings for the soul who would have come in to go into the creative project, and then to give it away, to let it go out into life. She did this, and the depression vanished.

It seems useful for both the mother *and,* if possible, the father to create something and give it out into life for each aborted pregnancy. This seems to furnish the "balancing" needed and removes the possibility of problems with guilt or self-punishment from occurring later in the life. It is advisable for each of the parents to discuss past abortions fully with his and her Inner Guide.

134)   Q. How do you define "soul?"

A. For me, "soul" is the combination of the water (emotional) and air (mental) bodies, while Spirit is the fire (spiritual) body alone, the deathless body that continues life after life.

135)   Q. You mentioned that you have your Moon in Gemini and work with two *High Priestess* figures. Why is this?

A. Gemini in your horoscope indicates an area of duality. Gemini or the *Twins* in tarot always want to be two or more things. Therefore I recommend that people who have Sun in Gemini work with two Solar Center or Power Alien figures, those with Moon in Gemini, with two Lunar Construct or Vessel Alien figures, and those with Gemini or Sagittarius rising (the Ascendant) in their horoscopes work with two Shadow figures. When the Gemini factor is condensed into one form, it becomes too contradictory and too hard to understand. By asking for two figures the dualistic needs of the Gemini factor are clearly perceived.

136)   Q. How do you read AIDS as a message to us about ourselves?

A. As one of the leaders of the American macrobiotics movement says, "The disease is always the cure." We are experiencing AIDS now because nature is telling us that we must be conscious of how we use our sexual energy. To use sexual energy unconsciously during this time of kundalini activation will bring painful results, no matter what the sexual preference. A further message seems to be that we must become more aware of our health and bodies.

Macrobiotics is the only diet or treatment I have heard of which heals the immune system by improving the blood and gets early cases of AIDS to remit, when used in conjunction with a spiritual or meditative practice.

137) Q. What are "Protectors"?

A. I call Protectors those individuals who have no Alien patterns in their natal horoscopes, but who find themselves surrounded by people who do. They seem to function in a protective way towards the Aliens, warning them when they get too "far out" or scary for other people, and acting as "translators" for them. They generally have not suffered the social rejection and alienation that the Aliens have experienced, and those people who have Alien patterns don't frighten the Protectors or make them nervous as they do others.

138) Q. How do you explain *déjà vu*, the feeling of having experienced an event or situation previously which in fact you are experiencing for the first time?

A. There seems to be a lag between the time when the archetypes create the reality we will be experiencing in what we call the real world and when the event they have created actually occurs. I think *déjà vu* has to do with a subliminal bleedthrough into ego consciousness at the time a situation is being created on the archetypal level. Then, when the event or situation occurs, we "recognize" it, even though we don't remember the actual bleedthrough occurrence.

139) Q. My mind keeps drifting or sometimes I fall asleep while meditating. What can I do about this?

Figure 33. The *Moon* or Pisces is one of the forces that hold the secrets of the archetypes and the keys to the physics of the inner dimensions and past lives. Trump of the *Moon* from the tarot deck in *Seed*, published by Crown Publishers, New York, 1969. Used by permission.

A. This is usually caused by the archetypal forces called the *Hanged Man* and the *Moon* in tarot (Neptune and Pisces in astrology). If you ask your Guide to take you to the images of these two energies within, and talk to them about the problems of concentration and alertness, you should be able to obtain a solution to the problem. The phenomena you mention seem to indicate a repression of one or both of these energies or a repression of energies connected to the twelfth house, which have to do with our escapist urges: spacing out, fantasy, day-dreaming, and addictive behavior.

The archetypes often suggest a more *active* fantasy life, with you *entering* the fantasy with your Guide and *participating* rather than merely watching yourself on an inner movie screen or stage. Fantasizing and day-dreaming, where you are only the observer, are among the greatest thieves of life energy. The remedy for this seems to be *getting into the fantasy and living it* on the inner planes with your Guide. Then you provide a doorway for the energy to come into your daily life on the earth plane.

140) Q. What is the difference between a shaman and a priest or priestess?

A. The word "shaman" is Siberian and means in English "one who knows." Different kinds of shamanism are found all over the world and are still actively practiced in Brazil, Haiti, Africa and among the Indians of North America. The English word "wizard" also means "one who knows." The Persian astrologers or *magi*, who gave their name to magic, are still called "Wise Men" in the Christian tradition.

Traditionally, the shaman is an associate of the Gods and Goddesses, the possessor of extraordinary magical and psychic abilities, a channeler of potent archetypal energy, a worker with the dead, a descender into the underworld, a shape-shifter, counselor, healer, artist and poet. The shaman develops his or her powers in the first three energy centers along the spine, the three lower *chakras*, and sometimes in the fourth or heart center. Virginity or celibacy are not requisite for these powers, except for those powerful individuals who elect to be shamanic priests or priestesses.

A priest or priestess must be virgin, celibate, metasexual or practice coitus interruptus to develop his or her powers in the upper centers also, usually with the seat of power located in the heart for balance. They strive to gain access to all the awakened centers. Thus, they can safely channel the kundalini and the archetypes' undiluted spiritual powers through themselves.

Inner Guide work initiates one into shamanism with all its attendant powers. Continued deep-level work with the Guide finally leads one into priest or priestess training, whether in this life or many lives down the line, to development as a fully awakened shamanic priest or priestess.

141) Q. I seem to have more resistance to being receptive in the meditation than others have. I have trouble hearing, seeing and feeling things on the archetypal level. Can you suggest anything I might do to get my ego more out of the way?

A. You might try working naked when you meditate. Clothes seem to carry a heavy investment of the ego's energy and serve to help the ego maintain itself at its current awareness level, resisting that which is new or that which would cause it to change and transform. Nakedness brings vulnerability, but also receptivity. Aquarius and Uranus (the tarot *Star* and *Fool*) have to do with both freedom and nudity.

142) Q. How do marijuana and alcohol affect the Inner Guide Meditation and the rest of life?

A. Marijuana effectively blocks initial contact with the true Inner Guide for up to ten days following its use, and it takes about a year for heavy smokers to totally rid the body of its effects (although a macrobiotic diet speeds up the detoxification). It affects the ego in such a way that those unconscious elements which presently control or manipulate the ego are further distorted or blocked from being understood, allowing inflation of the ego and increased separation from the heart center, one's true nature. The fear mechanism that strives to keep the current ego from growing and changing is strengthened by marijuana, its derivatives, and by alcohol. Alcohol and marijuana are the two drugs which pull us into the unconscious Collective Mind or Mass Mind, the mind that fosters and perpetuates the illusions of separation and non-unity, and attempts at all costs to maintain the *status quo,* the mind of mediocrity. They keep us internally and externally bound to and dependent on the unconscious mother-father (Moon/Saturn, Cancer/Capricorn) archetypes and away from the development of our own freedom, creativity, and individuality.

In astrological terms, alcohol suppresses the Lunar (tarot *High Priestess*) and the Cancerian (tarot *Chariot*) energies in the reality-generating system, while marijuana suppresses the energies of Saturn (tarot *World*) and Capricorn (tarot *Old Pan* or *Devil*). This can be demonstrated through an individual's horoscope. Of those people related to you through blood, law, or role, the ones that correspond to the astrological houses containing your Moon and Cancer energies will suffer in their lives or create problems in your life as you use alcohol, and the ones that correspond to the houses containing the Saturn and Capricorn energies, will suffer or cause problems for you as you use marijuana. This includes the fourth house of the horoscope, the natural house of Cancer—mother, home, reality base, feelings and emotions, family as a unit, security, father's third sibling, as being responsive negatively to alcohol; and the tenth house, the natural house of Capricorn—father, employer, authority figures, policemen, reputation, honor, career, public success, "the powers that be," the Establishment, mother's third sibling, as being negatively responsive to marijuana.

Marijuana seems to be the more insidious of the two drugs, because it is a drug that "lies" to the individual, telling the person's ego that his or her abilities to love and create are becoming greater, when, in fact, it takes away these abilities and replaces them with the *illusion* of having these increased abilities. The illusion is defended with a paranoid ego stance—"I'm right, and they're wrong," "Nobody really understands," "I'm surrounded by enemies" and the like.

If you regard the Cancer/Capricorn pole of a horoscope as a seesaw, marijuana smoking suppresses the Capricorn end, resulting in the Cancerian end raising too high and becoming unbalanced—the emotions go out of control, the personality becomes grandiose, all limits dissolve into the boundless, and the ego goes into a manic

Figure 34. Trump of the *Chariot* based on Aleister Crowley's Thoth Tarot Deck. Used by permission.

phase, often quite severe. If a physician is consulted, he will often prescribe some mood balancing drug, through ignorance of the mechanics of the four-body system. This results first in stabilization, but then in increased desire or need for the marijuana, which in turn produces depression, paranoia, exhaustion, fear, and guilt. Thus a classical manic-depressive syndrome is created and maintained until both drugs, the marijuana and the mood stabilizer, are no longer used and the four-body system returns to its own natural health and balance. This is the seesaw effect often observed in marijuana users. It takes away the individual's ability to love and create—to do the work of his or her own heart center—and it substitutes the mind and rationalization in its place, sealing off spirit. It makes invisible to the ego the true purpose of the life, and it injures all those around the person, generally those who love the person most and are the closest (family, friends, lovers). Marijuana also clogs the seven energy centers (or chakras) along the spine, so that awakening kundalini energy becomes quite dangerous to the individual's life or sanity.

I find marijuana use deleterious, because it prevents a person from contacting the true Guide, but doesn't prevent contact with the archetypes and with false guides, which makes deep-level meditation dangerous. But like everything, marijuana isn't all "bad." It probably prevented World War III back in the late 60's and early 70's. ("Stoned" soldiers aren't too interested in fighting wars.) It seems a useful drug for people to "go through," but not to get habituated to.

It is a tragedy of our time that alcohol and marijuana are so poorly understood. In this era we live in of vast changes on all levels of reality, fear of change is prominent. Only meditation—some form of going within safely—effectively deals with these fears.

143) Q. What is the *Divine Androgyne* I hear you speak of?

A. This is a figure produced by a combination of primary energies. You can bring it to form by asking your Inner Guide to bring your Solar Center Construct figure (or Power Alien), your Lunar Construct figure (or Vessel Alien), and the archetypes of your Mercury (the tarot *Magician*) and the archetype that represents the sign your Mercury is in, e.g., a person with Mercury in Virgo would ask for the *Magician* and the *Hermit*. Then ask these four figures to dissolve into an oval of light and to become one androgynous figure. The resultant figure represents your central essence, that which is beyond polarity or duality. It represents the general theme of this life, and perhaps the central theme of many lifetimes. This figure represents the Primary Original within you that can help teach you how to get beyond the pull of the opposites and how to achieve the "Alchemical Marriage," the union of the masculine and feminine principles within yourself which results in the experience of Oneness and union with Deity.

In his book *Visionary Love*, Mitch Walker describes this spiritforce: "The Androgyne, the union of masculine and feminine, personifies the harmony of opposites. It's the paradigm of *healing*, embodying all the diverse traits of masculinity and femininity together in oneness. When a person allies himself with the Androgyne, he becomes a force for wholeness, for gentle balance, tapping into the endless nurturance of the primal Great Mother and the infinite energy-power of the primal Sky Father". . . and he "becomes an agent in the transformation of a conflicted, unbalanced humanity."[9]

This is an extremely powerful energy form. Be sure to ask your Guide just how much to initially interact with the *Divine Androgyne* figure, and heed your Guide's advice.

144)   Q. Is there a spiritual hierarchy that our Guides reflect?

A. It is my belief that understanding or structuring things in terms of hierarchy is no longer useful to human evolution. Certainly, the Guides seem to reflect no hierarchical structure. I believe we are in a cycle, this last portion of the Piscean Age, when hierarchies will no longer work. We see it in the fall of kings, gurus and corporate heads. We must take our judgments out of concepts like "higher" and "lower." For instance, can one say that the brain is

---

[9]Mitch Walker and Friends, *Visionary Love* (San Francisco: Treeroots Press, 1980), p. 19.

better than the heart? Remove either, and death ensues. Is one cell of the body more "holy" than another? I believe that the final lesson of Pisces that each of us must learn is to see the common thread that spiritually connects each and all of us, and to deal with each other with sensitivity and compassion. Today, any organized body of people must learn to be "leaderful," to have each person concerned about the spiritual whole—the physical, emotional, mental, and spiritual bodies of the group—and his or her part in it, without the judgements of "better" and "less good," or "higher" and "lower" entering as factors. Otherwise, I think we will find the group will become "sick" and stop functioning, or will become something lifeless and robotic that will nourish neither itself nor any of its parts.

145) Q. Should the Inner Guide accompany you when archetypes want you to leave the meeting place and go somewhere else in the inner world?

A. Yes, definitely. Never go anywhere in meditation without your Guide. Remember, you don't really know what the "rules" are on the inner planes. Your Guide does. In a strange country it's best to have both interpreter and protector.

146) Q. Is what is called the "double" the same as the Shadow?

A. I believe the Shadow often contains the "double," but the double is more akin to what I call the Solar *Center* in a man and the Lunar Construct in a woman.
In Europe there is a folk belief about the double or *Doppel-gänger*: You see your double and you die. This seems to be psychologically true when speaking of the Shadow. As you work in the Inner Guide Meditation with your Shadow man or woman, the figure will come to look more and more like you. The day the figure looks *exactly* like you, as if you were looking into a mirror, is the day you will experience an ego death and rebirth. When the death-rebirth process is completed, your Shadow will again look unlike you. You can always tell where you are in your own transformation process by looking at your Shadow.

The "double" used in this sense, akin to or identical with the Shadow, differs from the "*Double*" described by Mitch Walker in his book, *Visionary Love*:

Within an individual person the myth of masculine/feminine splits the unconscious psychic unity into two halves. Besides embodying the Primal Parents (the Earth Mother and the Sky Father), these halves also form the basis for sex-role identity, for the roles of "man" and "woman." In this regard, that half which underlies a person's appropriate sex-role personality is called the *Double*, the source of masculinity in a man and of femininity in a woman. That half which is left out of the person's identity is called the *Anim* [akin to the *anima* and *animus* of Jungian psychology], the source of femininity in a man and masculinity in a woman. The Double and the Anim contain many spirit-forces and kosmic values, depending on the mythology which has shaped them. In particular, Double and Anim contain both erotic and destructive forces in relation to other individuals.

The social myth system seeks to regulate and control these forces through their suppression or projection onto other individuals. Mythic patterns are set up to channel what's often called "love." "Love" is the projection of an erotic aspect of Double or Anim onto another person. When this happens, the projecting person sees in the other the kosmic wonder, beauty and magick inherent in that spirit-source. This is the cause of great happiness and sexual yearning, and may lead to kosmic revelations seen in the sacred source of the projections.

When the Anims of a man and a woman are shared in this "love," there is a heterosexual union. Such unions have been told of in stories like "Tristan and Isolt" and "Romeo and Juliet." When the Double of two men or two women are shared in "love," there is a homosexual union. Relationships of this kind have been described in tales like "Epic of Gilgamesh" and "Apollo and Hyacinthus."

These love and sex patterns are closely regulated by the social myth system. Who you can love and/or have sex with, how and when you can, are all controlled by myths, which manipulate these forces, encouraging some aspects and discouraging others. As can be seen, "love" and sex roles are very closely tied together.

All societies institutionalize Anim-love in some form such as marriage, concubinage or rape, since heterosexual union is necessary to the survival of the species. However, Double-love can be institutionalized or condemned in a myth system. Two examples are ancient Sparta and the Jews: in Sparta Double-love served the state in the education of young men and the strengthening of warrior-traits, while in Jewish mythology Double-love was tabooed (although the story of David and Jonathan is a notable exception in the Bible).

When the social mythology shapes Anim and Double, it incorporates as part of the Double a spirit-energy called *Magickal Twinning*. When we see a pair of identical twins, we sense in their identicalness a common source or essence. This sense is a manifestation of Magickal Twinning, which is the numinous process that makes two things out of one or one thing out of two. The action of Magickal Twinning is a kind of duplication where the spirit-essence of one object is infused into another, making spirit twins, yet where the two duplicates are bound together through their common spirit-essence into a third object, an indivisible unity. The Greek tale of Narcissus, who fell in love with his reflection in a pool, is a story describing this Magickal Twinning-force. Through the action of Magickal Twinning, a person's sex role identity is formed as a vague reflection or twin of the unconscious Double. In this way sex-role identity gains solidity and substance through rootedness in the life-giving spirit world.

Because sex-role identity is based on the Double, when a person projects their Double onto another there's an unconscious sense of twinning or reflection of their ego, leading to the notion of identity or equality with that other person. In this way the Magickal Twinning-force is evoked between two people. Thus Double-love is distinguished from Anim-love by uncanny feelings of unity, strength and reinforcement of personal identity. This can create an atmosphere between lovers of profound familiarity, a mysterious, joyful sharing of feelings and needs, a dynamic, intuitive strength and understanding. Confucius describes this in his commentary on Fellowship in the *I Ching*:

> *But when two people are at one in their innermost*
> *   hearts,*
> *They shatter even the strength of iron or bronze.*
> *And when two people understand each other in their*
> *   innermost hearts,*
> *Their words are sweet and strong, like the fragrance of*
> *   orchids.*

This aspect of Double-love was exploited by many warrior societies such as the Dorians and the Japanese, since it increased the bravery, vigor and unity of soldiers.

Since Magickal Twinning inheres in the Double, Double projections involving others invoke the Twinning-force between people. When this happens, there's a sense (usually unconscious) of being identical to the other person. If two things are identical, they must be perfectly equal. Since Double-love involves the most intense projections of Double, it gives rise to the clearest, strongest sense of Magickal Twinning. Because of this, Double-love is the source of ideals concerning equality. Double-love, for example, is the basis for that harmonious rapport between people sometimes called "brotherly love." It's also the source for the ideal of political equality referred to as "democracy." In the so-called birthplace of democracy, ancient Greece, pairs of lovers were often proclaimed as tyrant murderers, and highly respected. Examples include Harmodius and Aristogiton, and Melanippus and Chariton.

Since all social myth systems have hierarchies, Double-love can become an equalizing force dangerous to a system which can't control it. This control is provided through myths condemning Double-love, or by institutionalizing it as an acceptable aspect of sex-role identity. However, if Double-love can break free of social control, it gives rise to an insolent, vigorous opposition to mythic hierarchies. This equalizing force was celebrated by Walt Whitman in a poem:

> *The prairie-grass dividing, its special odor breathing,*
> *I demand of it the spiritual corresponding,*
> *Demand the most copious and close companionship of*
> *   men . . .*

> *Those that go their own gait, erect, stepping with free-*
> *dom and command, leading not following,*
> *Those with a never-quell'd audacity, those with sweet*
> *and lusty flesh clear of taint,*
> *Those that look carelessly in the faces of Presidents and*
> *governors, as to say **Who are you?***
> *Those of earth-born passion, simple, never constrain'd,*
> *never obedient . . .*

In addition to these characteristics, there's also a destructive aspect of the Double called the *Competitor*. The Competitor is a negative Magickal Twinning, Double-hatred, and it seeks to destroy a person's identity. When the Competitor is projected onto another person, that person is seen as a threat and an enemy to be destroyed. In ritualized form this is the basis for most "sports" such as boxing, football, tennis and so on. The Competitor has great potential in furthering the human activities of murder, war and genocide. It brings about the pattern of the "hero" and his "enemy," the two men or the two armies that struggle against each other for victory. Achilles and Hector in the *Iliad*, and the war described in that story, are a good example of this pattern. As Achilles says to Hector: "Lions and men make no truce, wolves and lambs have no friendship—they hate each other for ever. So there can be no love between you and me; and there shall be no truce for us, until one of the two shall fall and glut Ares with his blood." Western culture has given an exalted place to the Competitor, who served the western god in his ambitious plans. . . .

The kosmic energy of Magickal Twinning, when not split up and projected as positive (love) and negative (hate) aspects of the Double, manifests in the spirit-realm as a being whose energy is catalytic, who interpenetrates other spirit-forces and brings them together. This spirit-being resembles an ancient Greek God called Hermes, who was a God of sexuality, travel, and magickal energy. He was a merry trickster-figure who pulled clever pranks, and he was also the messenger of the other Gods. His wand of two snakes or white ribbons twined about a rod—symbolic of the Magickal Twinning force—was the wand of the magician; his altar was the *herm*, a stone post with an erect cock (see Norman O. Brown, *Hermes the Thief*). Hermes was an important figure in medieval alchemy. His

Figure 35. The trump of *The Last Judgement*, which relates to Pluto, ruler
of the sign Scorpio (tarot *Death*), is the central archetypal energy associated with human sexuality and the kundalini force. Pluto's stay in the sign
Scorpio from 1983 to 1995 gives a humanity a major lesson in the conscious uses of sexuality. Its motto is: Change or die! Illustration shown here
is an original drawing by Leigh McCloskey ©1987. Used by permission.

alchemical element was mercury (quicksilver) and his principal magick was the bringing together of the male and female elements to form the philosopher's stone, the supreme alchemical goal.

This Hermes-being is not male or female, but a catalytic force which can reunite the kosmic duality of masculine/feminine. In ancient Greek mythology, the union of Hermes and Aphrodite, Goddess of Love, produced Hermaphroditos, the Androgyne. Hermes' erect cock symbolizes her alive penetrating essence, sexual in origin. Her magickal silvery laughter melts barriers and carries her far and fast through the spiritworld. She unlocks spirit-powers, and when she's summoned against a falseself system she leads the seeker to magickal forces which can transform that person into a healer and shaman of great beauty and strength.[10]

A third kind of "double" that may be encountered in literature is the "double" referred to by Carlos Castaneda in his writings. This "double" is the projected emotional or astral body. It usually is identical in appearance to the actual physical individual, but is less substantial—more an illusion, although it can look and act quite real. It is the body one is in when he or she is astral projecting or dead—the "ghost" body.

147) Q. What is "the physics of sex" I've heard you talk about?

A. I received the teaching about the physics of sex as the second part of the dream in which I was given the information about the Alien patterns in horoscopes. This occurred in Houston, Texas, on November 8, 1974. I was told in the dream not to talk about any of the sexual material for seven years—just to observe the physics at work in the world, and not to write about this physics in any detail until Pluto established itself in Scorpio, after August 27, 1984.

Because sexuality is an area where ignorance, prejudice and "morality" hold sway, we have lost the knowledge of the physics of sex. Sex operates by natural and universal law, as does all else in the universe, no matter what the current social persuasion. Certain

---

[10]Walker, *Visionary Love*, pp. 22-25. Used by permission.

abilities are available to people who utilize certain sexual modes and not to others. The path of the shaman, priest or priestess and the path of the householder are truly different, but equally sacred. This has nothing to do with "better" or "less good" but with an operating physics. The human physical, emotional, mental and spiritual systems operate according to the laws of physics as does everything else. The kundalini energy operates according to physics. In this new phase of the Piscean Age (which began in 1817) where we have the freedom, information and techniques available to cure our ignorance of the Earth and her mysteries, as well as the mysteries of our inner dimensions, this physics can be brought once again into consciousness.

For instance, children and adults who are and remain virgin seem to be *unprogrammed* and are like gelatin which has never set. That is to say, they seem to be easily able to develop the talents and abilities of *any* of the Alien patterns, so long as the condition of virginity is maintained; and they are able to safely handle a full kundalini arousal. Their horoscopes tend to be more difficult to read than those of individuals who have "earthed" through normal sexuality. When a person loses his or her virginity through normal heterosexual expression, an "earthing" takes place, the horoscope "sets," and their horoscopes become easy to read. They become predictable according to their degree of consciousness, and any Alien pattern (along with its abilities) tends to go unconscious. They lose the full spectrum of their Alien powers until they return to a state of virginity through celibacy, coitus interruptus or same-sex expression.

Heterosexual intercourse in which a virgin male has no orgasm during penetration does not appear to interfere with the state of virginity or the availability of the powers or Alien abilities in the man, unless the woman has orgasm while penetration occurs. If neither the man nor the woman have orgasm while penetration occurs, the virginity of both is maintained. Penetration in the foregoing instances refers to either genital sex, oral sex or anal sex where orgasm or ejaculation occur. More information on this can be found in a book dealing with tantric sex.

Unfortunately, there are not many good books on this subject. Tantra has always been a secret tradition passed orally from master to student. Probably the most useful book would be Mantak Chia's

Taoist Secrets of Love (Aurora Press, New York, 1984). But when reading this or any book, especially books dealing with metaphysics and sexuality, trust your heart and your intuition. If information in any book doesn't *feel* right to you, check it out with your Inner Guide. All of us who write books include all of our ego prejudices, beliefs, and opinions in our writings. Always believe your own heart over any written word.

Masturbation and same-sex expression also do not seem to interfere with the virgin state. This is probably the reason that celibacy, metasexuality and/or a virgin condition were, and often still are, pre-requisite or at least permitted in many religions and spiritual practices in the world. Normal heterosexual expression prevents access to or renders dangerous the spiritual powers that the true priest or priestess invokes. This is probably why the shamans and magic makers throughout the world are drawn from the metasexuals—virgins, celibates, gays, lesbians and some bi-sexuals. This 10 to 20 percent of the human population with a sexual *otherness* (a different kind of "wiring") have the ability to allow energies, which would be dangerous to the normal man or woman, to come through them. Lesbians and gay men seem to have better access to both the male and female aspects of themselves. They don't seem to project the inner opposite (Anim or Jungian anima or animus) as do the majority of people. Therefore, the inner union of the male and female principles, so vital in spiritual work, is almost a "given" for this group. They develop rapidly when they focus on and work toward achieving the abilities of shaman, priest or priestess, as do all individuals whose spiritual path is "solo" and who avoid the normal partnering process of society.

In the West, because we have suppressed the function of priestess for so many thousands of years, the most common example of sexual physics in a religious context is found in the Roman Catholic priest. A celibate priest serving the mass is performing an act of energy magic which brings spiritual energy from other dimensions into this one, then extends it out to touch a congregation through the doorway of himself. Should the priest, through ignorance, think he can have a heterosexual affair, confess it to another priest, and then go on serving the mass, he is quite wrong. Should this happen, he will become gravely ill, go insane or die. What he is bringing through himself in the mass is a real energy—a potent

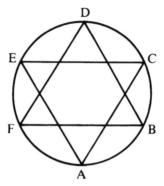

Figure 36. The six-pointed star illustrating psycho-sexual development.

energy. If he has grounded or "earthed" himself and continues to serve the mass, correctly, as designed, he will react as a short-circuiting wire does — he'll burn out. Only men and women who are not "earthed" through physical union with the opposite sex can be true priests and priestesses. Only they can handle and sustain a full kundalini awakening. The East knows this. The West has yet to learn. Religion without its real priest or priestess is form without content, structure without God or Goddess.

Virginity and celibacy must be given back to the youth of today as viable options. Channels for potent spiritual energy must become available in the world once more.

Psycho-sexual development can be diagrammed using a six-pointed star or "Star of David" drawn within a circle, the circle containing two interpenetrating equilateral triangles, one pointing up, the other, down. (See Figure 36.) The down-pointing triangle is the triangle of the feminine, the up-pointing, the triangle of the masculine. If we label the bottom point A and continue counter-clockwise left around the circle with the points marked $B, C, D, E,$ and F, then A represents the individual at birth where no polarity exists, the infant existing in the Oneness. B, then, is the first stage in human development, the autoerotic, where there is arousal of sexual feeling without external stimulation or with self-stimulation. C is the next stage, the homoerotic, where the sexuality projects out onto persons of the same sex, and D is the socialized, "normal" heterosexual stage, where the sexuality projects out onto persons of the opposite sex. This last stage is what most people strive for and where most people stay for an entire lifetime.

The path of spiritual return to Oneness continues along the circle reversing the previous stages. Thus, *E* becomes the point where the sexual energy is withdrawn from the opposite sex and attaches again to persons of like sex, the homoerotic stage of the return. We see this in our culture in monasteries and convents where individuals of the same sex group together. *F* is then the autoerotic stage on the path of return, where the individual becomes singular, no longer seeking the support of the same-sex group—the "hermit" stage. And, finally, *A* on the path of return is reached, the final goal of Oneness or Union with God, where the opposites are reconciled and the individual becomes truly androgynous. An individual *can* move directly from point *C* to point *E* along the circle, as Catholic priests often do, but then the inner opposite (male or female) *must* be worked with directly in some way to prevent psycho-sexual problems from developing and creating imbalance in the person's four-body system. This movement from *C* to *E* seems to be easier for women than for men, because women have easier access to their feeling natures.

Anyone can return to the state of physical virginity by becoming celibate or by practicing coitus interruptus. The amount of time it takes varies depending upon one's pattern. Power Aliens get back to a state of virginity in seven years, Vessel Aliens in fourteen years, Instrument Aliens in twenty-one years, and all others in twenty-eight years. But during the stay of Pluto in Scorpio which lasts until 1995, *anyone* can get back to the virgin state in seven years, seemingly a special dispensation brought by the sex/kundalini planet, Pluto, in the sex/kundalini sign, Scorpio. This is evidenced by those individuals I work with who have experienced the return of their "lost" abilities because of celibacy, coitus interruptus or same-sex expression since Pluto entered into Scorpio. This exception to the rule will probably also be true during Uranus' stay in Aquarius from 1996 to 2003.

In sexual physics the orgasm is the key. At orgasm, powerful energy is released into the physical plane. If this energy isn't directed in some way, ideally with love, toward the sexual partner, any of the archetypes can use the energy to manifest with on the material plane. If the person is using sex without love purely for physical gratification and "spaces out" at orgasm, his or her most unconscious archetypes can take this energy and manifest something with it, usually what the individual's ego would least want manifested. This seems to be why the world's so-called swingers often have such "horror show" lives. So when you have orgasm, remember to direct the energy into some positive manifestation. If you're masturbating, direct the energy consciously at orgasm—to your houseplants, to the healing of Mother Earth or to one of the archetypes, or, if with a partner, to each other with love. Don't waste sacred energy.

148) Q. Why do I sometimes react extremely negatively to people and situations in my life? It's like I'm possessed. I become a terrible person to be around.

A. It's not "you"—the real you—who you're judging to be a "terrible person." Your heart Center is *always* loving and giving. The negative roles we occasionally fall into are produced by one or more of the archetypes temporarily taking over or manipulating the ego. Try to take the behavior as information about parts of yourself that need attention in meditation—that need new expressions for their energies. Don't blame yourself or put yourself down. The consciousness process is organic. Love and accept yourself wherever you are, negative role behavior and all. Try to learn to lift above the ego and laugh at the negative roles you fall into. And work with the manipulating archetypes with your Inner Guide. You'll find that the negative role playing will finally fall away.

Remember, you're responsible for what the ego does—in the sense of responding to the archetypal messages you're acting out or sending yourself, but *you're not to blame*. Blame taking is ego arrogance. You would never have consciously chosen the negative roles. Don't confuse responsibility with blame.

149) Q. Is there a way to initiate a group of people into the Inner Guide Meditation all at the same time? Always working one-to-one seems so slow. It doesn't seem to serve enough people.

A. Early on in our experience with the meditation we attempted to introduce groups to their Guides *en masse*. We quickly learned the dangers of doing this and stopped. False guides seemed to favor this group process, and much ego inflation resulted. We felt lucky that inflation was the worst we encountered.

It is too dangerous to take a group into this particular meditation. The archetypes are too potent. Although some people did reach their true Guides, it occurred to us that we were being irresponsible. We've learned to insist on the safer, one-to-one initiation with the individual's horoscope as reference. In this way you can both see (through the horoscope) and feel (by focusing only on one person) what is happening in the meditation.

150) Q. What do I do to get off the "Wheel of Birth and Death" and not have to incarnate again?

A. I believe you must spend an entire lifetime as a virgin and neither kill anyone nor cause anyone's death during such a life. Sex and death seem to be what most keep us tied to the cycles of rebirth.

• • •

If you have further questions relating to any aspect of the Inner Guide Meditation, or, if you would like to share some of your own meditations, kundalini experiences, or personal insights, please send them to:

D.O.M.E.
The Inner Guide Meditation Center
P. O. Box 46146
Los Angeles, California 90046, U.S.A.

We'll try to publish the shared information and answers to questions in D.O.M.E.'s journal, *White Sun*.

Part 4

TECHNICAL ASPECTS

How to Translate a Horoscope into Tarot Terms

In this section, we will go more in-depth with the material I have presented up to now, and I will show you how to apply it to your own horoscope to use in your work with your Inner Guide. It should enable you to create your own worksheet to use as your map of your inner world, and should give you, the ego, some knowledge of how your energies structure and relate to one another. The worksheet is divided into sections, each representing a particular way of approaching or relating to the energies involved in a personal horoscope pattern. It gives you a particular and useful schematic of the reality-making energies at your core. It also facilitates your Inner Guide's work in teaching you.

First, you'll learn how to recognize the relationships between archetypes that both give you energy and create problems and pain in your life, so that you'll have the keys to solving your own deep conflicts. As you and your Guide work with these pairs, you'll find that your problems begin to solve themselves and your energy begins to increase in a more balanced way.

Second, there will be an explanation about those energies that you were born with in a union or other harmonious relationship, so that you and your Guide can bring these positive, and usually easy, inner relationships into consciousness in your life.

Third, you'll be shown how to discover those archetypes in your particular horoscopic pattern that have the final say in your life, so that you can become aware of and work with them and, along with your Inner Guide, become a conscious member of your own inner board of directors.

Next, you'll be shown how to bring specific energy groupings in your horoscope together for further balancing and harmonization of your overall pattern, and then, how to combine certain archetypes into single figures, so that you can bring into form each of your basic cast of important inner characters, such as your Higher Self, your Inner Mother and any Alien figures you may have in your horoscopes – the primary aspects of your being.

And last, you'll learn how to discover which archetypes in your horoscope resist consciousness and need more attention and work using the Inner Guide Meditation than the others, so that your unconscious talents and abilities, represented by these consciousness-resistant archetypes, can be brought more quickly into the light and incorporated into your life.

Figure 37 gives you a sample horoscope and worksheet derived from it (translated into tarot archetypes) to refer to as you go through the various sections of the worksheet analysis discussion. It would be useful for you to follow the sample horoscope and worksheet as you read through each section, so that you are clear on how to utilize the information presented there. When you understand how to create a worksheet from the example chart, obtain a copy of your own horoscope from a reputable astrological computer company or from D.O.M.E. Center in Los Angeles, and try your hand at making a worksheet for yourself or others. (Remember to request horoscopes using Koch Birthplace House Cusps – not Placidian, Equal House or other systems – and *tropical*, not sidereal astrology. Try to obtain the birth data you use from a birth certificate because parents' memories aren't always accurate as to the exact hour and minute of birth, and horoscopes can often change dramatically in just a few minutes.)

The "Horoscope-Tarot Equivalents" which follow this section list the tarot equivalents for the eight planets, Sun, Moon, and the twelve signs of the zodiac. (For instance, Aries = the *Emperor*; Mercury = the *Magician*, etc.) Utilizing these tarot equivalents, the worksheet is designed to give the astrological relationships in image form, between the energies in an individual's natal horoscope, so that the inner planes may be approached in a structured way. (In calculating aspects in the original horoscopes, an orb of influence of 15°, plus or minus, is allowed for solar aspects, 12° for lunar aspects and 8° for planetary aspects, if the aspect is a conjunction, square, opposition or trine; and 6° for solar and lunar aspects and 5° for planetary aspects, if the aspect is a quincunx or sextile; and 3° for a quintile. Parallels of declination are allowed an orb of 1° for the planets and 1¹/₂° for the Sun and Moon.)

High Energy Relationships

These pairs of tarot archetypes represent the *squares* (90° relationships or aspects), the *oppositions* (180° relationships) and the opposing zodiacal fields: Aries/Libra, Taurus/Scorpio, Gemini/Sagittarius, Cancer/Capricorn, Leo/Aquarius, and Virgo/Pisces. All these pairs represent energies that the individual was born with in an unconscious non-cooperation, polarization, or conflict relationship. They function to create the pain, difficulties, and problems of the life, but they also give the most energy and indicate the horoscope's greatest positive potential.

To bring these energies into balance, begin by getting to know each member of a particular pair. Ask the two recommended initial questions suggested in the section "How to Contact Your Inner Guide:" 1) "What do you need from me and from my life to work with me and to be my friend?" and 2) "What do you have to give me that I need from you?"—the symbolic object that represents talents or abilities having to do with the archetype presenting the gift. (It may be useful to review this section when you begin a regular meditation program.) Then really get to know each of the figures in the same way you would get to know new people in outer life. Ask what each has to do with in your outer reality—what aspect of your reality does each create and sustain? In the same way as getting to know a new person in your outer life, the more time you spend with each of the archetypal energy forms, the more you will begin to know the figure and understand its needs within you. Ask the figure to acquaint you with its territory in the inner world—where it lives in your inner landscape. Question things you don't understand. Why has the *Fool* no fixed abode? Is he happy with this, or would he like a base to operate from? Why does your *Empress* figure always appear to be sad? What is the message to you about you that the *Hanged Man* carries by always appearing in rags? Why is the *Temperance* figure always difficult to see? Why won't the *Twins* quit jumping around? What can you do or how can you change so that each of the figures can evolve into their most beautiful, most spiritual forms within you? If a figure frightens you or makes you uncomfortable, tell it so, and ask what you can do to allow it to change within you.

Let each of the figures tell you more about the gift it gave you—the symbolic object it put in your hand on your first meeting.

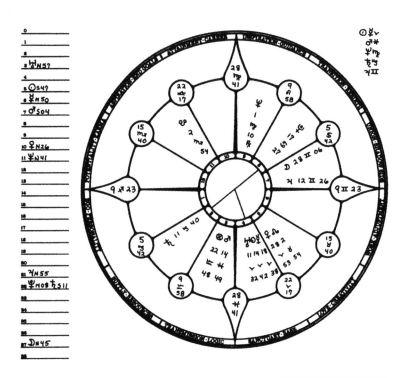

Cardinal	☿♀⊙♄♅♇
Fixed	
Mutable	☽♂♃♆ Asc.

Fire	☿♀⊙♅ Asc.
Earth	♄♆
Air	☽♃
Water	♂♇

☽ Moon in Gemini
☿ ⊙ Mercury in Aries
✳ ♀ Venus in Aries — Detriment
☿♂♂⊙ Sun in Aries — Exaltation
♂ Mars in Pisces
✳□♃ Jupiter in Gemini — Detriment
□□✳♄ Saturn in Capricorn — Rulership
♂♂✳□♅ Uranus in Aries
✳△♆ Neptune in Virgo — Detriment, Accidental Exaltation
□□△♂□♇ Pluto in Cancer — Accidental Rulership
♐ Sagittarius Rising (Ascendant)
☊ Moon's True North Node in Taurus
☋ Moon's True South Node in Scorpio
⊕ Part of Fortune in Aquarius

Figure 37. Edwin Charles Steinbrecher, born April 4, 1930, in Chicago, Illinois, at 10:55 PM. Chart has been erected using Koch houses and the form the author uses at D.O.M.E. On the facing page you can see how this

*HIGH ENERGY
RELATIONSHIPS:*

Temperance and *Twins* (*Lovers*)
Magician and *World*
Magician and *Last Judgement*
Sun and *World*
Sun and *Last Judgement*
Tower and *Wheel of Fortune*
World and *Fool*
World and *Last Judgement*
Fool and *Last Judgement*
Emperor and *Justice*
Chariot and *Old Pan (Devil)*
Hermit and *Moon*
Strength and *Star*
Death and *High Priest* (*Hierophant*)

CHECK UNION BETWEEN:

High Priestess and *Sun*
High Priestess and *Magician*
High Priestess and *Empress*
High Priestess and *Hanged Man*
Magician and *Sun*
Magician and *Tower*
Magician and *Wheel of Fortune*
Magician and *Fool*
Sun and *Wheel of Fortune*
Sun and *Fool*
Tower and *World*
Wheel of Fortune and *World*
Wheel of Fortune and *Fool*
Wheel of Fortune and *Last Judgement*

BASIC ARCHETYPES:

Sun	*Magician*
Tower	*Moon*
Hanged Man	*Hermit*
World	*Old Pan*
Wheel of Fortune	*Twins*
Emperor	

FIRST QUESTIONS TO ARCHETYPES
(WITH GUIDE):

1. What do you need from me and from my life to work with me and be my friend?
2. What do you have to give to me that I need from you? (Ask for a symbolic object, its interpretation as to what it represents, its powers and uses as a tool, and where in the body to absorb and carry it.)

CIRCLE OF HANDS WITH:

1. *Hermit, Temperance, Moon* and *Lovers*
2. *World, Fool, Sun, Magician* and *Last Judgement*
3. *Justice, Old Pan, Emperor* and *Chariot*
4. *Strength, Death, Star* and *High Priest*
5. Shadow man/men (1 or 2 male figures)
6. High energy and union pairs
7. Basic archetypes ("board of directors" with Shadow man/men and the Inner Guide)

CONSCIOUSNESS RESISTANT FACTORS:

Empress	*Death*
Wheel of Fortune	*Twins*
High Priestess	*Hermit*
Hanged Man	

"ALIEN" ENERGY CONSTRUCTS:

Uranian Power (masculine-creative principle, higher Self, Solar *center* & primary purpose) = *Fool* + *Sun* + *Magician* + *Emperor* + *Empress* (male figure)
Fixed Adept = *High Priest* + *Strength* + *Death* + *Star* (male or female figure)
Lunar Construct (feminine-receptive principle & inner mother) = *High Priestess* + *Twins* (1 or 2 female figures)
Cardinal T-cross energy balancing construct:

would be translated into a worksheet showing the tarot archetypes. This worksheet is discussed step-by-step on pages 209 through 233.

(Only accept one object from each of the archetypes when you first meet that particular figure, not a gift every time you see the figure, unless your Guide makes an exception to this rule. Otherwise you will be overwhelmed with objects, and the gifts will become confusing and meaningless.)

After coming to terms individually with each member of a particular pair, ask your Inner Guide to bring the two archetypes together with you and your Guide. Explain to the archetypes that when they fight, act separately, or refuse to cooperate as energies within you, it causes pain, injury, and destruction in *your* life and in the reality around you. Ask each what each needs from the other to begin working together in harmony and to cooperate as energies within you. It may be that the *Sun* in a *Sun-Tower* pair says that it needs the *Tower* to stop being so pushy before it will agree to cooperate and work in harmony with it. Then ask the *Tower* what it needs in return to agree to what the *Sun* asks and to agree to start working in harmony with the *Sun* from then on.

When each of the archetypes says what he or she wants, ask if they agree to give each other what each has asked for, and if they agree to work together in harmony as energies within you from then on. If an impasse occurs, remind them again that *you* are the one who is injured by this disharmony. Sometimes the best you can get from a stubborn or an antagonistic pair is "We'll *try* to get along." Accept this for the present, but give more attention to that particular pair in subsequent meditations.

As each pair becomes more conscious and begins cooperating within you, this constructive energy flows into your life, changing and harmonizing both inner and outer realities. Therefore, the squares and oppositions are, in potential, the "best" aspects of your horoscope, because they have the most energy.

After the two archetypal energy forms have communicated what they need from each other to begin cooperating within you and have agreed to each other's terms, ask them both what you can do (or can stop doing) in your everyday life to help them stay in harmony within you. When they have communicated what is needed from you and you agree to it, ask them to join hands with each other and with you and your Guide. When you have made this circle of hands, and you can *feel* the grip of each entity holding your hand, and can feel the texture and other qualities of the skin of the hands you hold — be sure to be in your body and not watching yourself at this point — give the two archetypes permission to balance their energies *with* each other and *in* you. At this point you will feel strange sensations in different parts of your body as the energies shift and rebalance within you. Note which specific body areas you feel being affected. Allow the energies to flow until your Guide breaks the circle.

Do this with each of the "high energy relationship" pairs. When you have balanced each of the pairs, start at the top of the list again, get to know them better, and find out what more you can do to keep each of the pairs working in harmony. Keep going through these pairs again and again until your Guide tells you that each pair is working together enough for you to continue with the worksheet. The balancing of these energy pairs brings the four-body system into harmony and balance and makes it safe for the kundalini energy to begin activating.

Unions

The "check union between" section of the worksheet includes the *conjunctions* (0° relationships), *parallels* (0° relationships of declination), *sextiles* (60° relationships), *quincunxes* (150° relationships), and *quintiles* (72° relationships) of a natal horoscope. These unions represent energies in the pattern that, according to theory, *should* be working together. They seldom are in conflict, but often through the process of living they have been pushed into acting separately. It's easy to get these pairs back into working in a united way. When you and your Guide are with the two figures which make up a pair, ask what they need from each other and from you (in terms of action, thought or behavior) to aid in their harmonious union and to keep them working together.

This part of the worksheet can be done last, because generally these pairs cause no problems in the life.

Basic Archetypes

The basic archetypes are the *final dispositors* of the horoscope along with the Sun and its sign and the ruler of the sign on the

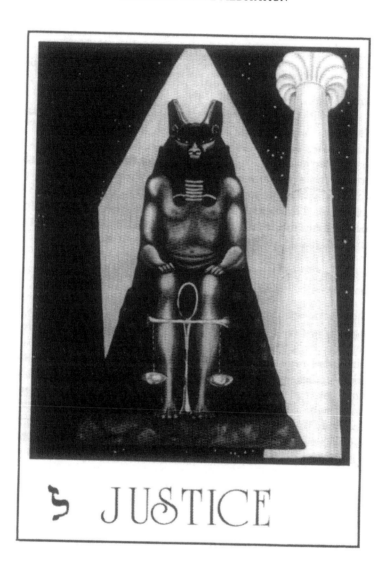

Figure 38. *Justice*, the archetype associated with Libra, is concerned with harmony, balance and union. Trump of *Justice* shown here is from the Servants of the Light Tarot Deck, Jersey, Channel Islands, UK. Used by permission.

Ascendant and its sign added if they are not included in the group of final dispositors. These represent the "last vote" forces within an individual. No matter what the current ego may desire, these are the energies that receive the final say over every area of your individual reality. Treat the basic archetype group, your Shadow and your Guide as your "Board of Directors" or "Board of Advisors." Bring life questions and life projects in to discuss with them. This way you, the ego, keep your one "vote," and, if any of them are going to fight you or block you on a specific project, they will say so and you can work out a compromise. The final dispositors always include planets in their rulership, e.g., Saturn in Capricorn, planets in mutual reception (which means each planet in the sign ruled by the other, e.g., Sun in Scorpio and Pluto in Leo), and all planetary chains, e.g. Saturn in Libra, Venus in Aries and Mars in Capricorn. For more information on final dispositors, see Thyrza Escobar's fine book, *Essentials of Natal Interpretation.*[1]

The Circles of Hands

The section labeled Circles of Hands identifies specific *energy groups* in your natal chart and always includes the cardinal, fixed and mutable grand cross groupings: e.g., the cardinal signs: Aries, Cancer, Libra and Capricorn; the fixed signs: Taurus, Leo, Scorpio and Aquarius; and the mutable signs: Gemini, Virgo, Sagittarius and Pisces. Also included in this section are the planetary groupings formed by the classical astrological patterns of the T-cross, the grand trine, the grand square and the yod cross (or finger of God) configuration.

In addition to these, individual groupings consisting of three or more planets forming high energy relationships that connect to one another in the natal chart are included for a circle of hands. For instance, if the planet Saturn were squaring a conjunction of the Sun and Mars in the natal pattern, included in this section would be a circle of hands with the tarot *World*, *Sun* and *Tower*.

The Shadow man or woman, the "high energy relationship" pairs, the "unions" and the figures making up the "basic arche-

[1]Thyrza Escobar, *Essentials of Natal Interpretation* (Los Angeles: Golden Seal Research, 1978).

types" or "board of directors" also are included in the circle of hands section.

It is recommended that these circles of hands be done on a periodic basis. The planetary, zodiacal and combination forms are living energies each of us carries within that are creating and sustaining our realities. As we go through the various cycles and rhythms of our lives, some of the energies may go out of balance with the others. For instance, in a mutable sign grouping of the *Twins*, the *Hermit*, *Temperance*, and the *Moon*, whenever you meditate with them and ask them to do a circle of hands, the *Hermit* may be out of balance, not cooperating, or antagonistic to the others in the group. In such an instance ask the entire group what *you* can do new (or stop doing) in your everyday outer life in terms of action, thought, or behavior to allow them all to remain in balance and cooperating with each other within you. Ask also what you may be doing or not doing in your life that keeps the *Hermit*, in this instance, out of balance with the rest of the energies.

End each interaction, whether with a pair, your Shadow or with a larger group, by asking the participants to take hands with each other and with you *and your Guide* forming a circle of hands. It is important to really *be there* in your body looking out of your eyes and not watching yourself in the scene when you do this circle of hands. Feel the textures of the hands you hold, your Guide on your right (if right handed) and the archetypes or energy combinations to your left. Reverse this if you are left handed. Give them permission to balance their energies *with* each other and *in* you. You will *feel* the energy shift and change within your body as the archetypal energies balance themselves in your system. Each pair or group will cause sensations in specifically different areas of your body, and each circle grouping will have a different energy quality than the others. Feel the sensations and note their locations in your body. If the sensation or feeling flow is weak, ask for increased intensity, and give them permission to penetrate any blockage you may have to receiving their balanced energy, always making sure that you are *in* your body and in full possession of *all* your senses. If you are not *in* your inner world (or astral) body and find yourself watching an image of yourself, you are disconnected and will feel nothing, nor are you furnishing a conduit for inner world changes to flow out and change your outer world. Let your Guide be the one to break the circle.

The Alien Energy Constructs

The Alien patterns are specific planetary placements and unions, or absences of planets, Sun, Moon and Ascendant in certain zodiacal signs which produce highly specialized individuals:

The Alien Powers are those with the Sun in conjunction with Saturn, Uranus, Neptune or Pluto (allowing a 15° orb). They have the ability to *extend* or *radiate* their specialized energy field out into the physical plane, affecting and changing whatever or whomever it touches. Theirs is a *high priest* function, in the ancient sense, whether in a male or female body. They act as "doors" to bring energy to the physical plane from other dimensions. The effects on others take place whether or not the individual Powers have consciousness of the energy they carry.

The *Saturnian Powers* are the masters of time, space, dimension, government, history, form, rocks, crystals, permanence, structure, and the secrets of geometry and natural law as they function on the earth plane. They have innate knowledge of the energies produced, transmitted, or contained in three dimensional forms. Their energy brings to form and stabilizes whomever or whatever they focus their attention on; and they have the ability to accurately visualize and build anything. They are the oldest of the Aliens, along with the Saturnian Vessels and Instruments, having manifested in humankind as soon as awareness of the solar system and its movements occurred in human consciousness. They function as testers and guardians of humanity, and they have the gifts of humor and mirth. Resistance to consciousness of their abilities takes the forms of rigidity, oppressiveness, feelings of inferiority, aloofness, work-aholism, depression, tyrannicalness, despair, marijuana or alcohol addiction, uptightness, dictatorialness, anxiety, judgmentalness, ennui, power-tripping, mono-level awareness, apathy, loneliness, fear, paranoia, grandiosity and a general separation from the All in word and deed.

The *Uranian Powers* are the masters of freedom, empathy, friendship, uniqueness, eccentricity, the unexpected, altruistic love, astrology, electricity and all vibratory phenomena, invention, innovation and group process. They tend to have little understanding of normal human time, seeing tomorrow more easily than today. They bring forth projects and ideas that are generally three to seven years

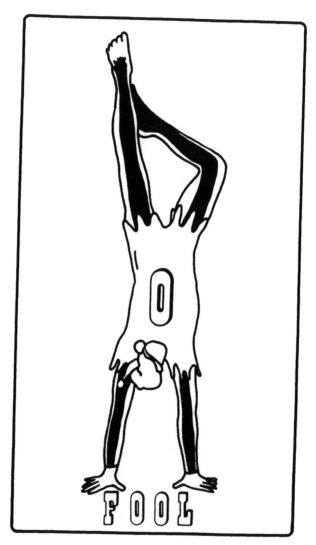

Figure 39. The *Fool* (Uranus) represents the energy of one of the four planetary factors that create the main Alien groups along with the *World/ Saturn*, the *Hanged Man/*Neptune, and the *Last Judgement/*Pluto. Trump of the *Fool* shown here from the D.O.M.E. Meditation Cards by Sheila Ross, ©1978. Used by permission.

ahead of the rest of humanity (if not more), and they often focus on the futuristic or the ancient. They have what is called "instant empathy," generating in others the feeling that the other person has known them forever—that they are old friends and confidants beyond time. They have few, if any, of the normal prejudices of the world and can even forget what sex, religion or color another person is, relating always to the person's central essence. They are friends to the whole world and tend toward non-discrimination. They are non-judgmental and are often considered to have genius because of their abilities to perceive innate patterns in things and situations, and because of their multi-level awareness. Information comes to them in sudden "knowing." Their job is to make sure that natural law on earth conforms to and changes with universal law. They are the illusion and projection breakers, and they free locked-in conditions and destroy outmoded forms. They have elements of surprise and unpredictability in their behavior. They are born "conscientious objectors," because it is impossible for them to kill another without dire consequences to themselves. They are masters of the release and control of the descending aspect of the kundalini energy, the evolutinary energy in humankind, called "the Descent of Grace" in the West. Any kind of confinement or restraint is crazy-making for them. Resistance to consciousness of their abilities takes the forms of rebelliousness, iconoclasm, flakiness, lawlessness, chaos, coldness, antisocial or shocking behavior, revolution, reporting the ideal instead of the real, anarchy, electrical overcharges in their bodies, and acute nervousness.

The *Neptunian Powers* are the masters of magnetism, mysticism, mystery, illusion, invisibility, sympathy, compassion and the archetypal reality levels. They dissolve things and situations no longer useful to the planet's evolution. They are the sensitives and the psychics. Their love is pure compassion, because they are able to perceive the common thread that connects all things. They are the illusion makers, because they are also the masters of the process now understood as psychological projection. They are the knowers of the movements of Sacred Dance that reflect and draw into the earth plane energies and patterns of the universe from other reality dimensions. They are natural musicians, poets, dancers, film makers, clairvoyants, mystics and weavers of fantasies. Information comes to them in feelings and pictures, and they feel everything, like raw nerves in the world. They tend to be extremely light sensitive, and need to protect their eyes. They need to shower immediately whenever they feel down or feel they have picked up a "bad vibration" from somewhere, water acting to cleanse the aura quickly. All the Neptune Aliens need periodic physical privacy in order to stay centered, and, if they can find it in no other way, going to a movie theater will take care of this need. Resistance to consciousness of their abilities takes the forms of spaciness, super-sensitivity, confusion, fogginess, seduction, deception, fears of the unreal, absentmindedness, masochism, victimization, escapism, addiction, degeneracy, weirdness, delusion, dissipation, gullibility, wishful thinking, weakness, impracticality and isolation from others.

The *Plutonian Powers* are the masters of metamorphosis and irreversible change. They move people, things and situations from one level of vibration to the next one above it, often using the acceleration of time or sexuality to accomplish this. They destroy the old and outmoded through silent, relentless, often invisible, processes. They have knowledge of the workings of levitation, out-of-body experiences (astral projection), sex energy and the physics of sex, birth, death and rebirth. They have an innate understanding of the force called gravity, and they have to do with the release and control of the ascending aspect of the kundalini energy (or serpent power) which sleeps at the base of the spine, the evolutionary energy in humankind. They are the natural remodelers of the universe and have great powers and abilities relating to working with the masses because of their powerful charisma. They are natural sleuths and finders of hidden or lost things. Resistance to consciousness of their abilities takes the forms of compulsions, obsessions, rage, jealousy, vengefulness, sex without love, nihilism, criminal thought, outrageous behavior, debauchery, sex-related disease, sadism, sarcasm and stubborn blindness.

The *Mixed Powers* are those individuals who have two or more of the planets (Saturn, Uranus, Neptune or Pluto) in conjunction with the Sun. They have the innate abilities of each of the planetary factors.

The Alien Vessels are individuals born with the Moon in conjunction with Saturn, Uranus, Neptune or Pluto (allowing a 12° orb). Their action is *magnetic*, drawing specialized energies out of themselves and those around them. They also function as "doors" to other spaces. They are able to receive or take through themselves specific energies from others and return these as heightened, more conscious energy forms. These effects take place in others whether or not the individual Vessels have consciousness of their magnetic effect on others. Theirs is a *high priestess* function, in the ancient sense, whether their physical vehicles are female or male.

The *Saturnian Vessels* stabilize and bring to form those they are with. They inspire practical, earth plane ideas in others. They bring to consciousness knowledge of time, space, dimension, government, history, form, permanence, structure, construction, humor, mirth, and the secrets of geometry and natural law in others through their magnetism. They also inspire knowledge of the energies produced, transmitted and contained in three dimensional forms, especially in rocks and crystals. The Saturnian Vessels along with the other Saturn Aliens are the oldest of the Aliens on the earth plane. They are testers and guardians of humanity. Resistance to consciousness of their abilities takes the forms of rigidity, oppressiveness, feelings of inferiority, aloofness, work-aholism, dictatorialness, depression, tyrannicalness, despair, marijuana or alcohol addiction, uptightness, anxiety, judgmentalness, ennui, power-tripping, mono-level awareness, apathy, loneliness, fear, paranoia, grandiosity and a general separation from the All in word and deed, but in addition can unconsciously project these forms onto those around them and not see them in themselves.

The *Uranian Vessels* draw freedom, unpredictability, the unexpected, surprise, genius, uniqueness, eccentricity, the breaking of illusions and projections, friendship, empathy and altruistic love out of themselves and those around them. Their presence in a group allows the group to function in a friendly, cooperative way. They inspire ideas relating to astrology, vibratory phenomena, invention, innovation and the futuristic or the ancient in others. They are friendly, non-judgmental and have few prejudices, if any. They have the ability to free the descending aspect of the kundalini or any other blocked energy in others. Any kind of confinement or restraint is crazy-making for them. Resistance to consciousness of their abilities takes the forms of rebelliousness, iconoclasm, flakiness, lawlessness, chaos, coldness, antisocial or shocking behavior, revolution, reporting the ideal instead of the real, anarchy, electrical overcharges in their bodies, and acute nervousness, but in addition they can unconsciously project these forms into those around them and not see them in themselves.

The *Neptunian Vessels* draw compassion, sympathy and deep mystical feelings from themselves and others. They inspire knowledge relating to magnetism, illusion, the psychic, invisibility and the archetypal reality levels in others. They are sensitive and profoundly psychic, their psychic information coming to them in feelings and pictures. Those around them also become more psychic and visionary. They draw information about music, poetry, dance and film from those in their environment. They tend to be light sensitive and need to protect their eyes. They should shower or bathe immediately whenever they feel down or feel they have picked up "bad energy" from somewhere, water acting as a quick cleanser of the aura. They have strong physical privacy needs, and, if they can get their privacy in no other way, going to a movie theater seems to take care of this need. Resistance to consciousness of their abilities takes the forms of spaciness, confusion, fogginess, supersensitivity, seduction, deception, fears of the unreal, absent-mindedness, victimization, masochism, weirdness, escapism, addiction, degeneracy, delusion, dissipation, gullibility, wishful thinking, weakness, impracticality and isolation from others, but in addition they can unconsciously project these forms into those around them and not see them in themselves.

The *Plutonian Vessels* draw transformation energy from themselves and others. They inspire knowledge relating to irreversible change, sex energy and the physics of sex, transformation processes, astral projection, healing, levitation, metamorphosis, birth, death and rebirth. They have the ability to free the ascending aspect of the kundalini or any other blocked energy in others, hence their healing powers are great. They have great charisma. They are natural sleuths and finders of hidden or lost things. Resistance to consciousness of their abilities takes the forms of compulsions, obsessions, rage, jealousy, vengefulness, sex without love, nihilism, criminal thought, outrageous behavior, debauchery, sex-related disease, sadism, sarcasm and stubborn blindness, but in addition they can unconsciously project these forms into those around them and not see them in themselves.

The *Mixed Vessels* are those individuals who have two or more of the planets Saturn, Uranus, Neptune or Pluto in conjunction with the Moon. They have the innate abilities of each of the planetary factors.

The Alien Instruments are people who have Saturn, Uranus, Neptune or Pluto in the first house of their natal horoscopes or *conjunct the Ascendant* (cusp of the first house) *from the twelfth house* (allowing an orb of 10°). They function as broadcasters, amplifiers and receivers of one of the four primary planetary energies in those around them. Their abilities are intrinsic to their physical bodies. Nerve pathways and even bodily organs often are in atypical anatomical positions, enabling them, without injury, to act as specialized energy amplifiers, receivers and broadcasters.

The *Saturnian Instruments* broadcast and amplify energy having to do with time, space, dimension, form, permanence, government, history, construction, structure, humor, mirth, knowledge of rocks, crystals and all three-dimensional forms, the secrets of geometry, natural law as it functions on the earth plane, stability and safety. They are the oldest of the Aliens, along with the Saturnian Powers and Vessels, having manifested in humankind as soon as awareness of the solar system and its movements occurred in human consciousness. They are testers and guardians of humanity. Resistance to consciousness of their abilities takes the forms of rigidity, dictatorialness, feelings of inferiority, aloofness, workaholism, depression, tyrannicalness, despair, marijuana or alcohol addiction, uptightness, oppressiveness, anxiety, judgmentalness, ennui, power-tripping, mono-level awareness, apathy, loneliness, fear, paranoia, grandiosity and a general separation from the All in word and deed which they either live out themselves or project onto those around them.

The *Uranian Instruments* broadcast and amplify energy having to do with freedom, uniqueness, eccentricity, genius, altruistic love, electricity and all vibration, invention, innovation, non-discrimination, surprise, the unexpected, group process, empathy, friendship, non-judgmentalness, multi-level awareness, the breaking of illusions, unpredictability, the futuristic, the ancient, brotherhood/sisterhood, and the descending aspect of the kundalini. Any kind of confinement or restraint is crazy-making for them. Resistance to consciousness of their abilities takes the forms of rebelliousness, iconoclasm, flakiness, lawlessness, chaos, coldness, antisocial or shocking behavior, revolution, reporting the ideal instead of the real, anarchy, electrical overcharges in their bodies, and acute nervousness, which they either live out themselves or project onto those around them.

The *Neptunian Instruments* broadcast and amplify energy having to do with magnetism, mysticism, mystery, sympathy, compassion, invisibility, sensitivity, music, dance, projection, fantasy, poetry, clairvoyance, psychic ability, illusion and the archetypes. They tend to be extremely light sensitive and need to protect their eyes. They need periodic physical privacy to stay centered, and, if they can get it in no other way, going to a movie theater will take care of this need. They should shower or bathe immediately whenever they feel down or feel they have picked up a "bad energy" from somewhere, water acting as a quick cleanser of the aura. Resistance to consciousness of their abilities takes the forms of spaciness, supersensitivity, deception, confusion, fogginess, fears of the unreal, absentmindedness, victimization, weirdness, masochism, escapism, addiction, degeneracy, delusion, dissipation, gullibility, wishful thinking, weakness, impracticality and isolation from others, which they either live out themselves or project onto those around them.

The *Plutonian Instruments* broadcast and amplify energy having to do with irreversible change, transformation, sex energy and the physics of sex, charisma, birth, death, astral projection, healing, rebirth, metamorphosis and the ascending aspect of kundalini. They are natural sleuths and finders of hidden or lost things. Resistance to consciousness of their abilities takes the forms of compulsions, obsessions, rage, jealousy, vengefulness, sex without love, nihilism, criminal thought, outrageous behavior, debauchery, sex-related disease, sadism, sarcasm and stubborn blindness, which they either live out themselves or project onto those around them.

The *Mixed Instruments* are those individuals who have two or more of the planets (Saturn, Uranus, Neptune or Pluto) in the first house or in conjunction with the Ascendant from the twelfth house. They have the innate abilities of each of the planetary factors.

• • •

Some Alien patterns may be the result of mutual reception (two planets each in the rulership sign of the other), e.g., Moon in Aquarius, Uranus in Cancer, a mutual reception Uranian Vessel.

The planets become interchangeable and act like a conjunction, each also functioning in the house of the other. Another example would be Sun conjunct Mercury in Aquarius, Uranus in Virgo. This would be a mutual reception Uranian Power. Another would be Saturn conjunct Venus in Aquarius in the first house and Uranus in Libra. This would be a mutual reception Saturnian-Uranian Instrument. The Mutual Reception Aliens have the same abilities as the type of Alien which the mutual reception of two planetary factors (including the Sun and Moon) creates in them: Power, Vessel or Instrument. The difference between the natural Aliens and the mutual reception Aliens seems to be that the latter can allow their inherent talents and abilities to lie quiescent while the natural Alien internal constructs push from within for awakening and must be dealt with in some way.[2]

All the before-mentioned Aliens have the ability to contain and to radiate energies which in a non-Alien being would "blow the circuits" unless the body and psyche had been trained and prepared to receive and radiate them. Sometimes the Aliens have trouble with their abilities, which often frighten and disturb them — especially when these abilities awaken unexpectedly. It is interesting to note that individuals with non-Alien patterns, who are drawn to work and be with Aliens — those I call the Protectors, develop paranormal abilities much more rapidly than the Aliens. This may be because they have not developed the early suppression and defense mechanisms that the Aliens have.

Another group of Aliens, termed the Adepts, are individuals born with neither the Ascendant nor planets in a particular quality (cardinal, fixed or mutable signs) or element (fire, earth, air or water signs). These individuals have an expertise, not a lack, in the particular quality or element *missing* in their birth pattern, and they don't seem to suffer the alienation and the feeling of being different that the other Aliens experience.

The Adepts (an absence of one element or quality for the planets, Sun, Moon and the Ascendant).

Fire Adepts (neither the Ascendant, Sun, Moon nor any planet in fire signs) are experts in matters having to do with Aries, Leo, Sagittarius, the first house, the fifth house and the ninth house (e.g., spirituality, initiation, love, creativity, performing, appear-

---

[2]This Alien factor was discovered by Norma Gremore of Cedar Crest, NM.

ance, play, joy, all new beginnings, higher education, children, way-showing for others, philosophy, foreign travel, religion, theater) in terms of helping others with concerns of these life areas. However, their expertise cannot be applied to their own lives until the Adept is brought into consciousness within themselves.

Earth Adepts (neither the Ascendant, Sun, Moon nor any planet in the earth signs) are experts in matters having to do with Taurus, Virgo, Capricorn, the second house, the sixth house and the tenth house (e.g., income, money, talents, food, time, reputation, perfection, resources, earth-plane stability, health, diet, healing, magic, work methods, career, worldly achievements, fatherhood, structure, humor, rocks and crystals) in terms of helping others with concerns of these life areas. However, their expertise cannot be applied to their own lives until the Adept is brought into consciousness.

Air Adepts (neither the Ascendant, Sun, Moon nor any planet in air signs) are experts in matters having to do with Gemini, Libra, Aquarius, the third house, the seventh house and the eleventh house (e.g., the three modes of thought—logic, comparison and gestalt, partnership matters, learning, the social graces, lawsuits, compromise, arbitration, communication, connection making, ceremony, transportation, brotherhood, sisterhood, networking, political matters, giving intellectual tools and methods, group processes, friendship, altruistic love, conciliation, clear end goal formulation) in terms of helping others with concerns of these life areas. However, their expertise cannot be applied to their own lives until the Adept is made conscious within them.

Water Adepts (neither the Ascendant, Sun, Moon nor any planet in water signs) are experts in matters having to do with Cancer, Scorpio, Pisces, the fourth house, the eighth house and the twelfth house (e.g., matters pertaining to home and family, security concerns, the ways to end things, sex energy, the physics of sex, birth, rebirth, death, metamorphosis, archetypes, debt, change, motherhood, emotional matters, psychic abilities, astral projection, taxation, secrets, dreams, film, dance, poetry, music) in terms of helping others with concerns of these life areas. However, their expertise cannot be applied to their own lives until the Adept is brought into consciousness within themselves.

Cardinal Adepts (neither the Ascendant, Sun, Moon nor any planet in cardinal signs) are experts in matters having to do with starting new projects, initiation, home, family matters, partnership matters, lawsuits, career, professional concerns, time, management, the social graces, politics, reputation, appearance, worldly achievement, conciliation, arbitration, security concerns, the ways to end things and matters having to do with Aries, Cancer, Libra, Capricorn, the first house, the fourth house, the seventh house and the tenth house in terms of helping others with concerns of these life areas. However, their expertise cannot be applied to their own lives until the Adept is made conscious within themselves.

Fixed Adepts (neither the Ascendant, Sun, Moon nor any planet in fixed signs) are experts in matters to do with money, talents, resources, food, all varieties of love, creativity, children, sex energy, the physics of sex, birth, rebirth, death, transformation, change, fixed conditions, persistence, perseverance, life goals, friendship, groups, play, joy, theater, income, stability, manifestation and matters having to do with Taurus, Leo, Scorpio, Aquarius, the second house, the fifth house, the eighth house and the eleventh house in terms of helping others with concerns of these life areas. However, their expertise cannot be applied to their own lives until the Adept is brought into consciousness within themselves.

Mutable Adepts (neither the Ascendant, Sun, Moon nor any planet in mutable signs) are experts in matters having to do with communications, logic, connection making, health, service, healing, magic, all forms of education, travel, transportation, spirituality, psychic ability, the archetypes, secrets, film, dance, music, poetry, perfection, way-showing, religion, philosophy, work methods, employees, dreams and with matters having to do with Gemini, Virgo, Sagittarius, Pisces, the third house, the sixth house, the ninth house and the twelfth house in terms of helping others with concerns of these life areas. However, their expertise cannot be applied to their own lives until the Adept is brought into consciousness within themselves.

It is to be remembered that the Alien abilities function in the individual possessing them whether he or she is conscious of them or not, and they cause the life symptom patterns mentioned earlier.

To work with an Alien energy form, ask your Inner Guide to bring *all* the archetypes that make up one *Alien Energy Construct*, and then ask them to line up in a row in front of you and your Guide. Then ask them to dissolve into their raw energy components in an oval of light and to re-form as a single human or humanoid figure. Ask the Alien figure what it needs from you to facilitate its becoming conscious in you. Then ask the Alien if it would set up his or her kind of classroom and would begin teaching you all the mysteries, powers and abilities you were born with that the Alien represents, supervised by your Inner Guide. Meet in this classroom setting with your Alien on a regular basis so that the energy specialty it represents in you can rapidly become more conscious.

It seems useful to ask the Powers to take male forms, the Vessels to take female forms, and the Instruments to take the sex of the person possessing the construct. Let the Adepts become whichever sex they choose, male or female. Occasionally, an Alien figure will present itself as a hermaphrodite or an androgyne. Accept this, but ask the Alien to explain what the message is that its form is attempting to communicate.

No Alien Patterns in the Horoscope

Horoscopes without Alien constructs have the possibilities of the full range of human potential without the specialization of the Aliens. They don't seem to have the resistances in meditation which the Aliens have to push through, and, as a result, they tend to progress more rapidly with the meditation and with change than do the Aliens. They often strive towards being "far out" or weird, in contrast to the Aliens who are always trying to "fit in" and look like everyone else. Those individuals I call the Protectors are in this group. They have no fear of the Aliens and are drawn to them and work with them in a protective, understanding way. They also seek out information about the unusual, occult and the esoteric, having few fears of being thought to be different, often, in fact, relishing it. They act as a bridge between the Aliens and the rest of humanity, learning the language of the Aliens and acting as interpreters and mediators for them to others.

• • •

Should you wish a computer print-out of the names of well-known Aliens and of people without Alien patterns, famous and infamous (grouped by specific Alien type, approximately 30 pages), send an inquiry to D.O.M.E. Center, P.O. Box 46146, Los Angeles, CA 90046, U.S.A.

The Solar *Center* and Lunar Constructs

If there is neither a *Power* Alien construct nor a *Vessel* Alien construct in your horoscope, it is important to form and work with the figures of your Solar *Center* construct and your Lunar construct in meditation with your Inner Guide.

The Solar *Center* construct is formed by the Sun—the central core of the construct, its sign, and any planets conjunct the Sun and their signs. For instance, if you have a horoscope with the Sun conjunct Mercury and Venus in Virgo, you would ask your Inner Guide to bring the *Sun*, the *Magician*, the *Empress* and the *Hermit* to where you and he are, asking them to line up before you and your Guide. Then ask them to dissolve into an oval of light and to condense into one male figure. Ask your Guide to help the figure come to form. This figure is called the Solar *Center*. He represents the primary purpose of your life—what you have come here to do, and is the *yang* or masculine-creative principle in both men and women. Ask him to set up his kind of classroom in your inner world, and ask him to begin by teaching you all that he represents in you—all the mysteries, powers and abilities that he represents. What are you here to do this life? What are the first steps you now must take toward accomplishing your central purpose and allowing him to be fully conscious within you? What talents and abilities that he represents must you allow to start coming into consciousness? Meditate with this figure on a regular basis. He is the energy form that gives life to you and to your entire reality, within and without. His home is in your heart center, and he is the source of love and creativity within you. Other systems call this figure the Higher Self or the God Center. (A *Power* Alien in a horoscope is a Solar *Center* construct, although it is a specialized form.)

The Lunar Construct figure is formed by the Moon—the central core of this construct, its sign, and any planets conjunct the Moon and their signs. For instance, if you have the Moon in Sagittarius conjunct Mars in Capricorn, you would ask your Inner Guide to bring the *High Priestess*, *Temperance*, the *Tower*, and *Old Pan* to where you and he are, asking them to line up before you and your Guide. Then ask them to dissolve into an oval of light and to condense into one female figure. Again, ask your Guide to help the figure come into form. This figure is called the Lunar Construct. She represents the *yin* or feminine-receptive principle in both men and women—the good mother within you and your emotional nature. She is your magnet for love and for the other things you need in your life. Other systems call this figure the Great Mother or the Mother Goddess. Ask her to set up her kind of classroom in your inner world, as you did with your Solar *Center* figure, and ask her to begin teaching you all that she represents in you—all the mysteries, powers and abilities that she represents. How should you feel or direct your feelings? What is she trying to communicate to you by getting you to feel certain ways? How does she wish to express in your daily life? What do you need to give yourself or to let others give you that feeds and nourishes her within you? What talents and abilities that she represents must you let start coming into consciousness? Meditate with this figure on a regular basis also. (A *Vessel* Alien in a horoscope is a Lunar Construct, although it is a specialized form.)

Consciousness Resistant Factors

Certain astrological factors in a natal horoscope produce internal energies which resist assimilation by the ego, creating problems from the unconscious in the individual's reality in the life areas ruled by or corresponding to these energies. These factors are planets in their *rulership* or *exaltation* signs (both real and accidental) in women, and planets in their *fall* or *detriment* signs (both real and accidental) in men, as well as the signs on the cusps of the seventh and twelfth houses (if there are no planets in those signs in the sixth or eleventh houses), intercepted signs with no planets in them, and all planets *in* the seventh and twelfth houses (not including the sign on the Ascendant). These are energies you are born with repressed, and the tendency they have is to fall back into unconsciousness if only superficial or sporadic meditation time is spent in bringing them and their needs to consciousness. If they are unconscious, the talents and abilities they represent project out into other people, who seem to have those talents and abilities and you don't, or who hassle you in your daily life. Those consciousness resistant factors that are also basic archetypes—your board of directors—are especially important, because, if they are unconscious in you, other people have the last vote over certain areas of your life and you don't.

Give your consciousness resistant factors attention in meditation. Find out what each of them needs from you in order to stay conscious and healthy in you so that it doesn't project out into others. Learn what it is you must do to keep each of them at home, within you. The following lists of planets in these signs are:

Consciousness Resistant Factors in Men

Sun in Aquarius: *Sun* and *Star*
Sun in Libra: *Sun* and *Justice*
Moon in Capricorn: *High Priestess* and *Old Pan* or *Devil*
Moon in Scorpio: *High Priestess* and *Death*
Mercury in Sagittarius: *Magician* and *Temperance*
Mercury in Pisces: *Magician* and *Moon*
Mercury in Leo: *Magician* and *Strength*
Venus in Scorpio: *Empress* and *Death*
Venus in Aries: *Empress* and *Emperor*
Venus in Virgo: *Empress* and *Hermit*
Mars in Libra: *Tower* and *Justice*
Mars in Cancer: *Tower* and *Chariot*
Jupiter in Gemini: *Wheel of Fortune* and *Twins* or *Lovers*
Jupiter in Capricorn: *Wheel of Fortune* and *Old Pan* or *Devil*
Saturn in Cancer: *World* and *Chariot*
Saturn in Aries: *World* and *Emperor*
Uranus in Leo: *Fool* and *Strength*
Uranus in Taurus: *Fool* and *High Priest* or *Hierophant*
Neptune in Virgo: *Hanged Man* and *Hermit*
Neptune in Gemini: *Hanged Man* and *Twins* or *Lovers*
Pluto in Taurus: *Last Judgement* and *High Priest* or
    Hierophant
Pluto in Aquarius: *Last Judgement* and *Star*

Consciousness Resistant Factors in Women

Sun in Aries: *Sun* and *Emperor*
Sun in Leo: *Sun* and *Strength*
Moon in Taurus: *High Priestess* and *High Priest* or
    Hierophant
Moon in Cancer: *High Priestess* and *Chariot*
Mercury in Aquarius: *Magician* and *Star*
Mercury in Gemini: *Magician* and *Lovers* or *Twins*

Mercury in Virgo: *Magician* and *Hermit*
Venus in Pisces: *Empress* and *Moon*
Venus in Taurus: *Empress* and *High Priest* or *Hierophant*
Venus in Libra: *Empress* and *Justice*
Mars in Capricorn: *Tower* and *Old Pan* or *Devil*
Mars in Aries: *Tower* and *Emperor*
Jupiter in Cancer: *Wheel of Fortune* and *Chariot*
Jupiter in Sagittarius: *Wheel of Fortune* and *Temperance*
Saturn in Libra: *World* and *Justice*
Saturn in Capricorn: *World* and *Old Pan* or *Devil*
Uranus in Scorpio: *Fool* and *Death*
Uranus in Aquarius: *Fool* and *Star*
Neptune in Sagittarius: *Hanged Man* and *Temperance*
Neptune in Pisces: *Hanged Man* and *Moon*
Pluto in Leo: *Last Judgement* and *Strength*
Pluto in Scorpio: *Last Judgement* and *Death*

The two energies which have to do with the planet and sign may be asked to combine into a third figure which represents both energies. For instance, if the Moon is in the sign Cancer, ask the two tarot forms — *High Priestess* and *Chariot* — to merge into a third form which contains the combined energy of both. Ask your Guide to supervise this process.

It is to be noted that accidental rulership, exaltation, detriment and fall have to do with house position. Therefore, the Sun in the first house would have the qualitites of a Sun in Aries, no matter what sign it is actually in, and would be its accidental exaltation, the Moon in the tenth house would be in its accidental detriment, Mars in the fourth house would be in its accidental fall, Pluto in the eighth house would be in its accidental rulership, and so on.

The Special Constructs

A circular diagram is drawn for each of the classical astrological patterns: the T-cross (as in the example horoscope and worksheet), the grand trine, the grand square and the yod cross. These are drawn to indicate how to position the archetypes for a circle of hands. The circle is viewed from above. In the example, the Guide is at the ninth house point; I, "Edwin," am to his left; the other archetypal forms are positioned around in a circle to my left. The *World*, in the example, would then be holding the Guide's right hand completing the circle.

These special constructs are titled: T-cross energy balancing construct, grand square energy balancing construct, grand trine activation construct (luck) and yod cross (finger of God) construct.

Horoscope-Tarot Equivalents

Each of the twenty-two astrological factors — the twelve signs of the zodiac, the eight planets, the Sun and the Moon — correspond to the twenty-two greater trumps or major arcana of the tarot, as has been said. But the tarot cards represent only pictures of these energies — different artists' representations of the twenty-two pure archetypes of the Western Mystery Tradition. Some of you may find the tarot names and images too limiting, too constrictive. So I present the list that follows as a way of suggesting a broader spectrum of understanding and insight into each of these forces. The names given after the astrological and tarot names are additional titles for each of the specific archetypes, each title suggesting different aspects of the same energy. Ask your Inner Guide to bring the archetypal figures in each of their many aspects as you progress in your inner work. Say, for instance, that the *Fool* (Uranus) is consciousness resistant in your horoscope. It would tend to be useful to work with this energy often to allow it to begin its assimilation into your ego. But you don't have to work with Uranus in only one of its aspects. Look at its other titles in the list below. Ask to see its *Holy Ghost* aspect one time, its *Green Giant of Spring* aspect the next, its *Krishna* aspect another time. As you see and interact with the many aspects of this energy, you will begin to understand it in *depth*, not only its surface aspects, and it will reveal new aspects of itself which may not be implied in any of the titles below. As you work with it (or any of the other archetypes) again and again in its many variations on a theme, and the superficial veils that cloak the archetype fall away, and slowly its deep spiritual aspect will reveal itself. You will realize that you are truly interacting with an aspect of Deity — a part of Husband/Mother God, that has all the power of the universe, and that you are a channel for this power, conscious or unconscious.

0 Uranus—*Fool*: Adam-Kadmon, The Babe in the Egg on the Lotus, The Vagabond, Breath, Lightning, The April Fool, The Invisible Point Which Is Not, The Green Giant of Spring, The Jester, Unity of Center-Circumference, The Knight-Errant, The Unconscious Self, The Stranger in a Strange Land, The Wanderer, Aboriginal Chaos, Tao, Spirit, The Joker, The Great Void, The Babe in the Abyss, Genius, Dionysius, Krishna, Divine Folly, Harparkrat, The Divine Bum, Freedom, The Redeemer, Everyman, The Holy Ghost, The Eccentric, Spirit of Aether, The Androgynous One, Fiery or Scintillating Intelligence, The Crown of Wisdom, The Green Man.

1 Mercury—*Magician*: The Magus, The Juggler, The Magus of Power, The Initiate, Tahuti, The Pagat, The Mountebank, Hermes, Saint Christopher, Loki, Hiram, Harlequin, The Trickster, The Fabricator, Thoth, The Messenger of the Gods, The Minstrel, The Being, The Wizard, The Conjurer, Prometheus, Logic, The Occultist, Creative Will, Intelligence of Transparency, The Crown of Understanding.

2 The Moon—*High Priestess*: Initiation, The Divine Sophia, Artemis, Bona Dea, Maia, Kybele, The Binary, The Female Pontiff, The Archpriestess, Hecate, Pope Joan, The Priestess of the Silver Star, The Wise Woman, The Witch, The Yoni, Door of the Hidden Sanctuary, The Vesica Piscis, Gnosis, Veiled Isis, The Virgin Mother of the World, Moira, The Holy Guardian, Hathor, Juno, Hera Anima, Diana, The Receiver of All, The Vagina, Soul of All Light, Artemis, Goddess of the Night, The Pillars Jachin and Boaz, The Spiritual Bride and Mother, The Huntress, Trivia, Nuit, Virgin Mary, The Veil of Maya, The Madonna, Eve Before Her Union with Adam, Uniting Intelligence, Memory, The Good Mother, The Crown of Beauty.

3 Venus—*Empress*: Aphrodite, Isis Unveiled, Eve After Her Union with Adam, The Devouring Mother, The Goddess of Love, Lilith, Mother Nature, Isis-Urania, Demeter, The Queen, Daughter of the Mighty Ones, Objective Reality, Alchemical Salt, Gate of the Equilibrium of the Universe, Kali, The Mani-

fester, Ma, The Corn Woman, The Magma Mater, Love, The Gate of Heaven, Astarte, The Love of Master and Student in the Mysteries, Wife, Luminous Intelligence, Imagination, The Wisdom of Understanding.

4 Aries — *Emperor*: Tetragrammaton, Sun of the Morning, The Grand Architect of the Universe, The Ancient of Days, God as Father and Maker, Osiris, Guardian of the Holy Grail, The Cubic Stone, Alchemical Sulphur, The Law of Four, The Daredevil, Conqueror, Mars, Ares, Lightning, Chief Among the Mighty Ones, Priapus, The All-Father, Athena, Minerva, Spiritual Illumination, The Beginning, The I Am, He Who Sees and Sets in Order, The Warrior, The Survivor, The First One, The Pioneer, The Initiator, First Logos, The Higher Self, Lord, Eternal Life, Father of the Sun, Husband, Hercules, Spiritual Governor, The Man of War, The Stone Cube, Constituting Intelligence, Reason, Sight, The Cube of Space, The Wisdom of Sovereignty and Beauty, The Ram.

5 Taurus — *High Priest*: The Hierophant, Pope, Grand Master, Master of the Secrets, The Builder, The Gypsy Prince, Hierarch, Archpriest, Magus of the Eternal, The Prince, The Silent One, He Who Hears and Teaches to Hear, Revealer of the Holy, Universal Law, Master, Voice of the True Self, The Listening of the Silence, The Physical Voice of Triumph and Eternal Intelligence, Divine Presence as Voice, The Pontifex or Bridge-Maker, Triumphant and Eternal Intelligence, Intuition, Hearing, The Earth Spirit, The Wisdom and Fountain of Mercy, The Bull.

6 Gemini — *Twins*: Lovers, The Parting of the Ways, Eros, Cupid, The Two Ways, The Dual Brain, The Children of the Voice, Oracle of the Mighty Gods, Logic, The Judgement of Paris, The Androgynous Twins, Anubis, Andromeda's Rescue, The Student, Thinking Perfected, Hermes, The Connection, Duality, Twinning, The Angel Raphael, The Creation of the World, The Servant of Pan, Perfection of the Mind, Castor and Pollux, Temptation, The Monkey, Choice, The Two-Edged Sword, The Witness, The Alchemical or Hermetic Marriage of

the Elements, Division, Separation, The Attractions of Opposites, Disposing Intelligence, The Journalist, The Reporter, The Understanding of Beauty, The Production of Beauty and Sovereignty, The Devil's Tool.

7 Cancer — *Chariot*: The King in Triumph, The Charioteer, The Chariot of Osiris, Chaos, Home, The Fence, The Box, The Children of the Powers of the Waters, The Driver, Lord of the Triumph of Light, The Conqueror, Unification, The Source, Reconciliation, He Who Bears the Holy Grail, Self Control, Progress, The People, The Masses, Intelligence of the House of Influence, The Well, The Crab, Victory, Birth-Death, The Chariot of Reincarnation, The Ark, Receptivity, Understanding, Acting on Severity, The Dog.

8 Leo — *Strength*: Force, Power, Lust, Fortitude, The Conquered Lion, Pan's Phallus, Lucifer Transformed into Light, The Muzzled Lion, The Daughter of the Flaming Sword, Samson, The Enchantress, The Strength of Love, Union, Ecstasy, The Actor, The Life Force, The Lover, The Snake of Knowledge and Delight, The Lion-Headed Serpent, Vital Power, Prana, Dichotomy Resolved, Neith, Intelligence of the Secret of Works, The Performer, The Child, The Emperor's Love, Mercy Tempering Severity, The Cat.

9 Virgo — *Hermit*: Truth, The Helper, The Sage, The Ancient One, Prudence, Occult Light, The Path to Initiation, Adonis, Attis, The Secret Seed, The Pet, The Spermatozoon, The Prophet of the Eternal, The Pilgrim Soul, The Perfectionist, The Veiled Lamp, The Critic, Magus of the Voice of Power, Perfected Love, The Virgin, Inner Knowledge, Light and Force, The Servant, The Analyst, Hygeia, Intelligence of Will, Capuchin, Diogenes, The Perfected Tool, The Harpy, Response, Coition, The Old Man, The Hunchback, The Supreme Will, The Mercy of Beauty, The Magnificence of Sovereignty.

10 Jupiter — *Wheel of Fortune*: Chance, Fortune, The Law of Karma, Tarot, The Sphinx, Lord of the Forces of Life, The Three Fates, The Gambler, The Guru, The Three-Headed One,

The Cycle of Events, Zeus, The Circle of Time, Excess, Rota, Rotation, Major Fortune, True Will, The Law of the Wheel, Wealth and Poverty, Intelligence of Conciliation, Rewarding Intelligence of Those Who Seek, Expansion, Lady Luck, The Guide Force, The Mercy and Magnificence of Victory.

11 Libra — *Justice*: Adjustment, The Sword and the Balance, Union of Opposites, Copulation, The Judge, Daughter of the Lords of Truth, The Jury, Ruler of the Balance, The Blind One, Karma in Action, The Mirror, Inner Truth, Nephthys, Athena, The Partner, The Shadow, The Peacemaker, The Scales, The Other, The Stranger, The Crystal Cube, Narcissus, Equilibrium, Transition, Faithful Intelligence, The Severity of Beauty and Sovereignty, The Dove of Peace.

12 Neptune — *Hanged Man*: The Sacrifice, Spirit of the Mighty Waters, The Thief, Judas, The Victim, Samadhi, The Acrobat, Crucifixion, Mental Purity, The Law of Reversal, Baptism, The Drowned Man, The Musician, Balder, The Divine Giving-Forth, Stable Intelligence, The Redeemer in the Waters, The Old Man of the Sea, The Example, The Sacrificed God, Dissolution, Poseidon, The Dancer, The Invisible One, The Severity of Splendor, The Masochist.

13 Scorpio — *Death*: The Grim Reaper, The Circle Completed, The Scythe, The Angel of Death, The Skeleton, The Angel Azrail, Transformation, Reincarnation, Change, Sunrise, Sex, The Tax Man, Liberation, Reproduction, The Dark Angel of the Doors, The Tunnel, The Eagle, The Child of the Great Transformation, Thanatos, Charon, Birth, The Detective, The Great Snake, Kundalini, Metamorphosis, The Scorpion, Motion, Imaginative Intelligence, The Three Manifestations of Matter, The American Indian, The Red Man, The Sovereignty and Result of Victory.

14 Sagittarius — *Temperance*: Art, Alchemy, The Two Urns, Adaptation, The Bringer-Forth of Life, Daughter of the Reconcilers, The Teacher, The Way, Preservation, Higher Spaces, Verification, Tentative Intelligence, Intelligence of Probation or Trial,

Divine Wisdom, The Fourth Dimension, The Angel Michael, The Rainbow's Promise, The Pointer, The Arrow That Pierces the Rainbow, The Gypsy, Iris, Universal Life, Consummation of the Royal Alchemical Marriage, Chiron, The Queen of Heaven, The Philosopher, The Operation of the Great Work, The Quest of the Universal Medicine, The Coniunctio Oppositorum, Mantra, Combination, Wrath, The Beauty of a Firm Basis, The Centaur.

15 Capricorn — *Old Pan*: The Devil, The Tester, The Establishment, Matter, The Cube of Imperfect Understanding, Lord of the Gates of Matter, Formless Form, Child of the Forces of Time, Typhon, The Electric Whirlwind, God as Perceived by the Ignorant, Satan, Fate, The Twins Chained by Time, Lucifer — Angel of Light, The Spirit of Discord, Master of the Coven, Old Nick, City Hall, The Goat of Mendes, Society, Guardian of the Key to the Temple, Janus, The Mountain, The Eye of the Father, The Temple of Universal Peace Among Men, The World Father, The Watching Eye, The Prime Minister, The Blackness of Ignorance, Argus of the Many Eyes, Eroticism, The Horny One, The Path of the Tradition of Darkness, The Scapegoat, The Clown, Opacity, Shiva, Two-Sexed Horus, Bondage, Mirth, Renewing Intelligence, The Climber, The Sovereignty and Beauty of Material Splendor, Lord of the Flies, The God of the Old Testament, The Virgin's Child.

16 Mars — *Tower*: The Force of Nature, Exciting Intelligence, The Fall of Adam, The Cities of the Plain, Preparation Through Destruction for the New Birth, Pride of Intellect, Infatuation, Catastrophe, The Dark Night of the Soul, The Ruined Tower, The Castle of Plutus, The Column Jachin, Megalomania, The Effect, The Opening of the Eye of Shiva, The Tower of Destruction, The Fire of Heaven, The House of God, The Tower of Babel, Lord of the Hosts of the Mighty, Phallic Energy, Grace and Sin, Anger, The Red One, The Descent into Hell, Awakening, The Crisis Point, The Lightning-Struck Tower, Husband, The Victory over Splendor.

17 Aquarius — *Star*: Star of the Magi, Sirius, Destiny, Natural Intelligence, Revelation, Meditation, Astrology, Hapi, Gany-

mede, Brotherhood, The Imagination of Nature, The Dog Star, The Star of Bethlehem, The Pool of Memory, Daughter of the Firmament, The Stars, Sattva, The Genius, Hope, The Dweller Between the Waters, The Friend, The Group, Humanity, The Revolutionary, Tinkerbell, The Unveiling of Nature, The Supernal Power of Divine Fire, The Scientist, The Exile, The Food of the Gods, The Grave of Death, Altruistic Love, Freedom, The Free Man, Soma, The Victory of Fundamental Strength, The Metasexual Lover, The Bear.

18 Pisces — *Moon*: Dreams, Twilight, Dusk, The Ruler of Flux and Reflux, Child of the Sons of the Mighty, Medusa, Hecate, The Fish-God, Body Knowledge, Trance, The Compassionate One, The Land of Dreams, Corporeal Intelligence, Organization, The True Base of Reality, The Land of the Gods, The Mystic, The Role Taker, The Dreamer, The Synthesizer, The Mermaid, The Gateway to Resurrection, The Dancer, Fantasy, The Hounds of Diana, Tamas, Music, Metaphysical Sleep, The Poet, Ast the Serpent, Basic Understanding, The Victory of the Material, The Two Fish, Master of the Mind.

19 The Sun — *Sun*: Eternal Youth, The Center of the Self, Lord of the Fire of the World, Ra, The Symbol of Tetragrammaton, Apollo, The Eternal Child, Christ, The Ceaseless Giver, Phaethon, Mithra, The Spiritual Phallus, The Central Fire, Continuous Energy, Illumination, Lord of the Aeon, Rajas, Collective Intelligence, Regeneration, Fertility and Sterility, The Splendor of Fundamental Strength, The Higher Self.

20 Pluto — *Last Judgement*: Perpetual Intelligence, Realization, Resurrection, The Day of Wrath, Vulcan, The Raising of the Dead, The One-Way Trip, The Horn, The Angel Gabriel, King of the After-Life, Hades, The Great Vocation, The Physical Phallus, Spirit of the Primal Fire, Lord of the Underworld, The Hidden One, The Apocalypse, The Swan of Leda, Shiva, Dionysiac Ecstasy, The Gangster, Rise, That Which Limits the Auric Egg, The Kidnapper, The Force of Gravity, Conscious Immortality, The Phoenix, The Splendor of the Material World.

21 Saturn — *World*: The Virgin Universe, The Cosmos, Aion, The Great Ones of the Night of Time, The Crown of the Magi, Kronos, The God of Fertility, The Old God, The Point of Now, The New Jerusalem, Dominion or Slavery, Reality, The Esoteric Side of Nature, Immortality, The Dancing Hermaphrodite, The Center of the Cube of Space, That Which Holds All Together, Administrative Intelligence, Cosmic Consciousness, The Initiated One, The Regents of the Earth, The Woman with the Penis, Guardian of the Times of Man, The Dance of Shiva, The Slain God, The Eternal Present, The Foundation of the Cosmic Elements and of the Material World.

The attributions listed here are in accordance with those of the Hermetic Order of the Golden Dawn, the Society of the Inner Light, the Builders of the Adytum (B.O.T.A.), the Servants of the Light, D.O.M.E., the Inner Guide Meditation Center and my own personal research. I have settled on these after years of experimentation, as they seem to be verified by the human psyche.

Color and Tone Vibrations of the Twenty–Two Archetypes

Each of the twenty-two archetypes pictured by tarot or represented by the major trumps of the tarot has to do with vibrational energy, and each of them corresponds to specific vibrational frequencies. In the list below, I give some of the color and sound frequencies traditionally associated with each of the archetypes. Frequencies of odor (perfumes and other scents), temperature and taste might also be found and established through experiment for each of them. The color and tone vibrations listed below can be used to help invoke the archetype that you and your Guide plan to work with in more depth. You might sound a C-natural on a pitchpipe or musical instrument to get in clearer contact with the energy of the *Tower/* Mars or wear emerald green for an interaction with the *Empress/* Venus. Experiment with these in ways your Inner Guide or your imagination might suggest. You will find that incorporating knowledge of each archetype's color and sound into your meditation practice will give deeper contact with the archetypes you seek out and interact with.

The Fool (Uranus): Pale, clear yellow; E-natural
The Magician (Mercury): Yellow; E-natural
The High Priestess (Moon): Blue, silver; G-sharp, A-flat
The Empress (Venus): Emerald green; F-sharp, G-flat
The Emperor (Aries): Scarlet, pure red; C-natural
The High Priest or *Hierophant* (Taurus): Red-orange; C-sharp, D-flat
The Twins or *Lovers* (Gemini): Orange; D-natural
The Chariot (Cancer): Yellow-orange; D-sharp, E-flat
Strength (Leo): Yellow, gold; E-natural
The Hermit (Virgo): Yellow-green; F-natural
The Wheel of Fortune (Jupiter): Violet; B-flat, A-sharp
Justice (Libra): Green; F-sharp, G-flat
The Hanged Man (Neptune): Pale blue; G-sharp, A-flat
Death (Scorpio): Blue-green; G-natural
Temperance (Sagittarius): Blue; G-sharp, A-flat
Old Pan or *The Devil* (Capricorn): Blue-violet, indigo, black; A-natural
The Tower (Mars): Scarlet, red; C-natural
The Star (Aquarius): Violet; A-sharp, B-flat
The Moon (Pisces): Red-violet; B-natural
The Sun (Sun): Orange, gold; D-natural
The Last Judgement (Pluto): Scarlet, red, black; C-natural
The World (Saturn): Indigo, blue-violet, black; A-natural

Supplemental General Worksheet (for any horoscope)

In astrology there are six natural pairs that represent two ends of six particular poles in a horoscope and make up the twelve signs of the zodiac. The planetary or luminary rulers of these pairs also have this polarity aspect, as do planets or luminaries whose natures are opposite and complimentary. It is useful to check on the harmony within yourself of each of these pairs to make sure that the

the life areas of which they are the *general* rulers (your personal horoscope gives the *specific* rulers) are in balance. The natural opposites or polarities whose balances may be checked are:

Emperor and *Justice* (The ego-partner polarity)
High Priest and *Death* (The money-sex polarity)
Twins and *Temperance* (The logic-intuition polarity)
Chariot and *Old Pan* (The security-career polarity)
Strength and *Star* (The love-friendship polarity)
Hermit and *Moon* (The analysis-synthesis polarity)
Tower and *Empress* (The aggression-reception polarity)
Empress and *Last Judgement* (The manifestation-transformation polarity)
Magician and *Wheel of Fortune* (The wisdom polarity)
High Priestess and *World* (The mother-father polarity)
Sun and *Fool* (The spiritual love polarity)
Magician and *Hanged Man* (The magic-psychic polarity)
World and *Wheel of Fortune* (The contraction-expansion polarity)
Sun and *High Priestess* (The yang-yin polarity)
Fool and *Hanged Man* (The freedom-bondage polarity)
World and *Last Judgement* (The limitation polarity)

Horoscope – Tree of Life
Sphere Equivalents and Images

The Spheres or *Sephiroth* of the qabalistic Tree of Life represent energies that are not available to our ordinary perceptions on the material plane, but they are available to us through meditation. The ten Spheres correspond to the Sun, Moon and the eight planets. In the tarot they correspond to the number cards, Ace through Ten. The twenty-two paths of the Tree correspond to the tarot archetypes – energies and experiences that *are* available to us in our everyday lives on the material plane. The Tree of Life is a glyph describing the experiences that *anyone* will encounter on the inner planes, no matter what his or her path.

The four suits of tarot (Wands/fire, Cups/water, Swords/air and Pentacles/earth) correspond to the four-body system, as do the court cards (King/fire, Queen/water, Knight/air, Page/earth). For example, the Three of Wands would correspond to Saturn in the spiritual body (fire); the Three of Cups, to Saturn in the emotional body (water), etc.

There are, in fact, four Trees, the top of one meshing with the bottom of the next, each corresponding to one of the four bodies. In Western "path working" — the meditative experience of the Spheres and the tarot paths of the Tree of Life — you begin with your Inner Guide at *Malkuth*, the base of the Tree, and work your way up and back from *Malkuth*, to each of the spheres in turn.

Three resistance points are experienced as you do inner work. The first, called The Veil of the Lesser Mysteries, is encountered when you initially begin to meditate and move up the Tree from *Malkuth* to the next Sphere in order, *Yesod*. Here you are confronted with the necessity of immediately facing all your doubts and fears about meditation and the inner planes as you begin your own inner process. The next resistance point occurs after the Spheres of *Hod* and *Netzach* have been experienced and you progress towards *Tiphareth*, the heart center of the Tree. It is called The Veil of the Greater Mysteries, and a strong ego test in the outer world is encountered at this point. It is the place where you must truly decide whether or not you want to become your Higher Self and allow your ego to become its vehicle. The last resistance point is called The Abyss and occurs after the Spheres of *Geburah* and *Chesed* have been encountered. (An invisible Sphere called *Daath* is often described at this point.) Past this place no Guide can accompany you. Unwavering trust in Spirit is all you can take with you.

The images and colors below are given as suggestion for those who wish to work in meditation with the Spheres of the Tree. They are the traditional forms from the Western Mystery Tradition.

1. *Kether* (Neptune): An ancient bearded king seen in profile; the crown; the cranium; the thousand-petaled lotus; the divine spark; the Archangel Metatron; brilliance; a point of brilliant white light; white flecked with gold.

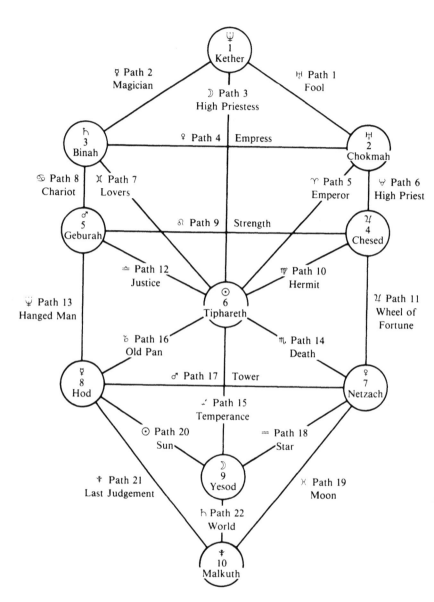

Figure 40. Horoscope/tarot equivalents as they appear on the qabalistic Tree of Life.

2. *Chokmah* (Uranus): A bearded male figure; an erect phallus; the left side of the face; the Archangel Ratziel; pure soft blue; grey; iridescent pearly-gray; white flecked with red, blue and yellow.

3. *Binah* (Saturn): A mature woman; a matron; the yoni; the cup or chalice; the right side of the face; the Archangel Tzaphkiel; crimson; black; dark brown; gray flecked with pink.

4. *Chesed* (Jupiter): A mighty crowned and throned king; the left arm; the Archangel Tzadkiel; deep violet; blue; deep purple; deep azure flecked with yellow.

5. *Geburah* (Mars): A mighty warrior in his chariot; the sword; the right arm; the Archangel Khamael; orange; scarlet red; bright scarlet, red flecked with black.

6. *Tiphareth* (Sun): A majestic king; a child; a sacrificed God; the heart; the breast; the Archangel Raphael; clear rose-pink; yellow; rich salmon-pink; golden amber.

7. *Netzach* (Venus): A beautiful naked woman; the bearded Venus; a rose; sexuality; the loins, hips and legs; the Archangel Haniel; amber; emerald; bright yellowish green; olive flecked with gold.

8. *Hod* (Mercury): A hermaphrodite; an apron covering the generative organs; the loins and legs; the Archangel Michael; violet-purple; orange; russet-red; yellowish black flecked with white.

9. *Yesod* (Moon): A beautiful naked man, very strong; the generative organs; the Archangel Gabriel; indigo; violet; very dark purple; azure flecked with citrine.

10. *Malkuth* (Earth and Pluto): A young woman, crowned and throned; the feet; the anus; the Archangel Sandalphon; yellow; citrine, olive, russet and black; citrine, olive, russet and black flecked with gold; black rayed with yellow.

How to Plug Your Relatives into Your Horoscope

Your relatives may be "plugged in" to your natal horoscope where they may be seen as outer aspects of specific areas of your life. They will function as barometers of these areas. By barometers I mean "gauges of change" that indicate what the "weather" of that life area is like. These relatives *as their ego personalities are perceived by you* (how they react to and handle the events in their lives in *your* eyes) will function to show you how you are handling that area of your own life for which they act as a barometer. They stand as symbols of particular life areas and show you how you are handling those areas of your life. To be a barometer has only to do with how *you* judge them to be dealing with their lives, not their own evaluation of themselves and their lives nor the evaluations of others as reported to you.

It is necessary to determine the correct pregnancy or fathering order of your relatives' (mother's, father's, grandmothers', brothers', sisters', aunts', sisters-in-law's, mothers-in-law's, etc.) pregnancies or children fathered in order to ascertain your barometers correctly. Try to obtain this information as accurately as possible. Miscarriages, stillbirths, children born out of wedlock and abortions each count as a pregnancy, and *where*, not when (actual dates aren't required), they occurred in the birth sequence is important. Twins count as two pregnancies, and which twin was first-born is important.

The basic "building block" roles are *father, mother, child, sibling* (brother or sister), and *partner*.

Father is always a tenth house role. Your perception of your father and the behavior *you* draw out of him will be described by your tenth house as his first house. The cusp of your tenth house is therefore the Ascendant of your father's horoscope *in your reality*, within your own horoscope. When you turn your horoscope around in this way, your eleventh house becomes his second, your twelfth house his third, etc. Your horoscope then will describe your father, his actions and behavior, and what happens to him in your reality. It can be read in the same way as if it were his actual horoscope, but only in your reality perception, not necessarily his own. So the father of any person in your horoscope through your perception of the person's role relationship to him will always be the tenth house from the house in which the person himself is. For instance, *the child of your mother's first pregnancy not counting you* will be your first sibling (your first brother or sister). This sibling will correspond to your third house. (In other words the first house (or Ascendant) of your first brother or sister in your horoscope will be your third house.) Then the tenth house from the third, your twelfth house, will be the relationship you will perceive between your first sibling and your father. So mother's father will be your first house; your first child's relationship to its father in your eyes will be your second house; your father's father will be your seventh house, etc.

Mother is always a fourth house role. Thus your fourth house cusp is the Ascendant of your mother's horoscope in your reality, and it will indicate to you her actions and behavior. By the same token, your mother's mother will be your seventh house or four houses from your fourth house; your father's mother, four houses from your tenth house or your first house (or ego barometer); your first child's relationship to mother, your eighth house (the fourth house from the fifth); etc.

Stepfathers and foster fathers, as well as stepmothers and foster mothers, are in the same areas as natural fathers and mothers, the tenth and fourth houses.

Sibling (brother or sister) is always a third house relationship, so your first sibling will be the third house from the first house or your third house. Your second sibling will be the third house from the third house or your fifth house. The third sibling, the third house from the fifth house or the seventh house, etc. Your father's first sibling will be the third house from the tenth house, so your first aunt or uncle on your father's side will be described by your twelfth house as that aunt's or uncle's Ascendant (or first house.) (Remember to check for miscarriages, abortions and stillborn children or children born out of wedlock in all birth sequences.) The second aunt or uncle on your father's side will then be your second house;

the third, your fourth house; etc. Your brothers and sisters in general and your first sibling in particular are all shown by your third house.

Child is always a fifth house relationship, so the first child you father or conceive will have your fifth house as his or her Ascendant. However, your second child is considered the sibling, or brother or sister, of your first child, and therefore will be your seventh house (the third house from the fifth); the third child, your ninth house; etc. As outlined before, *each pregnancy* is to be counted, whether the child was miscarried, aborted, given away, stillborn or born, as one slot. Say that your first pregnancy, or the first pregnancy you fathered was a set of fraternal twins, a girl, first-born, and a boy, second-born. Then the daughter would be your fifth house and the son, your seventh house. Your father's first sibling's first child by the same rule would be your fourth house (the fifth house from the twelfth). Your partner's first child by a previous marriage would be your eleventh house (the fifth house from the seventh), and should you legally adopt this child before you have any children of your own, the child would transfer to your fifth house. If you already had two children, the adopted son or daughter would then become your ninth house. Your children in general, and your first child in particular, are shown by your fifth house.

Partner, whether business or marriage, where it is a relationship of shared responsibility (this includes roommates and those you live with while you are living with them, all ex-partners, all persons you have contractual agreements with, and anyone you have impregnated or conceived a child by, whether the child was born or not), is a seventh house relationship. So your mother's partner (father or step-father) is your tenth house, the seventh house from the fourth. Your partner is the seventh house, the seventh house from the first. Your first child's partner is the eleventh house, the seventh or opposite house from the fifth. Your father's first sibling's partner, your aunt or uncle by marriage, becomes your sixth house, the seventh house from the twelfth.

With these five basic role concepts and the accompanying diagram shown in figure 41 on page 250, almost every person related to you through blood, role, or law can be put into one specific area of your personal pattern — relatives as distant as third cousins on your mother's side or great-great-aunts on your father's side. These barometers from the past can produce some fascinating family research and personal insight. What area of your life did great-great-uncle Joe, the horse thief, vibrate to? What life area did great-grandmother, the actress, vibrate to?

The following horoscope diagram gives a smattering of what each of the astrological houses has to do with and describes barometers that vibrate to each of the sections, as well as examples of some of the relatives which fall into each. I have included automobiles as barometers, because we have so many of them in our culture.

The following barometers are given for further example in addition to the diagram:

Cars are always a third house relationship (like siblings), as is any vehicle (as the mind is the vehicle of the ego or Ascendant). In lieu of a car, a bicycle, tricycle or just experiences encountered while walking will serve the third house function. Therefore, your mother's car is shown by your sixth house (third from the fourth); your partner's car by your ninth house; your father's car by your twelfth house.

Neighbors and acquaintances are also third house relationships; therefore your partner's acquaintances are shown in your ninth house; your first child's, in your seventh house; your eldest sibling's, in your fifth house.

Teachers as "method givers," like your grammar and high school teachers, are all described by your third house, and false guides are also described by this house.

Very personal friends (where there are many expectations of each other), lovers and clubs one belongs to vibrate with the first child and the fifth house; therefore your lover's first child is shown in your ninth house (the fifth house from your fifth house).

Co-workers, employees, pets, and the service personnel of life (the waiter at a restaurant, the clerk at the supermarket, your doctor, the person who fixes your car) are all barometers of your sixth house, the health/work methods area. Hence your neighbor's dog would be shown by your eighth house — the sixth house from your third; your partner's health by your twelfth house.

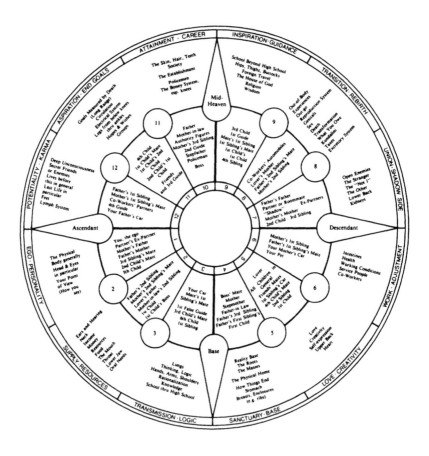

Figure 41. Keywords for each of the houses done on the chart blank we use at D.O.M.E. Note that the inner circle lists the keywords for each house as they relate to your relatives.

Your Shadow and all Shadow projectees are shown by your seventh house. Members of a jury would be Shadow barometers.

All grandchildren in general and the child of your first pregnancy are shown by your ninth house, as are all teachers who act as "way showers," not "method givers." College and university professors would be ninth house barometers, as would outer metaphysical and spiritual teachers. The first of the Guides is described by the ninth house, and he is the prototype and touchstone for all outer world teachers. The judge in a courtroom also functions as a ninth house barometer.

Authority figures, like your employer or a police officer you encounter, are all described by the tenth house, so your partner's boss would be described by your fourth house, your boss's boss, by your seventh.

Friendships (where the relationship is based on freedom and total acceptance for each of you) that don't have the expectations and obligations of a fifth house friendship are described by your eleventh house, as are groups you belong to that share as their goals the end goals of your life.

The males and females as barometers in the same house may not seem at all the same in the eyes of the ego, although the men will resemble each other as will the women. Each will serve to indicate to the individual how his male (*yang*, aggressive, outgoing) and his female (*yin*, passive, receptive) energies in the area being focused on are being handled. For instance, in the seventh house, if the wife is handling her life very well but the third sibling, who is a brother, is not, it would indicate that the feminine or *yin* energies in that life area are being assimilated into consciousness but the masculine energies are not. Working with the masculine aspects of that life arena in the Inner Guide Meditation will produce a positive change in the brother as you, the ego, bring the more *yang* aspects of your seventh house into the light of consciousness and act on them in the world.

Again, for astrologers wishing to read the details of an outer world person in their own charts, the horoscope must be turned so that the house that the particular person vibrates to in the horoscope becomes the first house of that person. For example, if you wish to see your mother's horoscope within your own chart, turn the chart so that your fourth house becomes your mother's first house (or Ascendant.) Then your fifth house becomes her second, your sixth house, her third, etc. Transiting planets to these houses and their planets will show up as events in both your own and your mother's lives. Reading transiting aspects to both your fourth and tenth houses (as twelve-house horoscopes within your own) will soon demonstrate that the father is always the tenth house, the mother, always the fourth. In the thousands of horoscopes I have read, I have never found a case where these house positions were reversed, although the roles as they play out in life may well be — mother acting as father and vice versa.

We are all connected, one to the other, by *projection*. Reality is in fact a Oneness. This projection, the two-way energy flow which connects us all, produces real action and behavior in others who unconsciously take roles for us in our realities, as we take roles for them. Those you project on are also projecting onto you, but, until you *experience* how your energies are manipulating the other's life, you will never understand how you receive and live out the projections of another.

Remember, for all practical purposes, *there's no one out there but aspects of yourself* that are being projected on everyone and everything. Once you make yourself more conscious, your entire reality and everyone in it become more conscious.

The Inner Guide Meditation and the *I Ching*

I recommend the *I Ching* as an excellent tool for getting through the "magic mirror effect" that occurs in meditation. It is the best "ego check" I have found to date. When you feel that the answer you have received in meditation, or the action that has been recommended, goes too much along with your desires or ego wishes (and doubt occurs), ask the *I Ching*'s advice on acting or not acting on the answer or request for action. The *coin method* for use with the *I Ching* is given.

I consider the Wilhelm/Baynes edition published by Princeton University Press[3] as the best version available, with the Carol K. Anthony, *A Guide to the I Ching* and Greg Whincup's *Rediscovering the I Ching* as excellent supplements. According to C. G. Jung's *Man and His Symbols*, when using pennies or other Western coins to cast the hexagrams, it is suggested that the following values be assigned:

$$
\begin{aligned}
\text{Heads} &= 3 \\
\text{Tails} &= 2
\end{aligned}
$$

Michael Secter, author of the *"I Ching" Simplified*,[4] has developed a new method for casting the coins that gives the same mathematical probability as the ancient Chinese yarrow stalk procedure.

Toss two of the three coins, then pick up the one that comes up tails if there is a head and a tail (or pick up either one if both are the same). Then cast this one and the one not yet cast. Now, count up the total on the three faces and note this total on paper. Repeat this six times. Have your question in mind when doing this. Build the column of totals *from bottom to top* (like building a house) as shown in figure 42.

The *odd* numbers are represented by a straight unbroken line and the *even* numbers by a broken line. Next to each number, place its corresponding line. Again, work from bottom to top as shown in figure 43 on page 254.

> 7 = 1 head, 2 tails (6th two throws)
> 8 = 2 heads, 1 tail (5th two throws)
> 6 = 3 tails (4th two throws)
> 7 = 1 head, 2 tails (3rd two throws)
> 9 = 3 heads (2nd two throws)
> 7 = 1 head, 2 tails (1st two throws)

Figure 42. Tossing the coins. You will be reading the totals from the bottom up.

---

[3]Cary Baynes and Richard Wilhelm, *The I Ching or Book of Changes* (Princeton University Press, 1967.)

[4]Michael Secter, *"I Ching" Simplified* (Santa Fe, New Mexico, Insight Press, 1981).

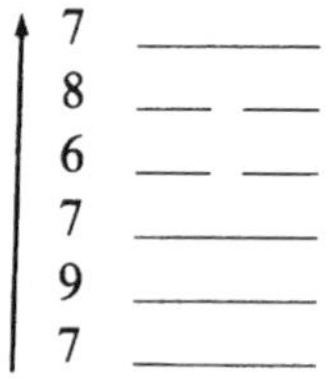

```
  7  _____
  8  __  __
  6  __  __
  7  _____
  9  _____
  7  _____
```

Figure 43. The resultant hexagram.

The pattern the six lines form is called a *hexagram*, and is composed of a top and a bottom *trigram*, or group of three lines.

Now turn to the chart of hexagrams at the back of the *I Ching* book. Notice that the first three lines in our sample hexagram are *straight, straight, straight* (reading from the bottom up). These bottom three lines are called the *lower trigram*. Find the corresponding *straight, straight, straight* lines on the hexagram chart in the column marked "Lower Trigram" on the left. You will find the pattern of lines called *Ch'ien*. Then notice the top three lines of the sample hexagram. They are *broken, broken, straight*. The top three lines are called the "Upper Trigram." Find the corresponding upper trigram on the hexagram chart across the top of the page where you will find that it is named *Ken*. The box where *Ch'ien* and *Ken* come together is the square numbered *26*. This is the number of the *first hexagram* of your answer.

The lines that total 6 and 9 *always change* into their opposites. Six, which starts out broken become a straight line, and 9, which starts out as a straight line, becomes a broken line. (7's and 8's always remain the same, not changing into their opposites.) The sample now looks like figure 44.

```
  7  _____   _____
  8  __  __    __  __
  6  __  __    _____
  7  _____   _____
  9  _____   __  __
  7  _____   _____
```

Figure 44. The final pattern.

Note that in the second hexagram, the lines corresponding to the 9 and the 6 are now opposite what they were in the first hexagram. Looking up the second pair of trigrams in the key in the back of the *I Ching* identifies them as *Li* over *Li* or hexagram *30*. Place this number at the bottom of the second hexagram. Now you are ready to read the *I Ching*'s answer to your question.

Turn to hexagram *26* in *Book I* of the *Text* and begin reading through "The Judgement" and "The Image" up to where it says "The Lines." The Lines refer to the *changing* lines in the *first* hexagram (6's and 9's, not 7's and 8's). Since, in our sample hexagram *26*, the first or bottom line is not a 6 or 9, we go to the line called "9 in the 2nd place." This is the first *sequential change* (relative to the question) that operates against the *background* of the "The Judgement" and "The Image" of hexagram *26*. Then skip to the 4th line of the hexagram (the *next* changing line) and read the paragraph which begins "6 in the 4th place means."

That is all there is to read in hexagram *26*. (Again, remember to first read up to where it says "The Lines" in *any first hexagram*, and then read only the *changing* lines of that hexagram). "The Judgement" and "The Image" give you the *background* of the situation being asked about, and the changing "Lines" give the sequential changes that will happen against that background. To complete the reading turn to the 2nd hexagram, *30*, and read only "The Judgement" and "The Image." *Never read any lines in a 2nd hexagram*. The 2nd hexagram indicates the *end result* of the question and never has "Lines" to read.

There is one other kind of hexagram to be considered. It occurs when all the totals turn out to be 7's and 8's. This is a *Fated* hexagram and never has "Lines" to read. It is a situation already *set* in time and space.

When wording your questions, it is best to avoid questions beginning with "Should . . ." *The Book of Changes* is set up to show sequential action in time. The clearest answers come as the result of *two separate questions* regarding any one situation: "If I *do* such and such what will be the end result?" and "If I *don't* do such and such what will be the end result?" This presents the two possible time flows. A simple "What's happening?" will serve to clarify confusing life situations.

Remember, the *I Ching* or *Book of Changes* always speaks to the "superior" or *conscious* person. Some suggestions for interpreting the *I Ching*'s words:

Superior = Conscious
Inferior = Unconscious
Man = Masculine, creative principle in a man or a
  woman
Woman = Feminine, receptive principle in a man or a
  woman
Great Man or Sage = The Inner Guide
King or Prince = The Self or Center in a man or a
  woman

The six lines making up an *I Ching* hexagram represent the six internal chakras or energy centers in the human body. They project and coordinate the reality your archetypes are creating and sustaining. The *I Ching* answers your questions based on how your archetypes are going to create the particular reality situation you are asking about.

Remember that the *I Ching* is not a substitute for your intuition, for the knowledge of your heart. Try to use it only for those situations where you get no "knowing" response, where your intuition seems to be shut down, or where ego involvement doesn't allow you to get a clear answer from your Higher Self or your Inner Guide. Don't misuse or become dependent on it.

APPENDIX

Transiting Positions of Pluto, Neptune, Uranus and Saturn from January 1, 1965 to January 1, 2000

Decans of any sign: 1st: 0°01' to 10°00',
2nd: 10°01' to 20°00', 3rd: 20°01' to 30°00'

Transiting planets affect planets in the natal horoscope by decan vibration, not by classical orb, so a planet in 20° 01' of any sign will affect planets in decans from 20° 01' to 30° 00', but will no longer affect a planet in 19° 59' of a sign.

Pluto: The Last Judgement (Brings irreversible change, transformation, metamorphosis, rebirth, remodeling, takes to the next level, shocks, outrages, invisible until its process is completed, unpredictable)

2nd Decan Virgo ♍	1/1/65–11/3/66; 2/12/67–9/1/67
3rd Decan Virgo	11/3/66–2/12/67; 9/1/67–10/5/71; 4/17/72–7/30/72
1st Decan Libra ♎	10/5/71–4/17/72; 7/30/72–10/25/75; 4/12/76–8/21/76
2nd Decan Libra	10/25/75–4/12/76; 8/21/76–11/3/79; 4/24/80–8/29/80
3rd Decan Libra	11/3/79–4/24/80; 8/29/80–11/5/83; 5/18/84–8/27/84
1st Decan Scorpio ♏	11/5/83–5/18/84; 8/27/84–11/4/87; 6/22/88–8/17/88
2nd Decan Scorpio	11/4/87–6/22/88; 8/17/88–1/16/91; 3/31/91–11/6/91

3rd Decan Scorpio	1/16/91–3/31/91; 11/6/91–1/16/95; 4/22/95–11/10/95
1st Decan Sagittarius ♐	1/16/95–4/22/95; 11/10/95–1/30/99; 4/27/99–11/23/99
2nd Decan Sagittarius	1/30/99–4/27/99; 11/23/99–1/1/00

Neptune: The Hanged Man (Dissolves, makes invisible, glamorizes, sensitizes, brings inspiration, increased psychic abilities or confusion, delusion, fog, victimization)

2nd Decan Scorpio ♏	1/1/65–11/19/65; 6/12/66–9/18/66
3rd Decan Scorpio	11/19/65–6/12/66; 9/18/66–1/5/70; 5/3/70–11/6/70
1st Decan Sagittarius ♐	1/5/70–5/3/70; 11/6/70–12/19/74; 6/17/75–10/22/75
2nd Decan Sagittarius	12/19/74–6/17/75; 10/22/75–2/8/79; 5/6/79–12/7/79; 8/13/80–9/20/80
3rd Decan Sagittarius	2/8/79–5/6/79; 12/7/79–8/13/80; 9/20/80–1/18/84; 6/22/84–11/21/84
1st Decan Capricorn ♑	1/18/84–6/22/84; 11/21/84–3/15/88; 5/10/88–1/3/89; 8/13/89–10/29/89
2nd Decan Capricorn	3/15/88–5/10/88; 1/3/89–8/13/89; 10/29/89–2/15/93; 7/3/93–12/19/93
3rd Decan Capricorn	2/15/93–7/3/93; 12/19/93–1/28/98; 8/23/98–11/27/98
1st Decan Aquarius ♒	1/28/98–8/23/98; 11/27/98–1/1/00

Uranus: The Fool (Causes rebelliousness, makes you iconoclastic, brings the sudden and unexpected, lightning-like change, events which free, but can pull the rug out from under you if not worked with)

2nd Decan Virgo ♍	1/1/65–9/12/66
3rd Decan Virgo	9/12/66–9/28/68; 5/21/69–6/24/69

1st Decan Libra ♎   9/28/68–5/21/69; 6/24/69–10/15/70; 5/12/71–7/23/71

2nd Decan Libra   10/15/70–5/12/71; 7/23/71–11/1/72; 5/6/73–8/15/73

3rd Decan Libra   11/1/72–5/6/73; 8/15/73–11/21/74; 5/1/75–9/8/75

1st Decan Scorpio ♏   11/21/74–5/1/75; 9/8/75–12/12/76; 4/24/77–9/30/77

2nd Decan Scorpio   12/12/76–4/24/77; 9/30/77–1/7/79; 4/15/79–10/23/79

3rd Decan Scorpio   1/7/79–4/15/79; 10/23/79–2/17/81; 3/20/81–11/16/81

1st Decan Sagittarius ♐ 2/17/81–3/20/81; 11/16/81–12/12/83; 7/15/84–9/20/84

2nd Decan Sagittarius   12/12/83–7/15/84; 9/20/84–1/9/86; 6/20/86–10/30/86

3rd Decan Sagittarius   1/9/86–6/20/86; 10/30/86–2/14/88; 5/27/88–12/2/88

1st Decan Capricorn ♑   2/14/88–5/27/88; 12/2/88–1/5/91; 8/30/91–10/9/91

2nd Decan Capricorn   1/5/91–8/30/91; 10/9/91–2/10/93; 7/17/93–12/3/93

3rd Decan Capricorn   2/10/93–7/17/93; 12/3/93–1/12/96

1st Decan Aquarius ♒   1/12/96–2/20/98; 8/23/98–12/11/98

2nd Decan Aquarius   2/20/98–8/23/98; 12/11/98–1/1/00

Saturn: The World (Brings things to form, changes Yes/No patterns, rewards or punishes, not unexpected, structures or re-structures, manifests)

1st Decan Pisces ♓   1/1/65–3/18/65

2nd Decan Pisces   3/18/65–3/11/66

3rd Decan Pisces	3/11/66–3/3/67
1st Decan Aries ♈	3/3/67–5/30/67; 9/20/67–2/20/68
2nd Decan Aries	5/30/67–9/20/67; 2/20/68–5/13/68; 11/12/68–1/28/69
3rd Decan Aries	5/13/68–11/12/68; 1/28/69–4/29/69
1st Decan Taurus ♉	4/29/69–4/16/70
2nd Decan Taurus	4/16/70–7/10/70; 11/1/70–3/29/71
3rd Decan Taurus	7/10/70–11/1/70; 3/29/71–6/18/71; 1/10/72–2/21/72
1st Decan Gemini ♊	6/18/71–1/10/72; 2/21/72–5/31/72
2nd Decan Gemini	5/31/72–9/6/72; 10/28/72–5/13/73
3rd Decan Gemini	9/6/72–10/28/72; 5/13/73–8/1/73; 1/7/74–4/18/74
1st Decan Cancer ♋	8/1/73–1/7/74; 4/18/74–7/13/74
2nd Decan Cancer	7/13/74–6/26/75
3rd Decan Cancer	6/26/75–9/17/75; 1/14/76–6/5/76
1st Decan Leo ♌	9/17/75–1/14/76; 6/5/76–8/25/76; 4/4/77–4/17/77
2nd Decan Leo	8/25/76–4/4/77; 4/17/77–8/10/77
3rd Decan Leo	8/10/77–11/16/77; 1/5/78–7/26/78
1st Decan Virgo ♍	11/16/77–1/5/78; 7/26/78–10/17/78; 3/8/79–7/8/79
2nd Decan Virgo	10/17/78–3/8/79; 7/8/79–10/2/79
3rd Decan Virgo	10/2/79–9/21/80
1st Decan Libra ♎	9/21/80–9/12/81
2nd Decan Libra	9/12/81–12/10/81; 3/25/82–9/4/82
3rd Decan Libra	12/10/81–3/25/82; 9/4/82–11/29/82; 5/6/83–8/24/83

1st Decan Scorpio ♏	11/29/82–5/6/83; 8/24/83–11/23/83; 6/23/84–8/1/84
2nd Decan Scorpio	11/23/83–6/23/84; 8/1/84–11/19/84
3rd Decan Scorpio	11/19/84–11/16/85
1st Decan Sagittarius ♐	11/16/85–11/15/86
2nd Decan Sagittarius	11/15/86–2/21/87; 5/8/87–11/14/87
3rd Decan Sagittarius	2/21/87–5/8/87; 11/14/87–2/13/88; 6/10/88–11/12/88
1st Decan Capricorn ♑	2/13/88–6/10/88; 11/12/88–2/9/89; 7/11/89–11/9/89
2nd Decan Capricorn	2/9/89–7/11/89; 11/9/89–2/7/90; 8/13/90–11/2/90
3rd Decan Capricorn	2/7/90–8/13/90; 11/2/90–2/6/91
1st Decan Aquarius ♒	2/6/91–2/5/92
2nd Decan Aquarius	2/5/92–2/1/93
3rd Decan Aquarius	2/1/93–5/21/93; 6/30/93–1/28/94
1st Decan Pisces ♓	5/21/93–6/30/93; 1/28/94–4/28/94; 8/19/94–1/22/95
2nd Decan Pisces	4/28/94–8/19/94; 1/22/95–4/17/95; 10/2/95–1/9/96
3rd Decan Pisces	4/17/95–10/2/95; 1/9/96–4/7/96
1st Decan Aries ♈	4/7/96–3/28/97
2nd Decan Aries	3/28/97–7/12/97; 8/22/97–3/17/98
3rd Decan Aries	7/12/97–8/22/97; 3/17/98–6/9/98; 10/25/98–3/1/99
1st Decan Taurus ♉	6/9/98–10/25/98; 3/1/99–5/23/99
2nd Decan Taurus	5/23/99–1/1/00

Recommended Reading

* Indicates books and materials giving further information on tarot and the archetypes.

Andersen, Hans Christian. *The Complete Fairy Tales*.* Many translations available.

Anonymous. *The Impersonal Life*. San Gabriel, CA: Willing c/o Sun Center Publications, 1963.

Anthony, Carol K. *A Guide to the I Ching*. Stow, MA: Anthony Publishing Co., 1982. *The Philosophy of the I Ching*. Stow, MA. Anthony Publishing Co., 1981.

Argüelles, José. *The Mayan Factor: Path Beyond Technology*. Sante Fe, NM: Bear & Co., 1987.

Arundale, G. S. *Kundalini: An Occult Experience*. Wheaton, IL: Theosophical Publishing House, 1972.

Avalon, Arthur (Sir John Woodroffe). *The Serpent Power*. New York: Dover, 1974.

Ashcroft-Nowicki, Dolores. *The Shining Paths: An Experiential Journey through the Tree of Life*.* Northants, UK: The Aquarian Press, 1983.

Bach, Richard. *Illusions*. New York: Delacorte Press, 1977.

Baynes, Cary F., and Wilhelm, Richard, trans. *The I Ching or Book of Changes*. Princeton, NJ: Princeton University Press, 1967. (Still the best.)

Bentov, Itzhak. *Stalking the Wild Pendulum: On the Mechanics of Consciousness*. New York: Bantam, 1979.

Bernard, Raymond. *The Serpent Fire: The Awakening of Kundalini*. Mokelumne Hill, CA: Health Research, 1959.

Blum, Ralph. *The Book of Runes*. New York: St. Martin's Press, 1982.

Brennan, J. H. *Astral Doorways.* York Beach, ME: Samuel Weiser, 1972; *Experimental Magic.* York Beach, ME: Samuel Weiser, 1972; *Five Keys to Past Lives.* York Beach, ME: Samuel Weiser, 1971.

Brunton, Paul. *A Search in Secret Egypt.* York Beach, ME: Samuel Weiser, 1984.

Butler, W. E. *How to Develop Clairvoyance.* York Beach, ME: Samuel Weiser, 1973; *How to Read the Aura.* York Beach, ME: Samuel Weiser, 1971.

Carroll, Lewis. *Alice in Wonderland** and *Alice Through the Looking Glass.** Many editions available.

Case, Paul Foster. *The Tarot: A Key to the Wisdom of the Ages.** Richmond, VA: McCoy, 1981; *The Book of Tokens: Tarot Meditations.** Los Angeles: Builders of the Adytum, 1974.

Castaneda, Carlos. All his books except *The Eagle's Gift.* New York: Simon & Schuster.

Cavendish, Richard. *The Black Arts.** New York: Putnam, 1967. (Poor title. Not so black. Good survey of the metaphysical field.)

Chia, Mantak. *Healing Love through the Tao: Cultivating Female Sexual Energy.* Hungtington, NY: Healing Tao Books, 1986; *Taoist Secrets of Love: Cultivating Male Sexual Energy.* New York: Aurora Press, 1984.

Crowley, Aleister. *The Book of Thoth.** York Beach, ME: Samuel Weiser, 1974.

Drury, Neville. *Don Juan, Mescalito and Modern Magic: The Mythology of Inner Space.* London: Routledge & Kegan Paul, 1985; *Inner Visions.* London: Routledge & Kegan Paul, 1979; *The Path of the Chameleon.* London: Spearman, 1973; *The Shaman and the Magician.* London: Routledge & Kegan Paul, 1982; *Vision Quest.* Chalmington, UK: Prism Press, 1984.

Edinger, Edward F. *Ego and Archetype.** Baltimore: Penguin, 1973.

Fortune, Dion. *The Cosmic Doctrine.* York Beach, ME: Samuel Weiser, 1976; *The Esoteric Philosophy of Love and Marriage.* York Beach, ME: Samuel Weiser, 1982; *The Mystical Qabalah.** York Beach, ME: Samuel Weiser, 1984; *Through the Gates of Death.* York Beach, ME: Samuel Weiser, 1972.

Golas, Thaddeus. *The Lazy Man's Guide to Enlightenment*. New York: Bantam, 1980.

Grant, Joan. *Winged Pharaoh*. Columbus, OH: Ariel Press, 1985. (All her books on "far memory" are excellent, e.g., *The Eyes of Horus, Far Memory, Life as Carola, Lord of the Horizon, Return to Elysium*, all published by Ariel Press.)

Greek Mythology.* Many good collections available.

Green, Celia. *Out-of-the-Body Experiences*. New York: Ballantine, 1968.

Grimm, Brothers. *The Complete Grimm's Fairy Tales*.* New York: Pantheon Books, 1972.

Halevi, Z'ev ben Shimon. *An Introduction to the Cabala: Tree of Life*. York Beach, ME: Samuel Weiser, 1972.

Harding, M. Esther. *Woman's Mysteries, Ancient and Modern*.* New York: Harper & Row, 1976.

Harner, Michael. *The Way of the Shaman*. New York: Bantam, 1982.

Jung, Carl G. *Man and His Symbols*.* New York: Dell, 1968. *Memories, Dreams, Reflections*. New York: Vintage, 1965.

Kaplan, Aryeh. *Jewish Meditation: A Practical Guide*. New York: Schocken Books, 1985.

Knight, Gareth. *Experience of the Inner Worlds*.* Cheltenham, England: Helios, 1975; *A History of White Magic*. York Beach, ME: Samuel Weiser, 1979; *Occult Exercises and Practices*. York Beach, ME: Samuel Weiser, 1969; *Practical Guide to Qabalistic Symbolism*.* York Beach, ME: Samuel Weiser, 1978; *The Treasure Houses of Images*.* Rochester, VT: Destiny Books, 1986.

Kotzsch, Ronald E. *Macrobiotics Yesterday and Today*. New York: Japan Publications, 1985.

Krishna, Gopi. *The Awakening of Kundalini*. New York: E. P. Dutton, 1975; *Kundalini in Time and Space*. New Delhi, India: Kundalini Research and Publication Trust, 1979; *Kundalini, the Evolutionary Energy in Man*. Boston: Shambhala, 1971.

Kübler-Ross, Elisabeth. *Death: The Final Stage of Growth*. New York: Prentice-Hall, 1975.

Kushi, Aveline, with Jack, Alex. *Complete Guide to Macrobiotic Cooking*. New York: Warner Books, 1985.

Kushi, Michio, with Blauer, Stephen. *The Macrobiotic Way: The Complete Macrobiotic Diet & Exercise Book*. Wayne, NJ: Avery, 1985.

Kushi, Michio, with Jack, Alex. *The Cancer Prevention Diet*. New York: St. Martin's Press, 1983; . . . and Kushi, Aveline. *Macrobiotic Diet: Balancing Your Eating in Harmony with the Changing Environment and Personal Needs*. New York: Japan Publications, 1985.

Lamy, Lucie. *Egyptian Mysteries*. New York: Crossroad, 1981.

Lao Tsu. *Tao Te Ching*. Many translations available. (Witter Bynner's is excellent: New York: Capricorn, 1962.)

Larsen, Stephen. *The Shaman's Doorway: Opening the Mythic Imagination to Contemporary Consciousness*.* New York: Harper & Row, 1976.

Laurence, Theodor. *The Sexual Key to the Tarot*.* New York: NAL, 1973.

Le Guin, Ursula K. *The Earthsea Trilogy. (The Wizard of Earthsea*. New York: Bantam, 1975; *The Tombs of Atuan*. New York: Bantam, 1975; *The Farthest Shore*. New York: Bantam, 1975.)

Leonard, George. *The Silent Pulse*. New York: E. P. Dutton, 1978.

Monroe, Robert A. *Journeys Out of the Body*. New York: Anchor, 1977.

Moody, Raymond A., Jr. *Life After Life*. New York: Bantam, 1976.

Plato. *Phaedrus* and *Symposium*. Many translations available. (Avoid Jowett.)

Regardie, Israel. *The Complete Golden Dawn System of Magic*.* Phoenix, AZ: Falcon Press, 1984; *The Tree of Life*.* York Beach, ME: Samuel Weiser, 1969.

Rendel, Peter. *Introduction to the Chakras*.* York Beach, ME: Samuel Weiser, 1981.

Richardson, Alan. *An Introduction to the Mystical Qabalah*.* York Beach, ME: Samuel Weiser, 1974.

Sams, Craig. *About Macrobiotics: The Way of Eating*. Northants, England: Thorsons, 1984.

Sanella, Lee. *Kundalini—Psychosis or Transcendence?* San Francisco: H. S. Dakin, 1976.

Schwaller de Lubicz, Isha. *Her-Bak, "Chickpea:" The Living Face of Ancient Egypt*. Rochester, VT: Inner Traditions International, 1980; *Her-Bak: Egyptian Initiate*. Rochester, VT: Inner Traditions International, 1982; *The Opening of the Way*. Rochester, VT: Inner Traditions International, 1982.

Schwaller de Lubicz, R. A. *Esoterism & Symbol*. Rochester, VT: Inner Traditions International, 1985; *Nature Word: Verbe Nature*. West Stockbridge, MA: Lindisfarne Press, 1982; *Sacred Science: The King of Pharaonic Theocracy*. Rochester, VT: Inner Traditions International, 1982; *The Temple in Man*. Rochester, VT: Inner Traditions International, 1981.

Shearer, Tony. *Beneath the Moon and Under the Sun*. Albuquerque, NM: Sun Books, 1977: *Lord of the Dawn: Quetzalcoatl*. Happy Camp, CA: Naturegraph, 1971.

Silberer, Herbert. *Hidden Symbolism of Alchemy and the Occult Arts*.* New York: Dover, 1971. (Also available as *Problems of Mysticism and Its Symbolism*, now out of print. York Beach, ME: Samuel Weiser, 1970.)

Sinetar, Marsha. *Ordinary People as Monks and Mystics: Lifestyles for Self-Discovery*. Mahwah, NJ: Paulist Press, 1986.

Tart, Charles. *Altered States of Consciousness*. Ann Arbor, MI: UMI, 1969.

Thompson, Mark, ed. *Gay Spirit: Myth and Meaning*.* New York: St. Martin's Press, 1987.

Three Initiates. *The Kybalion*. Chicago: The Yogi Publication Society, 1936.

Toben, Bob. *Space-Time and Beyond*. New York: E. P. Dutton, 1982.

Tripp, C. A. *The Homosexual Matrix*. New York: McGraw-Hill, 1987.

Walker, Mitch, and Friends. *Visionary Love*. San Francisco: Treeroots Press, 1981.

West, John Anthony. *Serpent in the Sky: The High Wisdom of Ancient Egypt*. New York: Harper & Row, 1979.

Whincup, Greg. *Rediscovering the I Ching*. Garden City, NY: Doubleday, 1986.

White, John, ed. *Kundalini, Evolution & Enlightenment*. New York: Anchor, 1979.

Wilber, Ken, ed. *The Holographic Paradigm and Other Paradoxes.* Boston: Shambhala, 1982.

Wilby, Basil. *New Dimensions Red Book.* Cheltenham, England: Helios, 1968.

Wilhelm, Richard, and Jung, C. G. *The Secret of the Golden Flower.* New York: Harvest, 1970.

Wing, R. L. *The I Ching Workbook.* New York: Doubleday, 1979.

Wolfe, W. Thomas. *And the Sun Is Up: Kundalini Rises in the West.* Red Hook, NY: Academy Hill Press, 1978.

Astrology

Arroyo, Stephen. *Astrology, Karma & Transformation: The Inner Dimensions of the Birth Chart.* Reno, NV: CRCS, 1978; *Astrology, Psychology and the Four Elements.* Reno, NV: CRCS, 1975.

Bacher, E. *Studies in Astrology* (9 vols.). Oceanside, CA: Rosicrucian Fellowship, 1973.

Bills, Rex E. *The Rulership Book.* Richmond, VA: Macoy, 1971.

Carter, Charles E. O. *Astrological Aspects.* London: Fowler, 1967; *Essays on the Foundations of Astrology.* London: Theosophical Publishing House, 1947; *The Principles of Astrology.* Wheaton, IL: Theosophical Publishing House, 1969; *Principles of Horoscopic Delineation.* London: Fowler, 1935.

Clogstoun-Willmot, Jonathan. *Western Astrology & Chinese Medicine.* New York: Destiny Books, 1985.

Davison, Ronald C. *Astrology.* New York: Arco, 1963.

Escobar, Thyrza. *Essentials of Natal Interpretation.* Tempe, AZ: AFA, 1982; *The 144 "Doors" of the Zodiac: The Dwad Technique.* Los Angeles: Golden Seal Research Headquarters, 1974.

Forrest, Steven. *The Inner Sky: The Dynamic New Astrology for Everyone.* New York: Bantam, 1984.

Garner, Robert. *What Sign Are You? (Tropical or Sidereal).* Bozeman, MT: author, 1971.

Greene, Liz. *The Astrology of Fate.** York Beach, ME: Samuel Weiser, 1984; and London: Allen & Unwin, 1984.

Hall, Manly Palmer. *Astrological Keywords.* Totowa, NJ: Littlefield, 1975.

Hand, Robert. *Essays on Astrology*. Gloucester, MA: Para Research, 1982; *Planets in Transit: Life Cycles for Living*. Gloucester, MA: Para Research, 1980; *Planets in Youth: Patterns of Early Development*. Gloucester, MA: Para Research, 1981.

Hickey, Isabel M. *Astrology, A Cosmic Science*. Watertown, MA: Fellowship House, 1970; . . . and Altieri, Bruce H. *Minerva/Pluto: The Choice Is Yours*, Bridgeport, CT: Altieri Press, 1973.

Jinni and Joanne. *The Digested Astrologer, Vol. 1: Signs, Houses, Planets and Aspects*. Seattle, WA: authors, 1972; *Vol. 3: The Spiral of Life: Psychological Interpretation*. Seattle, WA: authors, 1974.

Jones, Marc Edmund. All writings, for his incredibly beautiful command of the English language as well as his astrological wisdom. His work is available through Quest Books in Wheaton, IL, and the American Federation of Astrologers in Tempe, AZ.

Kempton-Smith, Debbi. *Secrets from a Stargazer's Notebook*. New York: Bantam, 1984.

Lewi, Grant. *Astrology for the Millions*. St. Paul, MN: Llewellyn, 1978; *Heaven Knows What*. St. Paul, MN: Llewellyn, 1985. *Your Greatest Strength*. York Beach, ME: Samuel Weiser, 1986.

Lowell, Laurel. *Pluto*. St. Paul, MN: Llewellyn, 1973.

Mailly Nesle, Solange de. *Astrology: History, Symbols and Signs*. Paris: Leon Amiel, 1981.

March, Marion D., and McEvers, Joan. *Astrology: Old Theme, New Thoughts*. San Diego, CA: ACS Publications, 1984; *The Only Way to Learn Astrology, Vol. 1: Basic Principles*. San Diego, CA: ACS Publications, 1981; *Vol. 2: Math & Interpretation Techniques*. San Diego, CA: ACS Publications, 1981; *Vol. 3: Horoscope Analysis*. San Diego, CA: ACS Publications, 1982.

Meyer, Michael R. *A Handbook for the Humanistic Astrologer*. New York: Anchor, 1974.

Moore, Marcia, and Douglas, Mark. *Astrology, the Divine Science*. York Harbor, ME: Arcane, 1978.

Robertson, Marc. *Time Out of Mind: The Past in Your Astrological Birth Chart and Reincarnation*. Tempe, AZ: AFA, 1972; *The Transit of Saturn: Crisis Ages in Adult Life*. Tempe, AZ: AFA, 1973.

Rudhyar, Dane. *The Astrological Houses*. New York: Doubleday, 1972; *An Astrological Mandala*. New York: Vintage, 1974; *Astrological Timing*. New York: Harper & Row, 1972; *The Lunation Cycle*. New York: Aurora Press, 1986.

Tierney, Bill. *Dynamics of Aspect Analysis*. Reno, NV: CRCS, 1983.

West, A. W., and Toonder, J. F. *The Case for Astrology*. Baltimore: Penguin, 1970.

D.O.M.E. Services

Calculated Computer Horoscopes (using the Koch Birthplace House Cusp System and tropical, geocentric astrology) with Astrology-Tarot Equivalent Worksheets and three Personal Transits Sheets may be ordered from D.O.M.E. Services at the address below. The cost is $35.00 postpaid (foreign orders add $5.00). This does not include an interpretation of the horoscope.

The LifeScan Astrological Personality Profile (a personal computer analysis of the horoscope written by John Woodsmall, Stephen Connors and Edwin C. Steinbrecher) is also available for $35.00 postpaid (add $5.00 for foreign orders). It includes possible Alien pattern interpretations.

If you would like a hand-drawn copy of the horoscope included with either of the above, add an additional $15.00.

Edwin C. Steinbrecher and the Staff of D.O.M.E., the Inner Guide Meditation Center, do Inner Guide initiations in Los Angeles and also are available to travel to your area for lectures, seminars, workshops, classes in astrology, tarot and macrobiotics, private past life sessions with the Inner Guide, and private astrology/Inner Guide initiation sessions. "Requirements for the Inner Guide Meditation Initiation" are available on request. There is also a three-week Inner Guide Meditation Initiators' Training Course Intensive offered twice yearly. Inquiries should be made to:

> The Secretary
> D.O.M.E.
> P. O. Box 46146
> Los Angeles, California 90046, U.S.A.

Subscriptions to D.O.M.E.'s journal, *White Sun*, and quality prints of Leigh McCloskey's original drawings are also available.

All D.O.M.E. services are tax deductible as D.O.M.E. is an IRS approved, non-profit spiritual organization.

About the Author

Edwin Charles Steinbrecher, originator and developer of the Inner Guide Meditation and founder and director of D.O.M.E. Center, is a second generation astrologer-metaphysician. He is editor of the D.O.M.E. journal, a consultant for the American film and television community and a frequent traveling lecturer on the Inner Guide Meditation. He lives and works at D.O.M.E. Center in Los Angeles, California, where he and his colleagues endeavor to refine and perfect the meditation and to train Initiators, shamans, priests and priestesses. His other interests are art, music, film, dance, poetry, collage, astrological research (collecting accurate birth data of well-known people for the use of students) and West Coast macrobiotics.

Photo courtesy of Joe Rizzo.

Index

Made in the USA